PLC 01

DATE			

Maria Rodale's
Organic Gardening

Maria Rodale's Organic Gardening

Your **Seasonal** Companion to Creating a **Beautiful** and **Delicious** Garden

Rodale Press, Inc.
Emmaus, Pennsylvania

We're always happy to hear from you. For questions
or comments concerning the editorial content of this
book, please write to:

Rodale Press, Inc.
Book Readers' Service
33 East Minor Street
Emmaus, PA 18098

Look for other Rodale books wherever books are sold.
Or call us at (800) 848-4735.

For more information about Rodale Press and the
books and magazines we publish, visit our World
Wide Web site at:

http://www.rodalepress.com

Editor: Ellen Phillips
Cover and Interior Designer: Karen Coughlin
Illustrators: Maria Rodale and Karen Coughlin
Interior Photographers: Maria Rodale,
    Don Fisher/*The Morning Call,* Anthony Rodale,
    and Kurt Wilson/Rodale Images
Interior Photography Stylists, Food Shots:
    Evelyne Barthelemy and Melissa Hamilton
Cover Photographers: Maria Rodale (front),
    Susan Pollack (back), David Rodale (back flap)
Photography Editor: James A. Gallucci
Copy Editors: Nancy N. Bailey and
    Jennifer Hornsby
Senior Research Associate: Heidi Stonehill
Manufacturing Coordinator: Melinda Rizzo
Indexer: Lina Burton
Editorial Assistance: Jodi Guiducci

Rodale Organic Living Books
Executive Editor: Ellen Phillips
Art Directors: Carol Angstadt and Patricia Field
Production Manager: Robert V. Anderson Jr.
Studio Manager: Leslie M. Keefe
Book Manufacturing Manager: Mark Krahforst

Library of Congress Cataloging-in-Publication Data

Rodale, Maria.
    Maria Rodale's organic gardening : your seasonal
companion to creating a beautiful and delicious
garden / Maria Rodale.
        p.   cm.
    Includes bibliographical references and index.
    ISBN 0-87596-799-X   hardcover
    1. Organic gardening. 2. Landscape gardening.
3. Gardens—Design. 4. Seasons. I. Title. II. Title:
Organic garden.
    SB453.5 .R6   1998
    635'.0484—ddc21   98-8913

Distributed in the book trade by St. Martin's Press

2   4   6   8   10   9   7   5   3   1   hardcover

To my husband, Lou, who is my best gardening
companion and friend;

To my two lovely daughters—Maya, for her wisdom
and inspiration, and Eve, for her companionship
both inside and outside of me while working
on this book;

To my father and grandfather, who taught me to see
gardening organically as a sacred responsibility and
an essential way to help make the world and us
healthier and happier;

And, finally, to my grandmother and mother, who
taught me that organic gardening can be
very, very beautiful

Contents

Summer 190

Fall 294

Acknowledgments

Special thanks to:

my summer gardening helpers, Alex and Andrew Norelli
and Andrew Jurkiewicz;

my summer assistant, Veronica Jurkiewicz;

my editor, Elly Phillips;

my designer and co-conspirator, Karen Coughlin;

the people who educated and inspired me: John Seymour,
Angela Ashe, Will and Hal, Bill Mollison, Scott Pittman,
John Brookes, Dr. Irving Dardik, and the farmers and gardeners
I have worked with throughout the years;

the people who let me photograph their organic gardens:
Louie Cinquino, Pat Corpora, Nancy Ondra, Ardie Rodale,
the Rodale Institute, the Rodale Institute Experimental Farm,
and Eileen Weinsteiger;

Fier Mill for bringing my wattle fence posthaste;

Gary's Tree and Shrubbery Service for all the big stuff and
anything involving power tools;

the Cinquino family, who have welcomed me into their
gardening and food-loving arms;

the Rodale family, for tolerating my eccentricities;

and everyone who was kind enough to let me interview
them for this book.

Oriental poppy

Introduction

Can truly beautiful gardens really be organic? Of course! Long before manufactured chemicals were invented, gardeners created some of the most beautiful gardens in the world.

Organic gardening is easy, safe, and delightful. You can create the garden of your dreams without resorting to anything toxic or ugly. (Admit it, you thought that if you were an organic gardener, you needed to have black plastic mulches and aluminum pie plates to scare the birds and rabbits, didn't you?)

The whole idea that organic gardening has to be ugly is a myth spread by well-intentioned gardeners who are more concerned about giant tomatoes than stunning views (not that there's anything wrong with that). But the reality is that you can have both giant tomatoes *and* stunning views.

Actually, you can have more. You can have giant tasty tomatoes, stunning tableaux, and a totally clear conscience because you haven't done anything in your garden to advance the degradation of the planet or impair your health or that of your family.

In fact, you can actually improve your health, your family's health, and the health of the planet. All it takes are a few of the things that make life worth living—curiosity, a sense of humor, and an enjoyment of nature and the great outdoors. I'd like to help you see just how easy (and beautiful) organic gardening can be through the simple step-by-step directions and stories in this book.

The Truth about Chemicals

Back when people started using chemical pesticides, chemicals provided impressive results. However, not many people could have foreseen the impact and consequences that chemicals have now and will continue to have on our health, our environment, and our future. Controversy rages around scientific studies that have shown chemical fertilizer and pesticide use linked to cancer, infertility, birth defects, water pollution, soil degradation, and erosion, just to name a few.

Most heavy chemical users will admit that what starts out as a quick burst of fertility and productivity quickly turns into an expensive and increasingly demanding habit that works less and less well over time—ultimately leaving the soil structure collapsed and the soil itself dead. The bottom line for you is this: Are you willing to risk your own and your children's future for a patch of weed-free lawn and chemically fed flowers and food?

Please don't fool yourself by thinking "just a bit here and there won't hurt anybody." According to the Environmental Protection Agency, in 1995 alone, American homeowners spent more than *1.9 billion dollars* on pesticides for the home and garden. A little bit used by a lot of people sure can add up.

Most weeds and pests (except, perhaps, the mighty woodchuck) can be controlled by such easy and harmless techniques that the only argument you may have for justifying the use of such poisons is simple ignorance of the alternatives. But with this book, you should now have *no* excuses!

What This Book Is . . . and Isn't

Although I have been an organic gardener for over 20 years, I have often yearned for a book like this—a season-by-season guide covering all the basics, the beauty, and the fun. After searching for it for years, I finally realized I would have to write that book myself. As a result, this is my journey—as well as yours—into creating a beautiful and delicious organic garden.

This book will show you how to create your beautiful yard totally organically and then enjoy the results—flowers, vegetables, fruits, and herbs—with delicious recipes that capture the "just-picked" flavor that can't be bought in any store. Once you have tasted vegetables, fruits, and herbs that you've picked and eaten the same day, you will notice that food is alive. The sooner you eat it out of the ground, the more alive it still is, and you can't help feeling more vibrant and alive yourself after eating it.

This book is selective and personal. It's selective because everything in it is geared toward creating and enjoying an aesthetically designed and maintained organic garden. (No pantyhose hanging from trees in this book!) But it's also personal because I am using my own experiences and my own garden in Pennsylvania as the basis for it and my own idea of what is beautiful. But whatever your concept of beauty is, you should be able to adapt the ideas and information in this book to suit your tastes.

Ultimately, gardening is about pleasure—the pleasure of creating, the pleasure of enjoying your home, and the pleasure of eating just-picked, delicious fruits, herbs, and vegetables. This book will give you everything you need to get started (or continue) designing, creating, and enjoying your own beautiful and delicious organic garden.

Sweet peas

Me & My

I grew up on the first organic experimental farm in America. It wasn't the first organic farm, since all farms before the 1900s were organic. However, it was the first one that specifically set out to test and experiment with organic gardening and farming practices, while most of the country became completely enamored of and addicted to chemical fertilizers and pesticides.

The farm was started by my grandfather J. I. Rodale who moved from New York City to Pennsylvania in the 1940s for both health and financial reasons. Land was cheap back then—he bought 65 acres and a house for $7,000. He had grown up in and above a grocery store on the Lower East Side; his family lived off the food that was too rotten to sell. Later, he became obsessed with fresh food that was grown without chemical fertilizers and pesticides. He called it "organic."

J. I. started *Organic Gardening* magazine in 1942 and *Prevention* magazine in 1950. He died when he was 70, but he lived 20 years longer than any of his brothers or sisters, who all suffered from heart conditions.

My grandfather J. I. Rodale visited Georgia O'Keeffe and her organic garden in Abiquiu, New Mexico, in 1967.

Both Georgia O'Keeffe and J. I. experimented with "electroculture," which was the belief that pulling electricity from the air into the soil would help plants grow. Experimentation is half the fun of gardening!

Garden

My father was the editor of *Organic Gardening* magazine for many years, but his true love was farming.

Photo by Don Fisher/*The Morning Call*

My father, Bob Rodale, continued the tradition, adding the focus of working with farmers, since he felt they could make the biggest difference. He started the Rodale Institute and proved scientifically that not only was organic agriculture more financially efficient than conventional farming but that it also actually improved the soil over time rather than depleting it. He called that "regeneration." Unfortunately, my father was killed in a car crash in Moscow at the age of 60, while starting up an organic farming magazine in Russian.

Growing Up on the Farm

When I was a kid, there was nothing unusual about living on the farm, other than the occasional visitor who would intrude on the imaginary play world of a farm kid. Most of the time, especially in summer, I spent the whole day roaming around the gardens. I played with the chickens, cows, cats, and pigs. I ate fresh berries and vegetables when I was hungry. I climbed trees, built forts in the hay barn, swam, and napped in the sun-warmed grass.

Eating sour cherries straight from the tree was one of my favorite activities when I was a kid.

My favorite places were the gardens next to my grandparents' house. Over the years they had created terraced formal gardens surrounding their house, which made excellent spaces for playing house, putting on plays, or just plain hiding!

My first job at age 13 was working on the farm. It was that year when I shoveled my first compost pile, drove my first (and unfortunately only) tractor, and pulled my first weed. I will never forget the first day, when I was squatting in the rock garden, having been assigned to pull weeds. Rock gardens are notoriously knuckle-damaging weeding problems, so I was just ripping the weeds off at the stem.

"No, no, no!" said Bob Hofstetter, the farmer with the Pennsylvania Dutch accent. "You have to pull weeds out by the roots!" I can't tell you how many times I have thought back to that moment of wisdom. I have thought about it when I'm lying on the ground exhausted from struggling and finally winning a tug-of-war with an especially stubborn and deep-rooted weed.

I have also thought about it when I've encountered personal or work problems in my life that I know will not go away just by cutting the problem off at the stem. To me, that is the true beauty and allure of working in the garden. It gives you time to learn and time to think and teaches lessons you can constantly apply to the rest of your life.

That summer I also learned how to become an excellent shot with dirt balls.

When I was 16, I was eager to get out of my parents' house (rebel that I was). My parents allowed me to stay out at the Rodale Institute Experimental Farm for the summer as long as I worked out there. Did I ever get the better end of the deal!

The Rodale Institute farm was where large-scale agricultural research was done. It employed scientists year-round and lots of student interns during the summer. I spent that summer weeding fields of test plots with other students while discussing philosophy, religion, and, of course, music.

It was on that farm, in those fields, that I had to confront my conflict about weeding. If all plants are good in their own way, I thought, is it right for me to kill plants that are not the "chosen ones"? Believe me, when you spend eight hours out in the middle of a huge field weeding all day, you start to think of such things. Eventually I got over it.

I did a lot of other interesting things that summer—like harvesting corn samples from hundreds of test plots, labeling and drying the samples, grinding them up in the 120°F drying house, and helping to analyze them. I planted amaranth, freeze-dried amaranth, and ground up amaranth seeds for testing. I smoked my first cigar (which, by the way, is an excellent way to repel gnats!).

Small-Town Living in America

I didn't really get my hands in the dirt again until 1980, when I rented a house on the main street of a small town. I was a young unmarried mother who was going to college and working part-time as a technical artist, so I didn't have too much time left for gardening. But still I dug, I planted, I designed, and I harvested a few meager things.

The house had been built in 1838, so there was a unique blend of old-fashioned trees and shrubs, crumbling cement walkways and terraces, dead overgrown plants, and depleted soil. Over the next few years I created a humble but lush yard that had so much work put into it I couldn't imagine ever leaving. So I bought the house.

When I met my future husband, gardening was one of the main things that brought us together. He was working for *Organic Gardening* magazine at the time. And although he had never had his own garden, that was only because he had never had the yard for it, for he came from a family of hard-core Italian gardeners. I let him have a corner in my vegetable garden, and the rest is history.

Not that it was easy. It was hard to forgive him when he thought he was doing me a favor by pulling weeds, when in reality he had just pulled out over 20 asparagus plants I had just spent five hours transplanting the week before. It was, however, a good test of our commitment to each other. He hates it when I tell people about that story, so I won't mention it again.

He was the one who suggested that we get our vegetable garden soil tested. I asked him to get it tested for hazardous metals and such, too, since we lived on a main street with lots of traffic.

It was one week before our September wedding when we got the horrible news.

Learning the True Meaning of Regeneration

"You're not eating anything from that soil you sent me a sample of, are you?" asked the soil tester over the phone.

"Yeah, why?" my husband asked.

"Your lead levels are really, really high."

"How high is that?"

"Was your yard ever a paint dump?"

When I heard the news, I thought of all sorts of scary things. Had it hurt my daughter all these years to make mud pies and play in the yard? Had it hurt me? Had we been poisoning ourselves with our fruits and vegetables? So much for gardening organically all these years! What could it be from? What were we going to do? Would we have to move? Were we healthy? Fortunately, my daughter was healthy, happy, smart, and neurologically well.

From that day forward, we didn't touch anything in our yard for over a year. That year was a long, ugly process of getting tests done all

This statue, The Organic Maiden, by Boris Bly, was commissioned by my grandfather in the early '50s. It now graces my grandmother's garden.

over our yard. We had samples of our fruits and vegetables tested. We did research into the options and possible solutions. We struggled with long-term decisions, such as what our commitment was to fixing it, our desire to keep living where we were living, and how much we were willing and able to spend to fix it.

We looked into the history of the house and why it had such high lead levels. I struggled with the thought of all those years of gardening, designing, eating—all the money spent on perennials, trees, shrubs, and other plants. What could be saved? The experience made for an interesting first year of marriage. But we came out of the other side the stronger for it.

What had caused the high lead levels? Although there was lead in the stucco that covered our house, that wasn't enough to cause it. Turns out that not only had the house next to us been a gas station up until the '50s (with leaking tanks of leaded gasoline) but it had also been a car repainting business. So we were, literally, growing our food in a paint dump. Just one reason why it's important to find out about the history of the land you live on. The industrial and agricultural revolutions were not kind to American soils.

What were our options? A lead level of 100 ppm or over is considered dangerous. A lead level of 500 ppm or over is considered hazardous waste. The only test result under 100 was an area in the front of the house next door that had had new soil brought in (after they took out the old gas tanks)! There were a few spots, with no rhyme or reason to them, that were well over 1,000 ppm.

This is my yard after the excavation, receiving its first load of fresh, clean soil.

The plant testing had shown us that the root and leaf crops were high in lead. So things like carrots, garlic, and lettuces were bad. But fruits (like the apple tree and our tomatoes) somehow filtered out the lead. So it wasn't going to be an unreasonable proposition to grow things again if we could bring in clean soil.

We had decided that not only did we want to stay in the house but also that we wanted to make it even better than before. My father's philosophy of regeneration really got me past the crisis mentality. His philosophy of regeneration was that there is an inherent healing process in the earth and in us, and after a crisis or disturbance, we have the opportunity to heal and grow into something stronger than before.

Some of the soil we needed to have placed in a special waste site. The less heavily contaminated soil was taken by the excavator to spread out on his woodland so that it would have the opportunity to be diluted even more over the years by fallen leaves. The soil we brought in was a local organic mixture of compost, mushroom soil, and sand.

But all this didn't happen until two years after we had found out about the problem. What did we do the second year? Redesign our yard. At first I was devastated by the thought of starting all over. But then I started becoming excited. How many times had I wished before that I could have access to a backhoe to mold the earth exactly as I wanted it? How many times had I thought, "If only I had more garden beds all over the yard . . . "?

A Detour to France

Around the time we were thinking about redesigning our yard, I saw an ad for La Napoule Garden Design Course in the south of France. The teacher was John Brookes, whom I had never heard of. All the designing I had ever done had been done by my own wits and art background and not by any book on garden design.

By this time in my life I had become a highly stressed executive desperately in need of a vacation. This course fit the bill, since it had always been a dream of mine to go to the south of France. So off I went.

What a joy! There were only nine of us, and we each had our own drafting table in a well-lit old artist's studio in an old stone castle right on the Mediterranean. The days were spent working on our designs and visiting the amazing and fabulous private gardens of the region. (All the rich old ladies wanted to show off their gardens to the famous John Brookes.) And, of course, we ate delicious French food and saw slides and heard lectures by John. My garden design turned out much better than I could have imagined, with his looking over my shoulder at times and making extremely wise and appropriate comments. It was fabulous.

I happily came back from France with my beautiful plan. My husband and daughter hated it. Well, not exactly. But while I had gone through a step-by-step process of design and planning, to them it just looked too different.

The industrial and agricultural revolutions were not kind to American soils.

Let's just say the process did not end there. In fact, it went on for another good eight or nine months. Hence, my hard-earned tips on garden design negotiations with family members in the "Spring" section of this book.

The end result was, and still is, just a beginning, of course. Recently I took a two-week Permaculture course with the founder of the concept, Bill Mollison (a rare and humorous treat). Learning about Permaculture has added a whole new set of ideas for me to think about—important ideas about fertility, productivity, efficiency, and learning about nature—rather than only thinking about beautiful design. Learning about nature and gardening is a lifelong education that can never be complete. Far from discouraging me, each new discovery just seems to reinforce the magic and mystery of life.

It has been two years since the last backhoe left the property, and there are still years of work to do. But gardening is about patience as much as anything.

Olive groves and redbud in the south of France

A Gardening Book Is Born

I am not an official Master Gardener. I would never be able to answer all the questions about chemical fertilizers on the test. And I am weak at remembering the Latin names for things. But I have been gardening for over 20 years—entirely organically. And as you have just read, I have had a few experiences that have forced me to stretch my range.

This is not a book about how fabulous my own garden is. It's far too new and immature—which is why you won't see a lot of vistas of my garden. Maybe in another 30 years I will do a book on my own beautiful yard.

Instead, this is a book I have wanted and had to write to find. Being born into a lineage of organic gardeners and farmers does not make a person automatically experienced and educated on what's good and what's bad, what works and what doesn't. I meet people all the time who are interested in gardening, and even gardening organically, but who don't know where to start or what to do.

Most important, I simply and purely love to garden. I love to talk about it, write about it, and more than anything, I love to do it. If you are reading this now, you probably love to garden, too. So please join me in this journey through the seasons of gardening. You will learn some interesting new things, get inspired, and make the world a better place by creating an organic Eden in your own backyard.

Eve the baby was born the day after I delivered the final manuscript!

The 6 Senses

# of Gardening

Your yard *is* your garden. Whatever its size—many acres, a small lot, or a windowsill—it represents your own personal connection with nature, with the outdoors, and with the outside world. We often think of our yards in a one-dimensional sort of way: how they look, for instance. We want our yards to look nice and be pleasing to us and to our families and neighbors. But there are many dimensions to our yards, and it takes all of our senses to truly understand them.

Once you understand how all your senses function in your garden, you can understand the full contribution you are making to your environment—beyond sight. How are you improving the quality of life for your family and your neighbors? How are you doing your part to return to the earth some of what it has given to you? It takes all your senses to know. Your senses can tell you different things about what you have and what you may need in order to create a healthy, thriving garden.

Whatever the season, whatever the time of day, before you go rushing out to landscape your yard, create your garden, or even build a home or structure, take the time to explore your land with all your senses.

An Exercise in Observation

When I attended a course on Permaculture at the Rodale Institute Experimental Farm, we were asked to go out and sit in one spot for an hour and use all our senses to perceive the environment. It was a cold and windy spring day, and we all grumbled about having to get chilled. But a funny thing happened. After the first 15 minutes of the usual distracted thoughts and minor gripes, I started to see things differently. Ironically, it was not a positive experience. For once I saw the farm not as I had always seen and loved it but as it actually was—stripped, raped, unprotected, and even wasted.

Here was an organic farm that suddenly seemed, except for the lack of chemicals, no better than a traditional farm. There were hardly any windbreaks left. I could see erosion occurring. I could also see all the space wasted growing grass. Even the buildings were not protected by trees. As the chilled spring wind whipped my hair and blew across the valley, I suddenly realized that something was missing in the landscape that I had once thought was beautiful.

The lesson, as Bill Mollison, the teacher of the course and founder of the concept, was eager to point out to us when we returned to the classroom, was this: Organic is not enough. You have to think about the whole system, everything in it, and how to make it thrive.

Try doing this exercise yourself in your own landscape. Do it during each season. Do it before reading this book and after. I don't know if I would have seen what I saw without the benefit of a teacher to open the window. Hopefully, this book will open some windows for you, too.

Go Outside and Sit for Awhile

Here's what to do. Go outside and let yourself be drawn to a spot in your yard—preferably one that you don't usually sit in. Take a tablet to record your thoughts or draw pictures. Take a blanket if you want, but I think it's important to sit on the ground and not in a chair.

After you have made yourself fairly comfortable, sit for an hour. Then, go through a rundown of all your sensory perceptions and see what they tell you. The list of questions and thoughts that follow will help you tap into the different aspects of each sense.

Sight

Sight is the most obvious sense we use to enjoy our yards. And the obvious questions are these: Does it look nice? Does it look pretty? Do all the plants look healthy? Are there birds, bugs, and animals? How

Oriental lily

does it look from the view inside your house? How does it look from your neighbors' yards? What views of the world do you have?

Now expand your sight and your range. Look at the surrounding landscape—what type of area are you in? Are you on a mountain or in a valley? Are you in the desert or in the forest? What is the slope of your yard? How do the rain and water flow off or onto your land? All these are things you might take for granted, but by looking at them all at once, you will get a new view of where you live.

Sound

When you go outside, what do you hear? Traffic or the rustling of trees—or both? Can you hear the chirping of birds, the buzzing of insects? Can you hear water? (Lucky you!) Nature has the ability to absorb sounds, reflect sounds, and create sounds.

We often think of being in the country as quiet. No traffic, no shouting neighbors. But in truth, nature is very loud—especially in spring, summer, and fall. If it's not the crickets or the birds, it's the wind in the trees. A healthy ecosystem is loud, filled with life.

Taste

What do you have to eat in your yard? Is your yard a forager's nightmare? Imagine that you have to live off your yard for one day, eating only things that are growing there. Would you go hungry? Let's say you do have food growing. Are your raspberries sweet or tasteless? Do your vegetables taste flavorful or bitter? The taste of food often reflects the quality of the soil. Some people can even tell about the soil by tasting it . . . but I won't recommend that.

We often don't think about tastes other than our own, but are there foods for birds and animals to eat in your yard? Are there berries on the trees? Nuts on the ground? Are your plants being overgrazed by insects or deer? Nature is one big cycle of eating and purging, growing and dying. Take a look around—there's sure to be a whole lot of eating going on.

Fresh fig

Touch

Run your hands along your vegetables, perennials, shrubs, and trees.
You may be amazed at the different textures and energies you'll feel.
For instance, it's one thing to look at a tree, but it's another thing to
feel the trunk—to feel the pulsating strength of the heavy living wood.
What about your feet? Is the ground hard and dry? Or is it moist and
spongy? Close your eyes and feel the touch of the wind. Which way is
it blowing? How does your soil feel? Sandy or sticky? Rocky or smooth?

So many of our senses are in constant use every day, but we barely
pay attention to what they are telling us. Paying attention is both a sen-
sual (literally!) and spiritual experience that can truly heighten your
appreciation of the world. Don't just rely on your hands, either. How
does the air feel against your skin? How does the ground feel against
your body?

Smell

What do you smell in your yard? Pine trees or car exhaust? Flowers, farm animals, or industrial fumes? Or all of the above? How does your soil smell? Healthy soil actually has a rich, sweet smell (kind of like coffee). How does the air smell?

Smells are perceived in the oldest part of our brains, and it's a key survival sense. Women tend to have a more sensitive sense of smell than men. And plants are actually fabulous air filters. Which smells predominate in your garden? Which ones come and go? How do *you* smell?

Intuition and Emotion

Last, when you put all these sensory impressions together, how do they make you feel? Do you feel safe and protected? Or do you feel exposed and threatened? Does the place feel lush or sterile? Does the area seem to be happy and healthy, or depressed and sickly?

What can you tell about your own personality from looking at everything? Are you a compulsive perfectionist? (Is everything pruned, swept, cleaned, and straightened up?) Or are you a compulsive slob? (Are there old abandoned cars, tools, and other stuff lying around? Are things in disrepair?) Try to look beyond your own personality and see Nature as *she* wants to be seen.

The Sensual World

There are perfectly beautiful landscapes that—when scrutinized with this exercise—reveal their true natures. Off the top of my head I can think of some of the American five-star resorts I've visited. Visually they are stunning. But when you apply the six-sense test, they fail miserably.

The grass often feels sticky and prickly from all the chemicals they put on it. The smells are of more chemicals (chlorine especially). And there is very little animal and bird life (unless they are maintained as pets). Everything feels so clipped, so primped, and so formal that I start to feel claustrophobic. I long to get out and see the *real* landscape. But more often than not, the sight of beauty predominates over our other senses. We think we are happy someplace because it is beautiful, but we end up with a vague sense of dissatisfaction and malaise.

My family had the totally opposite experience while staying in the Irish countryside visiting the "small holding" (three-acre farmette) of John Seymour, author of *The Complete Book of Self-Sufficiency*. Sense this: Walking down the middle of a long dirt road from his house (the river behind us) toward our lodgings. The road is lined with wild mint, foxglove, elderflowers, and berries.

Through the trees, we can see cows and calves grazing peacefully in the meadows, the air fragrant with hay, grasses, and cool shade. In our arms we carry eggs still warm from the chickens, a loaf of fresh-baked bread wrapped in a tea towel, homemade butter, and just-made strawberry jam. Occasionally a cow moos, the wind rustles through the trees, the birds squawk. In the distance, a dog barks.

Life is good. Life is more than good. A deep sense of peace and rightness with the world settles in my heart beneath my woolen sweater. We have traveled to many places in the world (although still not enough), and every one of us (Lou, Maya, and myself) remembers that vacation and that moment as one of the best of our lives. It makes me cry just to remember it.

Turning your yard into a beautiful, delicious, organic, and *happy* garden is not only easy and delightful but also it's good exercise for you and good for the planet. In the process of creating with all your senses, according to the cycles of the seasons, you will find yourself coming alive as much as the plants and animals around you. And that vitality will spread to those around you in a way that is truly joyful.

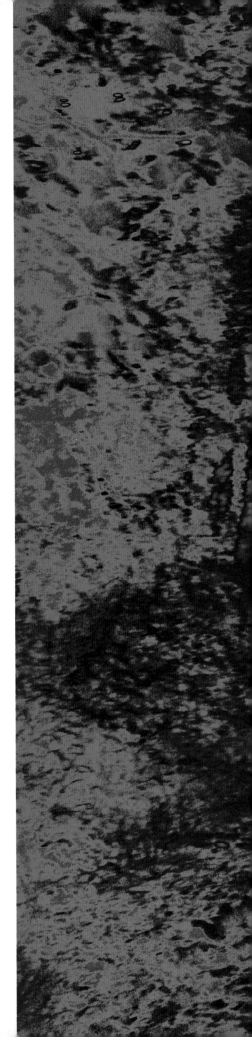

Winter

Winter is a time of stark beauty and contrasts.
The chill, contrasted with the warmth; the crunch
of snow, the smooth, hot comfort of a cup of tea; the crisp
night air, the steam that erupts from our mouths and noses like smoke;
cheeks burned from a day of outdoor fun, then warmed by a crackling
fire; cold feet stepping into a hot bath. It's also a time of rest, recovery,
and reflection. While the chipmunks sleep and we cuddle up in blankets, the rhythms of our lives slow. (Or we *wish* they would slow so we
could follow our natural urge to rest.)

Why start a gardening book with winter? Winter is when it all begins,
when the earth paints the canvas of creation white and you can truly
dream. And though the landscape seems dormant and spare, winter is
really one of the best times to see the true structure and form of your garden. Can your garden and yard be beautiful without blooming flowers,
green grass, leaves on the trees, and warmth? Yes! Winter is a key gardening season. It's also your annual chance to start over, improve, and re-
create your vision of paradise.

Designing

When I was a wild farm kid, the civilizing effect of my grandmother's garden let me fantasize and dream about all sorts of magical things—past, present, and future.

Your Garden

The best gardens begin, continue, and thrive with dreaming. What better time to dream than on cold, dark winter days sitting on your couch, by a window, or at your kitchen table, surrounded by garden catalogs, books, and magazines?

Nowadays, catalogs start arriving before the holidays—each direct-mail marketer trying to beat the others into your home. I personally prefer to wait until after Christmas to crack open the catalogs. Sometimes I wait until the new year. Sometimes I even wait until February, although at times, my procrastination is met with the disappointing news that an important choice is sold out.

For me, the holiday season is like the final harvest festival, with the well-deserved rest that follows. But once the festivities are over and you feel refreshed, let the dreaming begin! There's no dirt, no sore muscles, no poison ivy or bug bites, and no weeds. The time will come again when I can't wait to get my hands in the dirt, but for now, it's a welcome change. (Besides, the dirt is really cold in the winter—at least it is in Pennsylvania.)

Even before you start picking out your favorite plants or seeds, you need to take the time to design and plan for the coming year. Whether you are satisfied with your current yard, only satisfied with some of it, or starting from scratch, this exercise is fun and helpful. Here's what you need to do.

First, remember that when I say "garden," I mean your whole yard. That doesn't mean that your whole yard has to be planted in garden beds or vegetables. However, everything you have available should be considered part of the total garden environment you wish to create. And creation starts with a dream.

How to Dream a Garden

Here are the five steps you can use to dream a garden. Just find a few quiet minutes and let your imagination go.

1. **Spend some quiet time sitting and looking out your windows.** Make yourself comfortable, have some tea, and get a blanket if you're chilly. What do you see? Are you happy with what you see? What do you wish you could see out that window?

2. **Start wishing about what you'd really like to see.** Think big. Don't just relegate yourself to adding plants or trees. Imagine your ideal garden. The glorious thing about your garden is that your wishes can come true.

3. **Remember all the best places you've ever loved outdoors.**
The woods, the desert, a secret walled garden, the beach, a
tropical paradise, a lush British cottage garden, a farm, an arboretum . . . what made you love them? What do you remember most
happily from your childhood outdoor experiences? Where did
you feel best? Of all the things you have seen and places you
have been, what do you wish you could have outside your door?

4. **Now think of all the places in the world you'd love to visit.**
What seems to be drawing you there—water, mountains, your
ancestral home, the food, the light?

5. **Make a list of *everything*.** Include pictures from magazines, from
your travels, from catalogs, or even drawings. Tape or glue them
in a sketchbook or tablet.

By the way, now is not the time to be worrying about money or fea-
sibility. Most likely, you can't have everything you want unless you can
afford to have houses (and *gardeners*) all around the world. But when
you're dreaming is not the time to constrain yourself. You'll be amazed
at how you can make things happen once you allow yourself the freedom to think, unfettered by fear or self-restraint.

My philosophy is that everyone needs to be able to have goals that
will inspire them. Your goals may not be achievable this year, or even
next. But once you have a destination in sight, you can plan and build
and slowly work toward that goal—achieving far more than if you
never dared to dream in the first place.

Home Is Where Your Dreams Are

Most of us choose a place to live and try to make it home. The fun
comes when you can incorporate the things you love, and even the
things you can't have, into your own private paradise.

For example, I chose to make my home in Emmaus, Pennsylvania,
because that's where my family is and where my family's business is. I
don't regret making that decision. However, I have often *wished* I could
live in New Mexico, the south of France, England, India, Japan, Ireland . . .
I will probably never live in any of those places, but I can make my yard
feel as if I live there. One of the best compliments I ever received was
from a man who was dropping something off at my house one day.

"You live right on Main Street," he said, "but when I walk through
your gate and into your backyard, it's like being in another country. It's
like being in the south of France!"

No, I don't have climbing geraniums covering the side of my house,
cypress trees, fields of lavender, or the shimmering Mediterranean in
the distance. Some gravel and stones, arborvitae, nasturtiums, and
strategically placed patches of lavender give just the desired effect.
(Just wait till I get the grapevines put in.)

France is not the only country that calls my backyard home. Turn the corner behind my house and suddenly, you could be in Japan—with no jet lag.

Ultimately, it doesn't matter what inspires me. What matters is what inspires *you*. Your wish may be to feel as if you live on a farm in Iowa (picket fences, chickens, a patch of petunias). Or your wish may be to feel as if you live in the Alps in Switzerland (window boxes, wildflowers). Your lists should reflect your wishes. If you live with other people, it's good to check with them—especially your spouse. Don't hesitate to ask your kids, too. My daughter is often resistant to changes in our yard but then loves them once they're made. I've used a lot of her ideas, taken from drawings she has done, to create her ideal yard.

You have got your list of wishes and dreams, and hopefully even some pictures. Now what?

There's no place like home.

Peer Pressure in Suburbia

***Stop!* Before you go any further, check your internal peer pressure assumptions. Do you have symptoms of Peer Pressure in Suburbia? If you answer yes to one or more of the following questions, you may need a cure.**

1. Do you not want your house to "stand out" too much from your neighbors' houses?

2. Do you have a deep desire to keep a large lawn in your front yard, even though it gets absolutely no use other than to match your neighbors' and be mowed once a week?

3. Do you worry about increasing your property value more than it's worth with unnecessary and expensive landscaping?

4. Do you "hold up" your newly planted trees with those cords that are staked to the ground? (What are those stakes for, anyway?)

If you answered yes to even one of these questions, you may need to rid yourself of your peer-pressure fears before you go any further. Sure, you could get something out of this book. But you'll never really be free to dream. Your dreams will be put through a filter that says "I want to be just like everyone else so that people like me." Or "I don't want to stand out in a crowd because I don't want to embarrass anyone." Or "I want to fit in." Or "I want my kids to grow up normal." Sound familiar?

(What is a normal kid, anyway? Recently, after visiting friends in a new suburban development of house after house and empty yard after empty yard, my 14-year-old daughter said, "If I lived in a neighborhood like this, I would *have* to dye my hair purple and get my nose pierced." Kids have an innate and instinctive need to be different. Wouldn't you rather satisfy that need by landscaping your yard than by having your kids re-landscape their faces? Having said that, I do have to confess that my daughter *did* have purple hair for a brief time, and it matched my azaleas perfectly!)

Life is too short to worry about what other people think. Deep down you probably know it, too, but your fear may be holding you back. Or perhaps no one ever gave you permission to be different. Or perhaps you have been so subliminally conditioned that you can't see the benefit of doing anything differently. From here on out, you have permission to be different. You have permission to be fearless in the garden. And if you are not sure you want to be different and fearless, read on . . . read on . . . .

Or better yet, for the sake of this exercise, *pretend* that you have no neighbors, that you have no fears, that you have no constraints, and that you are going to live in your house forever and grow old watching your trees get big and gnarly and your children grow strong and independent.

Planting the Seeds of Your Dream Garden

The next steps get more practical but are still fun and should not be limited to reality.

1. **Make a wish list of favorite flowers, fruits, vegetables, trees, pets, wildlife, and birds.** Don't hold back. So what if you can't grow olive trees in your region? Don't worry about that now. I actually found an olive tree in a catalog that I can grow indoors in the winter and outdoors in the summer. There are also a lot of other trees that look like olive trees . . . get the picture?

2. **Make a list of all the things you want to do in your yard.** Here are a few to start with: entertain, relax, play football, play bocce, play fetch with the dog. My sister and brother-in-law built a campfire pit in a corner of their suburban yard. It is surrounded by trees, a hammock, and nice smooth rocks to sit on. It's become her family's favorite gathering place in the summer.

   In my case, I would have preferred the whole yard to be "grassless," with trees, woods, patios, and flowerbeds. But my husband, probably wisely, insisted that we have a large grassy play area for kids and dogs (and him). My design challenge became how to work that in without ruining the overall effect I wanted to create. In the end, having that open space really adds to the beauty of our yard. However, it also adds to the mowing.

3. **If you are so inclined, you can also make a list of things you *don't* want in your yard.** The things you may not want are ones that take a lot of work or maintenance, invasive plants that need to be constantly cut back, or certain types of wildlife. I personally like rabbits, but other gardeners spend hours trying to get rid of them. Woodchucks, however, are generally unwanted creatures in any garden when you are trying to grow vegetables or fruit.

4. **Make a list of important attributes.** Examples may be privacy, simplicity, formality, or wildness—basically anything that is important to you in your yard that hasn't shown up on any other lists. Since my family and I live on a main street next to a hardware store, important attributes for us are privacy, noise reduction, and pollution control. As it turns out, the same trees that are good for privacy—broadleaf and needled evergreens such as arborvitae, holly, boxwood, and rhododendron—are also good for reducing noise.

5. **Last, make a list of things you feel you *need* in your yard.** You may need a certain amount of space designated for vegetable gardening, a children's play area, a compost area, a trash area, a place for a shed or greenhouse, or a clothesline.

   After you have all your wishes, dreams, and lists compiled, take a break. Put your lists aside for a few days to "germinate."

These are a few of my favorite things...

Raindrops on roses

My dog

moss

persimmons

The Wasted Front Yards of America

When the great Japanese organic farmer and gardener Masanobu Fukuoka visited America for the first time, he was astounded by all the wasted land used for "front yards." In Japan, which supports over 12.5 million people on land the size of the United Kingdom, that kind of waste would be unthinkable.

To top it off, we then waste oil and nonrenewable resources mowing our lawns every week. We waste time pushing or sitting on our mowers. And we waste space that could be used for productive gardens. The next time you read an article that says that scientists think the only way to solve the future food shortage problem is through biotechnology, fertilizers, and pesticides, remember three important things.

1. The front yards of America alone could probably grow enough food to feed us for the next few hundred years.

2. The chemical companies and people who make a lot of money and profit from chemicals and biotechnology are the ones who pay scientists to do research.

3. Scientists don't want to lose their jobs.

So, here are six ideas you can try in your front yard that will turn it from an energy-, time-, and space-wasting pain to an effortless and remarkable space contributing to the beauty, health, and improvement of our world. (But there are as many other solutions as there are dreams—go back to your lists and see what other creative things you can do in your front yard.)

1. **Plant timber.** Oak, black walnut, cherry, and other large timber trees are all high-value items that can be grown and sold (in 50 to 100 years) for large sums of money relative to the minor investment. What other investment will both beautify your yard and help pay for your grandchildren's and great-grandchildren's educations? I heard a story of one college that built a beautiful building with giant wooden beams and then planted trees next to the building that could be used in 100 years if the beams needed to be replaced. Now that's smart, long-term thinking.

2. **Plant an orchard.** Grow your own fresh organic apples, peaches, cherries, grapes, pears, and exotic fruits. Not only do orchards look beautiful, but you can become very popular with your neighbors by sharing the excess. (Neighborhood kids will love your yard, too!) Many new varieties (and *old*

varieties) are very disease-resistant and require no chemicals or pesticides. And you can grow wonderful varieties you'll never find at the supermarket.

3. **Let your lawn return to forest.** After about three years of letting it go, you will notice a forest emerging. In about five years, you will feel as if you live in the wilderness. If your city's zoning board doesn't approve of it, go to court to fight for your rights to make a forest. Call it your very own wildlife conservation and ozone regenerating effort. In the 1970s, Rodale Press (publisher of this book and the company I work for) decided to let a portion of the company lawn grow into a natural meadow. The local zoning laws said you couldn't let your grass grow over a certain height. We went to court, won, and an article was written in *The New Yorker* about the case.

4. **Make a meadow.** Make sure your new wildflower meadow has paths for walking, spots for relaxing, and magical places for dreaming and pretending.

5. **Plant flowers.** Beautify your neighborhood and your world with lots of flowers to enjoy and share with family and friends. If you are so inclined, you can even start a cutting garden business, selling cut flowers to your local florists or drying flowers to sell to craft shops.

6. **Clean the air.** If you live along a busy street in an urban area, you may not want to turn your lawn into a forest or meadow, or maybe you can't (not enough space, for example). What you *can* do is do your part to clean the air—and keep dust and dirt out of your house—by planting air-cleaning and air-filtering plants. Some great trees for that are ginkgo (make sure you get a male), golden-rain tree, Japanese zelkova, oak, sycamore, and willow. As an added bonus, they cut down on street noise, too.

Some Scary Lawn Facts

- Thirty percent of water consumed on the East Coast goes to watering lawns; on the West Coast, it's 60 percent.

- The average suburban lawn is deluged with 10 times as much chemical pesticide per acre as farmland. In fact, over 70 million tons of chemical fertilizers and 70 million pounds of chemical pesticides are applied to residential lawns and gardens annually.

- Lawn care pollutes, too. Check out these statistics on hydrocarbons emitted from one hour of lawn mower, string trimmer, and leaf blower use compared to driving a car for one hour:

lawn mower:	10 to 12 times more pollution
string trimmer:	21 times more pollution
leaf blower:	34 times more pollution

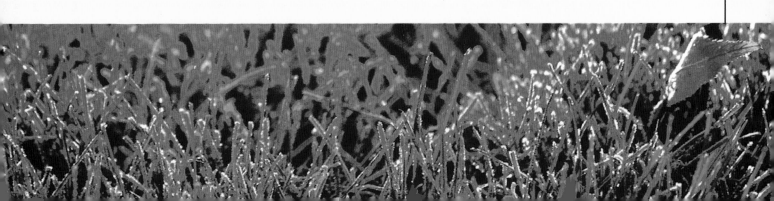

How to Bring Your Dreams to Life

You don't need a yard to have a garden.

To make your dreams and wishes a reality, you need a framework. For this project, your framework is your property or the space you have to work with. *Don't* get depressed. Whether you have a large estate or a small patio, there is space to build your dream garden. One of the most spectacular "gardens" I ever saw was in a shady back alley in Antibes, France. There was no yard, no dirt, nothing but a house right up against a narrow street—not even a sidewalk. But the whole front of the house was covered with hanging baskets filled with flowers and herbs. There were orange, yellow, magenta, pink, blue, and white flowers planted together with basil, rosemary, thyme, parsley, and sage. It took my breath away.

The goal here is to create an "outline" or map of your property to provide the backdrop to all your plans. You only have to draw it once, and then you will do all your dream planning on tissue paper placed on top of the framework. That way you don't have to keep redrawing your property lines. You can also make photocopies of the map or outline and have family members try their hands at designing, filling it in with their own dream gardens.

With all of these methods you'll want to include the things you know you want to keep for sure—like your house or special trees and bushes.

Of course, it's possible to create your dream yard without doing a drawing or a plan—to just do your building and planting instinctually. It depends on your style and your desires. Planning has often prevented me from making stupid mistakes. It has also not prevented me from making stupid mistakes. Planning is especially important, however, if you need to communicate your ideas to another person, such as a spouse or a landscaper.

There are three ways to create your basic plan or framework.

1. **The good old-fashioned way to create your map or framework is to do it on graph paper using a pencil and ruler.** At first, you don't have to draw it completely to scale and accurately, but later you may need to. I found out how important measuring was when I created a perfectly balanced formal garden on paper that fit what I thought an area of my yard looked like. But when I actually measured to give building directions, I found that it was impossible to create and had to start all over.

2. **The easiest (and most expensive) way is to hire a landscape architect or surveyor to draw your yard to scale for you.** It may be hard for the landscape architect

HALF THE PRESSURE TWICE THE SPEED

not to redesign your yard for you, but many will just measure and draw up a site plan for you for a nominal fee.

3. **There are also a number of good computer software programs specifically created for designing your own home landscape and garden.** These are especially handy in the final stages of planning, when you may need to give explicit instructions and/or very accurate measurements to someone. If you are comfortable using a computer, these programs are great. I hesitate to recommend any specific one since technology and software change so rapidly. But many garden magazines do regular reviews, and all the programs will be helpful in their own special ways. Try them out and see which ones you like best.

Once you have your framework, you are ready to start making your dream a reality . . . or as some would say, bring your dream back to reality. The truth is I will never have a gurgling stream with rocky waterfalls running through my yard. And as much as I would love to have a long, open view over fields, forests, and meadows, I've got a hardware store and big brick warehouse to look at. But I don't give up that easily, and neither should you. I know you are probably anxious to start ordering your seeds and plants, but there are a few more things that I suggest you do first. Then you can start your ordering.

Go for a walk: Observe, reflect & dream.

Designing with Duane Coen

Duane Coen is the landscape architect who created the Working Tree Center for my father. My father was interested in transforming the original organic farm into an arboretum. After many discussions, interviews, and research, Duane created a plan that incorporated my father's ideas on regeneration, the history of the farm, and the family's desire that the farm grow in beauty and value for future generations. Working with him on the Working Tree Center project and also on my yard (he did the initial drawings that I proceeded to totally redesign—the client-from-hell sort of thing) greatly influenced many of the ideas in this book.

What is the difference between a landscape designer and a landscape architect?

Well, there is a legal difference. In many states you can't call yourself a landscape architect or practice as one unless you are one. And to become one you have to have a combination of education and experience (totaling seven years in North Carolina) and take a comprehensive test. For many states, you need to be registered in the state in which you work.

Whereas, anybody can call himself a landscape designer.

8 Easy Steps to Make Your Dreams Come to Life

Ask not what you need but what you have.

—Robert Rodale

For all of these steps, you'll need to draw on tissue paper overlaid on your original drawing.

Step 1: Start Where You Are

Take your framework (plan) and draw in the natural environmental conditions that you have to deal with. Mark out the following general features:

- Sunny areas
- Shady areas
- Directionals: north, south, east, west
- Winter wind directions
- Sloping areas
- Wet and dry areas

Include problem areas you have to deal with. These could include sights you want to block out or neighbors' trees that have roots that invade your front lawn, making it hard to plant anything there, let alone dig through the thick matted roots. Once our toilets backed up, and we couldn't figure out what was going on. The plumber ended up digging up the pipes going out to the street—they were completely filled with our neighbors' maple roots. It wasn't the trees' fault. But in the "Spring" section, I talk about the importance of planting the right tree in the right place to begin with, so you can avoid such vexing (and expensive) problems.

So many problems can be avoided simply by knowing where your house and garden are positioned in relation to the sun.

Staying Warm, Keeping Cool

Some simple landscaping techniques can save you and the planet lots of energy.
Just try some of these tips.

Staying Warm

- To save energy and keep your house warmer in the winter, plant evergreen trees on the north side of your house. Also use evergreens to block the prevailing winter winds.

- Plant climbing vines on the north side of your house for further insulation. But be careful not to plant ivy and other invasive climbers unless your house can stand up to it (stucco is good, but ivy can invade the mortar and cracks in bricks and wood). A trellis mounted a few inches from your outer house walls provides a good climbing structure and an extra pocket of air to insulate your home from the cold.

- Keep evergreens away from the south side of your house. You want all the sun you can get hitting your house on that side during the winter months. Plant deciduous trees instead, since they'll lose their leaves in winter.

- If you plant vines for shade on the south side, plant vines that lose their leaves in the winter to allow more sun to enter your home.

Keeping Cool

- To keep your house cool in the summer without air conditioning, plant large shade trees on the south side of your house to keep the summer sun from hitting your walls and windows.

- As mentioned in "Staying Warm," plant deciduous vines on the south side of your house. They will lose their leaves in the winter but provide much-needed shade in the summer.

- Plant evergreens on the north side of your house to make cooling microclimates. They can cool your whole house if you open the windows in the summer on that side of the house. Around your evergreens, plant ferns, rhododendrons, azaleas, and hostas for a woodland look. You will be amazed at how much cooler the air is when it has to blow through your evergreen "forest."

Step 2: Know Where You Have Been

Try to learn as much as you can about the history of your land and region. What zone are you in? What are the geological attributes of your region? What are your unique environmental challenges (poor soil, desert conditions, rocky soil, or sandy soil)? Now is a good time to get your soil tested. Don't forget to check for hazardous metals, especially if you live in a place where people have lived for a long time before you.

Step 3: Know Where You Are Going

Next, draw flow lines through your yard. Flow lines are the natural paths that people make from the car to the door, from the door to the shed, from the deck to the bird feeder, and so on. How do people move through your yard? To a certain extent, you can control how people move through your yard, but if you make them go too far out of their way, people will tend to make their own paths.

I learned this lesson last winter. We had just put in a new, elaborate pathway through the garden with two sets of steps. All summer it worked beautifully, making a nice relaxing stroll to the door or the car. But this winter, after 3 feet of snow, we quickly began using a shortcut. My first spring project (as the ground thawed and the path got all

Make paths where
people really walk.

Purple basil

Permaculture Zone 1:

kitchen and herb gardens

Permaculture Zone 2:

fruits, larger vegetable

patches, chickens

muddy and slimy) was to make an official gravel path for the shortcut. After all, there are times when you don't want to take a leisurely ramble (when you're carrying groceries, for instance), and you just want to get to where you are going—fast. Any good yard design will accommodate the need to get where you are going.

Step 4: Put Everything in Its Proper Place

Divide your yard into zones of usage. Put the things that are used and needed most closest to your house and the things needed least the farthest away from your house. This is an idea from Permaculture, a system of making the most practical and ecological use of every inch of your property. For example, your kitchen garden and herb garden should be as close to your kitchen as possible so that you can pop out while you are cooking to gather some herbs. But you may want to have your compost pile farther away from the house in case of unsightly views or the occasional unpleasant smell (although a healthy pile doesn't smell bad at all).

Permaculture breaks the zones up like this (although you don't have to use all of them, of course)—Zone 1: kitchen garden, herb garden; Zone 2: fruits, larger vegetable patches, chickens; Zone 3: large animals; Zone 4: commercial; and Zone 5: wilderness, heritage trees, water, habitat for wildlife. You may not have all of these zones or even more than one, but it is an interesting way to think about organizing your garden that makes practical sense. It's common sense, really.

Purple pepper

Permaculture Zone 3:

large animals

Permaculture Zone 4:

commercial area

Permaculture Zone 5:

wilderness, heritage trees,

water, habitat for wildlife

Step 5: X Marks the Spot

On another piece of tissue paper placed on top of the previous two, identify the natural areas that seem to be self-contained or already marked off in some way. Perhaps you have a hillside, a rocky area, or a wooded site. Every yard has its natural spaces. You can create spaces, too, but sometimes there are spots already there that have some magic (or some problems). The challenge and beauty is to take your dreams and work them into what you already have to make it even better.

Design Tip If you are working on a specific area of your yard, you can take a photo of it, and do your drawings and sketches on tissue paper placed directly on top of the photo. Then your sketches will be really accurate.

Step 6: Take an Expedition

Find out what your native trees, wildlife, and birds are so you can incorporate them into your landscape. I am not a pure "nativist" who believes you should only plant things native to your region, since all things are, after all, native to the earth. But it does help to know what sorts of plants do well without much care. Native plants tend to feed

and shelter native birds and animals. Many plants native to your area are medicinal or useful as well. A walk in the woods or a stroll by some natural hedgerows (usually growing between fields) can provide you with insights into your native plants and landscape. Make it a point to go on some local native plant search expeditions. Take a notebook, a camera, guidebooks, sandwiches, and water.

Step 7: Commit to Your Dreams

Start applying your dreams, wishes, and favorite plants to their places, taking into consideration the specific areas you have outlined. Sections of this book will help you identify plants and designs, so you may want to read ahead before you finalize anything.

Try not to think too much about specific plants yet. You want to be thinking about the "bones," or the underlying structure, of your yard. (Remember, bones are things like walls and large trees—the skeleton that holds the body of your yard together.) Lots of good plants can hide bad bones, but if you have good bones to begin with, almost anything will look good.

This is where it is really helpful to go back to your sketchbook filled with pictures, and ask yourself: "How can I create something like this in my yard? How can I integrate what I know will work here and what I need here with my dream landscape?"

Bones are things like walls and large trees— the **skeleton** that holds the body of your yard together.

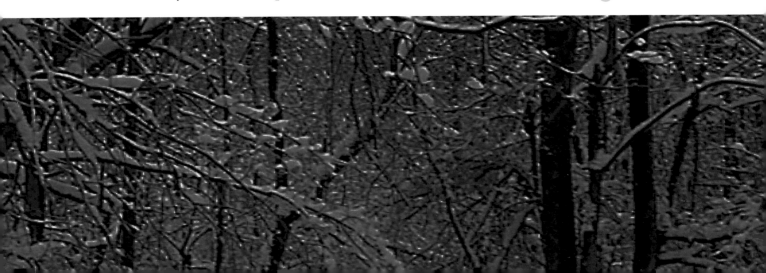

Free Your Mind

One of the best (though inadvertent) lessons I ever got—and also one of the most basic—came from renowned British landscape designer John Brookes.

When I attended his course in the south of France (I know, such suffering), the project I was working on was totally redesigning my yard. Even though I knew I would be tearing down a fence and building a garden wall closer to the street, I kept the gate in the same place as it was on the fence. When he looked at it, he said (in a very British accent), "Why on earth do you have the gate *there?* When it's open, you will feel so *exposed*. Put it *here*." And he pointed to the middle of the wall, rather than to the edge that had a clear view into our living room windows. He was so obviously right. And I had never even considered moving the gate.

My point? Don't limit your thinking to the way things are now or the way they have always been. Unchain your mind!

Take a step back, and look at how things could be instead. Anything can be changed. Sometimes for a big cost, sometimes for no cost. You can still be practical without being stuck in your thinking.

I applied that same lesson to the other areas of my yard. Why did the vegetable garden have to be pushed to the side? Why couldn't it be the centerpiece? Why do fruits and vegetables and flowers all have to be separate? Why can't they be together? Actually, that idea came when I found out I didn't have enough room to have everything I wanted and keep it separate. That's when I started squeezing things together into a beautiful and delicious organic garden.

Hellebores are one of the few plants that actually bloom in the winter.

Step 8: Pick Your Plants

Now take your list of favorite plants and start putting them where they make sense. You will probably need a good plant identifier book specifically for your region to help you. I'll tell you about some of my favorite plants in this book, but there are many good books that cover the whole gamut and cover different regions of the country. (See "Recommended Reading" on page 358 for a few of my favorites.) Put the shady plants you like in the shady places, and put the sun-loving plants in the gardens you have created in the sun. Can't fit the regular variety? See if it has a dwarf variety. The most important thing you can do to be a successful gardener is to put the right plant in the right place to begin with.

It's a lot easier to see where things should go after you have created your framework and marked out the spaces. With your framework, you can look at your whole yard as one big integrated area. You may not want to do everything at once. In fact, you may just want to choose one area each year to develop. But at least you have a plan that all fits together and flows from space to space.

What's Your Style?

Design your yard to suit *your* style, not mine. This book can help you to really identify and create your own personal style. You'll be much happier living in an environment that reflects your desires rather than someone else's.

However, this book can't help but reflect my style, since I am writing it. So I want to describe it for you so you'll know what you are looking at. I call my style "Wild Formal."

My Wild Formal Style

Wild Formal brings together the two conflicting aspects of my own personality. On the one hand I love order. I like things to be organized and balanced, and I like the looks of many fancy gardens I see (especially the European ones). On the other hand, as people who know me will attest, my life tends toward constant chaos, and I do not have the desire or inclination to be the obsessive-compulsive gardener it takes to maintain a formal landscape. Plus, I like nature wild and natural. So I have compromised.

The *structures* of my garden are formal. The garden beds, the pathways, the patios, the statues—everything that doesn't have to be maintained—reflect fairly formal and classical styles and materials. The *plantings* are more wild. I let things grow in their natural shapes rather than prune them. I let things overflow the formal boundaries. I mix things all together—flowers, herbs, vegetables, fruits. This year I had cantaloupes that planted themselves (from last year's compost pile, which I moved this year) and crept onto the paths. Cherry tomatoes pop up everywhere. These sorts of things make me happy. They may drive you crazy. That's fine. There's room in the world for all of us.

Wild Formal is truly a style made possible by being an American. As much as we long for the organization, the tidiness, and the harmony of our historical homelands, we are still pioneers—immigrants from countries that could not contain our hopes and dreams. As much as we reminisce about our pasts or worship royalty and affluence, we are still wild at heart and rough around the edges.

Sure, I love the pictures in books and magazines that show formal vegetable gardens with everything planted in gorgeous patterns—all balanced and organized (usually found in the British and French magazines). But then what happens when you eat some of those vegetables and fruits? Suddenly the pretty picture seems ruined.

The greatest thing about vegetable gardening, though, is that you can try it that way one year, and try it a totally different way the next. Just don't forget to *eat* your vegetables!

Now that you have all this information together and you know my personal bias, you will want to start putting your own ideas together. Find your own style. Play! Have fun! Have no fear!

Designing Especially

Ideally, your yard should look fabulous in all four seasons. But winter is one of the most ignored seasons, which is a shame, since winter can be a beautiful time outdoors. It's also the easiest for spotting design and planting problems—which makes it a good time to look at the underlying structure of the paradise you are creating.

Most garden designers, especially the British, talk about garden "bones." As I said earlier, bones are the structural elements that give your landscape substance. They can be manmade structures like walls or patios, or they can be trees and shrubs. In winter, all your garden's bones are revealed, and you can see the naked truth of your yard and garden design. (Is your garden emperor wearing no clothes?)

Here are some tips for improving the overall design of your yard throughout the year, especially in winter.

Check for exposure. One of the best things about gardens is that they can hide unsightly things. Are there eyesores in and around your yard that could be concealed by a well-placed bush, rock, or tree?

Check for privacy. If privacy is important to you (and it is to me since I live downtown), now is the best time to check for open areas that may need more shielding. When I designed my yard, I started with privacy first.

Yuccas make handsome specimen plants. They're striking even in winter since they hold their form all year.

This lovely hedge hides both a busy hardware store parking lot and piles of bags of mulch, compost, and road salt.

for **Winter**

Planting the perimeter with arborvitae and other shrubs and trees is like priming a canvas before you paint. Think of it as the backdrop to the scene you want to create.

I never used to like arborvitae screens until I figured out why they looked so ugly to me. Many people tend to trim and shear arborvitae so they end up looking like little green soldiers with flat-topped heads. (In fact, I've had to stop landscapers from trying to do this in my own yard.) But when left to grow naturally, arborvitae take on a very elegant shape with very fine needle structure, almost like the Mediterranean cypress. The only time I trim mine is when a branch weakens from snow or ice.

Check for a mix of textures. An all-evergreen planting is boring. And an all-deciduous planting looks scraggly in the winter. Do you have a nice harmonious mix of textures? Even among evergreens, you can get a pleasing mix of textures, such as trees with soft, long needles (white pine), short, sharp needles (Douglas fir), and flat needles (arborvitae). Among deciduous trees, textures vary from silky-barked sprawling trees (beeches) to gnarly and twisted rough trees (sycamores, shagbark hickories).

Check for color. When you really look, there as many colors of green in nature as there are varieties of tree. Play with the different shades by alternating them and mixing them up. In general, darker greens recede in the landscape, and lighter greens stand forward. Barks have different colors, too. It's fun to find surprising ways to fit color into your garden. The stems of some shrubby dogwoods are bright red, orange, or yellow—a beautiful sight in the winter landscape. And willow branches can be any color from red to purple to black. There are some beautiful berries in the winter—viburnums and hollies have especially brilliant winter fruit. And don't overlook the wheaten golds, reds, and oranges of ornamental grasses as they spread their feathery plumes in a snowy landscape.

The burgundy foliage of barberry bushes and the cool winter silver of lavender make for a surprising and lovely color and texture combination.

Trees and Shrubs for Winter Interest

You'll enjoy your winter landscape even more if you plant a few of these choice trees and shrubs.

Trees and Shrubs with Ornamental Berries

If more than one fruit color is listed, choose a variety with the color you like best.

Crabapples (*Malus* spp.)—red, yellow, and orange fruits

American cranberrybush (*Viburnum trilobum*)—red berries

Hawthorns (*Crataegus* spp.)—red berries

Heavenly bamboo (*Nandina domestica*)—red berries

American holly (*Ilex opaca*)—red or yellow berries

English holly (*I. aquifolium*)—red or yellow berries

Winterberry holly (*I. verticillata*)—red, yellow, or orange berries

Scarlet firethorn (*Pyracantha coccinea*)—orange or yellow berries

Mountain ashes (*Sorbus* spp.)—scarlet or orange berries

Cranberrybush viburnum (*V. opulus*)—red berries

Trees and Shrubs with Ornamental Bark

'Heritage' river birch (*Betula nigra* 'Heritage')

Red osier dogwood (*Cornus sericea*)

Tatarian dogwood (*C. alba*)

Lacebark elm (*Ulmus parvifolia*)

Shagbark hickory (*Carya ovata*)

Paperbark maple (*Acer griseum*)

Crape myrtle (*Lagerstroemia indica*)

Lacebark pine (*Pinus bungeana*)

Stewartias (*Stewartia* spp.)

Sycamores, plane trees (*Platanus* spp.)

Weeping willows (*Salix* spp.)

Sycamore

Check for safety. Are all your walkways easy to shovel? Do you have railings where you need them? The last thing anybody needs in winter is a broken bone or a bad bruise. Be safe, not sore.

Environmental Tip Do not use salt to de-ice your walkways. Salt causes groundwater pollution, corrosion, and plant stunting and disease. Also avoid the chemical de-icers. All that stuff ends up in your soil. For safety for you and your soil, use sand or fine gravel instead.

Check for interest. Does your yard look exciting or boring? Often statues and fountains can really save a winter scene from looking bleak. I am not a fan of over-ornamenting a garden with statues and gadgets, but done with restraint, it can make your winter landscape glow. Beautifully structured trees, especially weeping trees, really show off during the winter, too.

Check for resting spots. Even in winter, there should be a place to sit, rest, and reflect. Why stay indoors? Have at least one bench or chair that can withstand the winter (stone, sustainably harvested teak or cedar, and wrought iron are good choices). I find it is handy to have a nice place to sit while I am putting on or taking off my cross-country skis, or more likely, while I am waiting for my husband to come home with a key when I've locked myself out.

Once you have answered these questions and thought about all these design issues, take some time to sketch your ideas and develop your plan. A well-thought-out plan will save you future anguish and will also create the ideal space for your very own beautiful and delicious organic garden.

Once there was a statue on this pedestal in my grandmother's garden. No one knows where it went. The **emptiness** is both **beautiful** and **haunting** to me.

Tips, Tools &

Techniques

You could spend days, weeks, months, or years planning the design of your yard, and it still might never be finished. In fact, a good garden is never finished—because then there's nothing left to do, and that's no fun! Each season has its unique rituals, traditions, and time-tested techniques.

The winter season is the time to order seeds and plants, start seedlings, and rest up for the much-anticipated warmer seasons of activity. But no ritual is probably more symbolic or more welcome in the dark days of winter than ordering from mail-order seed and plant catalogs.

Ordering Seeds

Is it possible that you don't get seed catalogs in the mail? Oh dear! Subscribe to a gardening magazine or two, and you'll never have that problem again. You can also fill out order cards in magazines to send away for them.

Or are you one who buys your seeds in person at the local nursery or garden center? That's perfectly fine. The drawback is that you may find selections limited to only the most popular varieties (that are most likely nonorganic, treated, and hybrid as well).

Catalogs, of course, are also great places to go for buying trees, shrubs, flowers, herbs, and all sorts of gadgets for the garden. You could go on planning, dreaming, and designing for a few years or so, but eventually you have to make the commitment to placing that catalog order.

Seeds come in all shapes and sizes.

Unless, that is, you plan on buying everything from your local nursery, which can sometimes be preferable. Each has its pros and cons. Usually a mixture of both works best.

For seeds, the pros and cons are fairly simple. Catalogs offer a wider selection, competitive pricing, fresh seeds, and advance buying. Catalogs are especially good if you are looking for natural, untreated, organic, and heirloom seeds and plants.

Garden centers offer local favorites and impulse buys, and they are especially great once spring comes and you forget to buy something before you run out. I always end up buying from both catalogs and local stores. I also end up with far too many seeds.

Yes, but Which Seeds Should I Order?

If you have never had a vegetable garden before or have never planted seeds, it may seem like a daunting task to sit before the multitude of varieties and choices and commit to any one of them. I know it still overwhelms me every year. But that's half the fun of gardening. I mean, most seed packets are really inexpensive, so there is no big risk if something doesn't work out too well—but there is a *big* flavor payoff if it does.

Go back to your list of favorite vegetables, herbs, fruits, and flowers (and if you didn't make your list before, make it now). There are many things that are relatively easy to grow that taste 1,000 times better than store-bought: Tomatoes, lettuces, peas, peppers, string beans, potatoes, squash, basil, thyme, nasturtiums, and sunflowers are just a start.

There are also things that are not that easy to grow and don't taste too much different from store-bought that also seem like more work than they are worth. Lima beans, for example. Which doesn't mean you shouldn't grow them, but they can be frustrating if you are just starting out.

As I mentioned above, I like to plot out my vegetable garden on a tablet as I am ordering the seeds so that I can fit everything in. I also have my basic plan once things arrive.

So, settle in, go through those catalogs, and make some choices.

Freshly arrived catalog-ordered plants take a while to recover from their journey.

Tips for Seed- and Plant-Buying Success

Here's what I've learned about ordering from catalogs and buying from nurseries and garden centers. Avoid my mistakes and profit from my experiences—you'll enjoy buying plants and seeds a lot more.

Best Catalog Buying Tips

- **I finally found a solution to my biggest pet peeve about catalog ordering.** It turned out to be one of my best planning tools as well. Here's the peeve: The catalog has gorgeous pictures and vivid descriptions, including where the plant grows best, its common and Latin names, and its eventual size. But when the plants arrive, they are little wads of roots wrapped in plastic wrap with just the Latin name on them (usually). Here's what I do: After I have finished ordering, I cut out the pictures and descriptions of what I have ordered. Then I get a sketchbook and assign pages to the general garden areas that I want to work on. I keep it extremely simple and keep each page limited to a small area. Then I tape or glue the pictures and descriptions to the general area where I want to plant them. That way, not only can I figure out which balls of roots are which, but I can also remember where I wanted to plant them. My system also lets me fiddle around with color and plant combinations on paper, where I can see them.

- **Order fruits and other potentially finicky trees and plants from catalogs that are based near your region.** If a catalog is based in the Pacific Northwest, the South, or the Northeast, plants are most likely raised in those regions and will more likely thrive if planted in those regions. Not all catalogs clearly state if the variety is transferable to other regions of the country. In addition to the importance of plant hardiness zones in discovering what can grow in your region, there are other issues, such as rainfall, altitude, and soil type, that can make a big difference in how things grow for you.

- **Don't buy too many of one plant at first.** Try them out and see if they do well. You can always order more later.

- **If you are ordering seeds, plot out your garden and where you are going to plant them as you are ordering.** This is especially important for vegetable gardens. That way you don't end up with too many kinds of seeds and not enough room to plant. You can also work out companion- and succession-planting schemes in advance. (See the "Spring" section for information on companion planting and the "Summer" section for information on succession planting.)

Best Nursery Buying Tips

- **Visit nurseries throughout the year, not just in spring or early summer**. They often carry different stock at different times of the year. New shipments also arrive periodically. I enjoy going every month or so because I can see what blooms in my area throughout the season. For example, things that look like scrawny pathetic twigs in the nursery in the springtime can turn out to be the most beautiful summer or fall plants.

- **Visiting nurseries off-season can provide you with great bargains.** I just bought three trees this spring (before the spring shipment arrived) for the price of one of the same trees I bought last fall. Sure, there is a risk that they won't grow as well as the freshly shipped trees. But I feel as if I rescued poor orphans, and with a little love, care, and compost, I can nurse them back to health.

- **Develop relationships with one or two good nursery owners in your area for two reasons.** Typically, the owners know the most and can answer your questions better than the regular staff. More important, you can often order things through your local nursery that they don't usually have in stock. For instance, if you are looking for a specific tree or plant but can't find it in a catalog or in stock at a nursery, they can often find it for you.

Before You Start

Here are a few general things to think about before ordering and planning your spring planting:

Be careful not to overorder things you haven't tried yet. If you see an exotic plant or seeds that you want to try, buy one or two plants or packets, try them out, and see if they grow well in your garden. Then next year you can go all the way.

Be careful not to overbuy seeds. One packet can go a surprisingly long way. Buy too much, and you will end up with packets and packets of half-used seeds that will lose their fertility if not stored correctly. If you do buy too many, give the extras to friends or local community gardens. If you run out, you can usually run to your local seed store to buy extras.

Focus on growing vegetables and fruits that are difficult to buy, appeal to you intensely, or taste better when they are homegrown (tomatoes!). You can spend a lot of money and time growing some things that are available cheaply and easily from local markets. But there's a world of unique varieties that even gourmet stores don't carry.

Ordering from Catalogs Versus Buying from Local Nurseries: The Truth and Nothing But

Catalog or nursery buying for plants and trees, however, is not so simple. I have compiled this list of pros and cons after years of mistakes, successes, and disappointments.

Catalogs

Catalogs are best for ordering: seeds, unusual fruits, unusual varieties of perennials and herbs, roses, bulbs, and small or unusual trees.

Pros	Cons
Great pictures and descriptions	Often misleading pictures and descriptions
Many more varieties than your local nursery	Plants and trees arrive much smaller than ones from your local nursery
Can be less expensive than nurseries	Can be more expensive than nurseries
Orders arrive on your doorstep!	Orders can arrive while you are away
Return or replacement policies are usually very good	Success rate is highly variable

Nurseries

Nurseries are best for ordering: your basic annuals, vegetable transplants, herbs, common trees, shrubs, and perennials.

Pros	Cons
Can choose the specific plant specimen	Often limited varieties to purchase
Larger sizes available	Have to pay delivery fee or take it home yourself and get your car dirty
Can see exactly what you are getting	Inconsistent labeling of plant traits (in fact, some are nonexistent)
Higher success rate of planting	Not organic (unless specified)
Easy to impulse-shop	Have to wait till spring!

The Different Types of Seeds and What They Mean

Sometimes all the terms used in gardening can make you feel as if you need a science degree. Seed terms are one area where I often get confused. So both for my benefit and yours, I've put together this handy little glossary so you no longer have to feel stupid when reading or talking about seeds.

Heirloom seeds and plants: seeds or plants that are old or historic varieties. Heirloom seeds from open-pollinated varieties are often saved by individuals and passed down from generation to generation and neighbor to neighbor.

Hybrid: a plant or seed obtained by cross-fertilizing two different genetically uniform plant varieties. If you collect seeds from hybrid plants, they will not produce the same plant the next year. Hybrid seeds are often patented and owned by seed companies.

Open-pollinated: varieties that grow "true to type" when reproduced by seed (which means if you plant it next year, you'll be likely to get the same as this year).

Treated seeds: seeds that have a fungicide or preservative applied to them to facilitate germination. You can tell when seeds are treated because they are dipped in coloring. That's why you see pink pea seeds or purple corn seeds.

Untreated seeds: seeds that have no fungicide or preservatives applied to them.

Genetically engineered or altered seeds: seeds that have had their genetic makeup changed in order to incorporate pest- or disease-resistant properties. Primarily used by farmers and sold by large chemical companies, the effects of these seeds are largely untested, unproven, and controversial. Concerns exist over potential allergic reactions to the food that is harvested (which currently does not have to be labeled), the possibility of uncontrolled mutation, and actual effectiveness. For instance, recent studies have found that insects develop resistance to genetically altered plants at a much higher rate than scientists had thought possible.

Got your seeds and catalog facts all together now? Ladies and gentlemen, start your ordering.

Starting Seeds

To start or not to start; that is the question. Especially for newer gardeners who have never done it before, seed starting at home can seem an intimidating task. But the longer you garden, the more you are going to want to do it. You can only buy your plants for so long until you start yearning for tomatoes other than 'Big Boy'. Before you know it, you will covet the unusual flowers and herbs that can't be found at the local nursery. Most nurseries and garden centers have a limited selection. Most also use chemicals to make their plants look so lush.

Sooner or later, you're going to want to give seed starting a go. The truth is it's not hard at all. And though you may not end up with perfect seedlings the first time and every time, the reward is worth the effort. Here are the simple tools that you'll need.

- Pot maker

- Flat trays to hold the pots in

- Plant growth lights or good southern-exposure window light

- Organic potting mixture (sterile soil, vermiculite, and compost)

Environmental Tip Don't use peat moss or peat pots. Peat is harvested from bogs in Canada, Scotland, England, and Ireland. Harvesting peat destroys fragile ecosystems. Since World War II, 98 percent of England's lowland-raised bogs have been dug up for garden peat. Make your own pots with newspapers and a pot maker, or reuse containers like plastic, cans, or milk cartons. Use sterile organic potting soil mix instead of peat moss. (Check to be sure the potting mix doesn't contain peat moss as well.)

To tell you the truth, last year was my first year starting seeds. It had scared me before (vague memories of seeds planted in school milk cartons that keeled over when they got home from kindergarten). I relied on my husband (brave soul that he is) or friends to start seeds for me. I was also lucky enough to get seeds started at my parents' organic farm and greenhouse. But the stubborn independent in me was determined to try it myself. I mean, how can I write a gardening book without ever having started my own seeds? The shame of it all! So I tried it and was shocked (and relieved) by how easy it was.

First, I made pots from newspaper and a wooden pot maker. (It costs about $5 up front for the pot maker, but then the pots are free forever.) Making the pots is extremely easy, with the worst part getting your fingers dirty with newspaper ink. Children, such as nieces and nephews, make good helpers when it comes to making the pots.

Then I filled the pots with sterile, store-bought organic potting mixture. It's worth it to buy a sterile potting mixture—otherwise you can have problems with pests and diseases, especially fungal diseases. The most common one is "damping-off." That's when perfectly fine looking seedlings decide to keel over and die. Buying sterile potting soil should eliminate that risk. (And most nurseries and hardware stores sell organic soils, thank goodness.) Another trick to avoid damping-off is to keep the soil moist, but don't overwater.

After I'd filled the pots with the soil mix, I stuck one or two seeds in each pot. I set all the pots in the waterproof trays that came with our plant-light shelves. (A good plant-light setup is an extremely handy thing to have, but it's not totally necessary if you've got some good windows facing south.) Ideally, seedlings should have 12 to 14 hours of light a day. We put our grow lights on a timer. We set the pots right up under the light, then gradually increase the distance once they start to grow, keeping the light about 4 inches from the tops of the plants.

The hardest part of my seed-starting venture was fighting for space on the shelves with my husband, who starts the tomatoes, peppers, and other miscellaneous vegetables.

These wooden pot makers can be found in many gardening catalogs and stores.

A week or two before planting your seedlings outdoors, start bringing the trays outside during the day to "harden off." That lets them adjust to the strong outside light and temperatures. If you live in a very sunny spot, you will want to shade them at first. For, as some African friends told Permaculturist Bill Mollison, "You wouldn't leave your babies out in the sun, would you?" Africans usually build twig and leaf arbors to cover their baby plants, then remove them after they turn into strong plants. If you have a cold frame, you can keep the transplants in there at night for awhile. But you don't need to.

Once your seedlings have been hardened off, there's just one thing left to do: Plant them, newspaper pots and all.

Seed-Starting Tips and Wisdom

I've learned a lot from my seed-starting experiences—and from talking to lots of experienced seed starters, including my husband! Here's an accumulation of tips and wisdom to help make your seed-starting adventures successful.

- Some seeds do much better than store-bought plants. I grew stock (a very fragrant and beautiful English annual flower) from seed and then bought some stock at a nursery. The nursery stock took off quickly in the spring but then got all gangly and ugly. The stock I planted from seed got a later start, but it looked absolutely gorgeous up until the hardest of the hard frosts struck.

- Perennials planted from seed will not bloom the first year, but they will bloom the second year. If planting from seed, plant indoors in early February and March, or direct-seed in May.

- Don't let your plants get too close to the lights or they will burn and get white spots on the leaves.

- Tomatoes need to be *brushed*. I know this sounds strange, but studies have found that physically brushing tomato seedlings (with anything from a paint brush or piece of paper to your hands) will strengthen the stem of the plant and make it less "leggy."

- If you find your plants getting leggy, or too tall without being strong enough, they need more light and more air circulation.

- When to start what seeds depends on what region you live in. Check the back of the seed package for directions according to your plant hardiness zone or area.

- Don't plant your seeds too early. If plants are too big when you plant them outside, many will suffer shock and take a longer time to get established.

A classic book on starting seeds is *The New Seed-Starters Handbook* by Nancy Bubel. (See "Recommended Reading" on page 358.)

Interview with Bob Hofstetter

**Bob
KNOWS
gardening**

Bob Hofstetter knows how to garden. He's been gardening for the Rodale Organic Farm and for himself since 1970. He's a third-generation farmer, and his grandfather was an organic farmer and vegetable grower.

Bob was hired by my grandfather J. I. Rodale the year before J. I. died. He had subscribed to *Organic Gardening* magazine through the Publishers Clearinghouse. (You know, buy a magazine and you *may* win a million dollars.) The first issue he received had a job posted for head gardener. Since he had just been laid off from his factory job, and the Rodale farm was only a few miles away, he applied and got the job.

Bob was the one who taught me how to weed (always get the root out). Since then he's taught countless others. He also spent many years as an editor for *The New Farm* magazine, which taught farmers how to farm organically and regeneratively.

I sat down with Bob this winter—one of the few times when things are slow on the farm—to ask him some questions about starting seeds, gardening, and his history with the Organic Method. Here are his hard-earned words of wisdom.

You have now been associated with organic gardening and the farm for 27 years. What's changed?

Acceptance in the community. Today, there is more science involved. Fun science.

There is a lot more interest than there was in the 1970s (back then it was more a cult thing). People ask more questions and ask more relevant questions.

Your grandfather J. I. wanted to see organic farming as part of mainstream agriculture. He wanted to see this as a part of society. He wanted to see farmers making a good living, but not just for the farmer—it wasn't a personal, private thing; it was a whole life issue, with everything working in one big circle. And it was a beautiful circle, and it still is.

It's ironic that organic gardening became a hippie cult thing, since my grandfather was not a hippie at all. He was really more of a New York intellectual. Did you ever see him in anything other than a gray suit, white shirt, and tie?

No.

Of all the gardening trends and trials that you have seen, what still works and what works best?

Start with strong, reliable seeds.

Use crop rotation, which suppresses disease. (Don't put the same family of plant in the same place year after year.)

Use compost. Compost (with a little animal manure) is the best thing there is because it's slow-release, and it's in the soil structure, so the plants will only take what they need. And you don't need a fancy recipe—anybody can make compost!

What are some of your best tips and secrets for the home gardener?

Start small: Restrain yourself. Don't plant more than you need or can use.

Don't pick beans when they are wet (they get all 'rusty' and brown).

The hardest thing for me to do, but you need to do it, is thin things out.

The home gardener doesn't really need to worry about phosphates and potassium. Compost should take care of it.

If you are saving seeds, you also might be saving diseases. Only save the seeds from healthy, vigorous plants.

On lawn care: People come out to the farm and they say "Boy, you got a lot of dandelion and sorrel." And I say "Hey, it's green. I mow it, it grows, it's green!"

Yellow leaves indicate a lack of nitrogen. Add more compost or use a nitrogen-fixing green manure.

Speaking of green manures, could you please demystify them for me?

It depends on what you need and what you want to do. If you need more nitrogen, use clovers, annual sweet clovers (Huban), crimson clover. If you have a lot of nitrogen and you just want to suppress weeds, plant annual ryegrass. Plant the green manures in the late summer, and then turn them under, or plant right through them in the spring.

If you could have only one gardening tool, what would it be?

A Warren hoe or cultivator hoe. You can pull and chop weeds, make a furrow, cover seeds, till, use it as a trowel, and use it to kill groundhogs.

J. I. Rodale gave this knife to Bob almost 30 years ago. He keeps it in his back pocket and uses it every day.

Enjoying the

Enjoying winter, more than any other season, is a state of mind. It's easy to complain about the cold, damp, icy misery. There are so many ways, however, that you can turn that misery into a sweet, quiet joy. Here are some of my favorites.

- Sit in a rocking chair by a window, fix yourself a cup of herb tea, and watch the snow fall, the trees shiver, and the winter birds and animals at your feeders. I'm always amazed at how much activity happens out there in the cold. And I don't even live in the country. Write in a journal, write letters to friends, or just dream.

- As early as February, you can cut branches from forsythia to bring indoors to force them to flower. Just plunk them in a vase of water and wait. Other spring-flowering bushes such as pussy willows also work. Try them out.

- Make something warm and tasty with those tomatoes you canned last year. Chili, spaghetti, vegetable soup. Mmmm! Sit down at the table, and stay there for a long time. Talk.

- Cut out pictures from the gardening catalogs to do crafts—decoupage furniture, or make greeting cards and collages. This is especially fun to do with kids. My daughter became obsessed with cutting out roses, and she ended up decoupaging one of her electric guitars with them—it's gorgeous! Do this *after* you have ordered your plants and seeds, of course.

- Make a bouquet of winter greens and twigs. In fact, plant things in your yard specifically for your holiday decorating needs: evergreen boughs, pinecones, and twigs with berries.

- Take a walking tour of your yard, and look at it with winter eyes. Are there any ways you can make it more interesting in the winter? Are there places where you can create sheltered areas? Do you need more pines on the north side of your house to prevent drafts?

- Go antiquing for the perfect old garden sculpture or furniture. I also like to collect really old gardening books (ones written back before chemicals were used).

- Subscribe to gardening magazines or browse through garden picture books to get ideas for your garden. Look for European (especially British) gardening magazines at your local library, bookstore, or newsstand.

Season

Should You Feed the Birds?

Ideally, we shouldn't have to provide seeds, houses, and play centers for birds—our landscapes should provide all that naturally. But it's both fun and important to fill in any gaps with feeders, nest boxes, birdbaths, and so on. This is especially true in winter, when the going can be tough on our fine feathered friends. These are some of the most important elements for attracting birds to your yard.

- Are there places for the birds to hide from predators? Prickly bushes work well.

- Are there places for them to nest? Trees, shrubs, hedges, vines, eaves, and brambles work really well—especially if you don't fuss around with them too much by pruning and otherwise disturbing the bird peace.

- Is there protection from the elements? Evergreen shrubs and trees planted near walls or in protected, undisturbed areas can be veritable palaces for birds during inclement weather.

- Is there food and water? You should only need to provide food in the winter and early spring—the rest of the year, let your landscape provide flower nectar, seeds, fruits, berries, and plants that attract insects. (Remember, birds can be the most powerful "insecticides" around.) But you should make sure your birds have clean, fresh water all year.

With a few thoughtfully placed trees, shrubs, vines, and other plants, you should be able to enjoy a varied and lively bird entertainment show year-round. And you shouldn't have to feed them except in the coldest, darkest days of fall, through the winter, and until the bugs are back in spring.

This is the greenhouse that my grandfather built.

- Start seeds (be sure to try at least one unusual plant just for fun . . . and to impress your friends and neighbors).

- Feed the birds.

- Find a local greenhouse that is in operation for the winter, and breathe in the smell of soil and growing plants.

- Where to go for inspiration: garden shows, botanical gardens, arboretums, friends' gardens, florists, and nurseries.

- Plan a trip somewhere warm, somewhere foreign, and somewhere beautiful to get new ideas for your garden. Even if you can't afford to go this year or don't have the time to get away, research the place as if you were going. Planning a trip is a fun way to learn about different cultures, climates, and cuisines.

- Dream of spring!

And I wait for the wind to blow away madness

I wait for the snow to bury my grief

I wait for its blanket to wrap 'round my sadness

Its quiet to bring me relief.

—Lui Collins
"Awaiting the Snow"

My favorite first sign of spring is snowdrops.

Food for

A **key** part of enjoying any season, any day (or for some of the more hungry of us, any hour), is food . . . especially fresh, organic, delicious food. One of the absolute key motivations for gardening is to savor the taste of freshly picked fruits, vegetables, and herbs, either eaten right from the vine on the same day they've been picked or preserved to be appreciated during the dark months of winter, like bottles of sunshine. Mmmmm, I can feel the warm glow just thinking about it! In our house, winter is not entered into without frozen pesto and roasted peppers, bottled tomato sauces, and other treats from the garden.

Winter is the most difficult month for eating fresh foods if you live in a cold climate. Traditionally, people always ate more starches and preserved meats in winter. The food that always inspires the most warm winter thoughts in my family is Nana's kugel. My grandmother, Anna Rodale, came from a family of coal-mining Lithuanian immigrants. She had a hard life before she met my grandfather. Her parents were both dead by the time she was eight.

Nana (as we call her) left school after fifth grade and worked in factories until she moved to New York City at age 14 with one of her cousins. There she met my grandfather at one of those "dime-a-dance" halls. Given her background, it's amazing that she went on to become a very cultured and creative painter and patron of the arts. But she never lost her remembrance of where she came from and tolerance for hard work. For us growing up, kugel represented that tie to her past.

The Joy of Kugel

What is kugel? Traditionally, it's a sort of casserole or pudding dish made of noodles or potatoes in an egg custard. It can be savory or sweet, made with vegetables or fruit.

In our family, kugel was a little different. Everyone in the family agrees that the way Nana made it, it consisted of potatoes, carrots, onions, celery, a turnip, eggs, salt, and chicken fat, all grated extremely fine and then baked in a fairly thin layer until it got crispy and golden.

OK, so I don't remember watching Nana make it (I was out playing with the cats). But I do remember the taste of the warm, salty, fatty, thin, and crispy kugel satiating a hungry little tummy. This recipe is my attempt to re-create my *memory* of kugel, based on my sister Heidi's description of Nana's methods and ingredients—with no chicken fat, since I don't have a yard full of chickens to render (yet).

Winter

"Quality Time"
in the Kitchen

Until I met my husband, my image of the women I knew cooking was seeing them stand at the sink, backs turned, scrubbing, peeling, and chopping. No wonder the women of my generation turned to food processors to shorten the "back-time" (both back to the family and strain on the back from standing).

Then I went to meet my husband, Lou's, family, and I saw what I thought was the oddest thing. His father would sit at the kitchen table, right in the middle of the action, leisurely peeling potatoes, carrots, and whatever else needed to be done. I must say, for some reason sitting down to do chores didn't seem appropriate when I first saw it, perhaps because I had never seen anyone else do it.

But then, when I was pregnant and was tired and had backaches, I tried it. Here's what happened. All the kids in the house—my daughter and two nephews—flocked to the table to join me (they were doing homework, drawing, and just chatting). Suddenly, I was the center of the action, and we were all talking and laughing. I was almost sad when I had finished the peeling. Later, when we ate the mashed potatoes, I could feel the joy of the peeling experience infused in the food . . . or maybe that was just the gravy.

So, don't shy away from peeling and grating for this—or any other—recipe. Use the time to spend with your family, listen to music, meditate, or simply dream.

Nana's Kugel Recipe

Kugel goes exceedingly well with a roast chicken and salad.

5 medium to large potatoes
1 medium carrot
1 small to medium onion
1 stalk celery
1 turnip (optional—I confess I have a thing against turnips)
¼ cup olive oil
1 tablespoon Knorr condensed liquid chicken broth
2 eggs, beaten
¼ teaspoon kosher salt

1. Peel potatoes (soak in cold water while peeling everything else), carrot, and onion. Clean celery.

2. Dry and grate everything finely (sitting at the kitchen table). Combine grated vegetables. The final grated mixture should be really wet and mushy. The color will seem rather orange because of the carrots, but that will change during cooking. Total grating time if done completely by hand is about 20 minutes.

3. Mix olive oil with the broth and stir. Put 2 tablespoons on the bottom of a Pyrex pie pan or small square baking dish.

4. Put all but 2 tablespoons of the olive oil and condensed broth mixture in with the grated vegetables, add the eggs, and mix it all together. Add the kosher salt.

5. Spread the mixture thinly (no more than 2 inches deep) in the baking dish. Put the last of the oil on the top and spread it around.

6. Bake at 400°F until brown and crispy (approximately 1 hour).

Yield: 4 servings (with a few pieces left to reheat for breakfast)

Nana in the **garden** with her **poodle**

My sister Heidi learned to make kugel at Nana's side. When she makes it, she uses the larger grater setting and uses more eggs (for this size recipe, she might use up to six eggs). I've found that when you use the smaller grater setting, you don't need as many eggs to hold it together.

Recently, I asked Heidi a few questions about her memories.

Did Nana ever put anything else in it?

No, but I tried it once with red beets. Don't do that.

Did Nana ever use butter?

No butter, no milk, no cheese. (Nana was lactose-intolerant.) Just chicken fat and eggs. I use corn oil now.

My Philosophy on Food

Perhaps because I grew up eating farm-fresh foods and listening to my father's stories of travel, philosophy, and business at the dinner table every night, I associate good food with love, history, intellectual stimulation, and joy.

When I was growing up, people would be shocked to find out my family was not vegetarian. In fact, many people are still shocked. I have to put up with comments like "Whew, I thought you were going to make me eat raw carrots and tofu for dinner" when I had just served a nice dinner to new friends. Growing up in a family and business that deal with both health and organic gardening can put a lot of pressure on a person to be "perfect." Meanwhile, the definition of perfect is constantly changing: oat bran, fat and fake fat, "lite" foods and health foods. Even for people like me who are perpetually overinformed, it is nearly impossible to know what is the right thing to do.

That's why, over the years, I have developed my own theory of food. Some people might call it my own rationalization for eating anything I want, and I have no idea whether it will make me live any longer, or any better. But I have met vegetarians who exercise and meditate and do everything "right" but are totally unhealthy and totally cranky. Of course, I have also met vegetarians who exercise and meditate and do everything "right" and are the picture of health and well-being.

On the other hand, I have met totally healthy and vital people who, in their 80s and 90s, are thriving and fit (even with potbellies) and live on red meat, whole-fat milks,

cheeses, and alcohol. John Seymour, author of *The Complete Book of Self-Sufficiency,* for instance, is 85 and is fitter than I am (he can walk farther, climb a fence faster, and do crazier things—which are better kept between himself and the authorities in County Cork). He eats meat fat and drippings on his toast every morning, drinks homemade beer and wine daily, chugs full-fat milk, eats his strawberries with cream and sugar, and eats cheeses fresh from Polly the cow (whom he milks twice a day).

Low-fat living never seemed to have made it to New Ross, Ireland, and somehow I suspect they are much better off because of it. But everything they eat is organic, and they work hard every day just living. (As I mentioned before, though, the joy of their life is palpable. Lunches linger for hours. Naps are expected. And singing, accompanied by much laughter, often occurs after dinner.)

As in the rest of life, there are no guarantees of anything and certainly no magic formula. My father, for instance, did everything "right" but then died too soon in a car crash that wasn't his fault. So the bottom line seems to be: Live each day as well as you can, and enjoy life while you are here. And eat foods that are fresh, organic, and alive to make each day the best it can be.

Which leads me to my five-point theory of food:

1. **Eat food that's as fresh as possible (while the life is still in it).** Scientifically, this is important because the vitamins and nutrients in the food are more potent the fresher the food is. Spiritually, I can't help but feel as if I am gathering life strength and vitality from the aliveness of fresh food. Try it for a week or two and you'll see what I mean.

2. **Eat as organically as possible.** Scientifically, there may still be no conclusive proof that chemicals are *not* harmful to human health, but they are definitely harmful for the environment. Spiritually, you can eat organic foods knowing that you are not harming the earth, other people, or your children. When I can find them, I buy hormone- and chemical-free butters, milk, meats, and cheeses. Then I don't worry about the fat as much. I end up shopping mostly at our local farmers' market, where a few stands sell hormone-free products. I also make a monthly trip to a high-end organic supermarket chain about 45 minutes away, and I buy food through the mail. Walnut Acres is, of course, the classic source for mail-order organic foods.

3. **Eat food as unprocessed and close to its original form as possible.** The closer it is to its original form, the more nutrients, the more life, and the more fiber will be in the food. That doesn't mean I only eat brown rice and raw vegetables. But it means that I'll make more foods from scratch rather than relying on frozen, processed foods. And I'll balance the refined with the raw, always making sure that I'm getting some pure foods daily. For instance, I always put sliced raw fruit on the table at dinner. I think that the fact that it is cut up (grapefruit slices, melon balls, and so on) makes you feel as if you have to eat it or it will go to waste (as opposed to a bowl of apples). And it feels rather cleansing. Or if I am too lazy to make a salad, I will cut up a fresh red pepper or cucumber for everyone to munch on during dinner. There are never any leftovers of the vegetables or the fruit.

4. **Eat all things in moderation.** I don't think any one food has the secret to long life or health embedded in it. And I have never seen a benefit to food fanaticism of any sort, whether it's junk food faddism or health food fascism. Balance, moderation, and variety are key. If you think of your body as an ecosystem, one of the key signs of any healthy ecosystem is diversity of species. Of course, if I would ever be accused of fanaticism, it would be toward organic living. But eating organically doesn't cut back too much on diversity. And I get plenty of chemicals in my system just by walking down Main Street.

5. **Indulge yourself occasionally.** I also get my share of junk food. I have a weakness for chips and chocolate. And any modern lifestyle in America requires the occasional stop at a fast-food establishment (or diner), which I am not above actually enjoying. But if you have a strong base of healthy living and good food, a few indulgences won't hurt you. No one is perfect, nor should they try to be. It's too boring!

Calendar

Here's a winter checklist of
garden chores, activities,
observations, and just plain
fun things to do in winter.

December

Planting	Nothing to plant but the seeds of contentment and celebration!		

Harvesting	Cut pine boughs, other greens, berries, and branches, and pick up pinecones for holiday decorations.	

Pruning		Nothing to prune but damaged branches from storms.

Doing	Make sure your yard equipment (such as hoses), tools, and weather-sensitive pots and furniture are put away.	Feed the birds.	Order garden-related gifts.

Preparing	Review garden records.	Prepare your New Year's resolutions.

January

Planting	If you live in a warm-season area, start seeds of cold-season vegetables, like cabbage and broccoli, and perennials.	In warm-season areas, plant pansies and other spring annuals.	
Harvesting	When there is not too much snow on the ground (if any), walk around your yard and pick up twigs and dead branches for kindling.	Keep a basket or box handy for storage.	
Pruning			Nothing to prune but damaged branches from storms.
Doing	Inventory your old seeds before you order new ones.	Feed the birds.	Check perennials for frost-heaving; cover with more mulch if needed.
Preparing			Check your seed-starting supplies and make notes if you need potting soil, pots, flats, or plant growth lights.

Renew memberships in garden organizations.

Order seeds, perennials, herbs, trees, shrubs, and other plants from catalogs.

February

Planting	Set up your equipment to start seeds. Buy potting soil, make your pots, check your plant growth lights for burned-out bulbs.		
Harvesting	In warm climates, harvest peas, lettuce, and other salad crops.	If you've forced endive indoors, harvest heads as needed.	
Pruning	If you can find them, prune back raspberries.		Repot and fix up your indoor plants.
Doing	On the first nice day that you have time, get out and clean up winter debris. But don't be too fastidious. Dead perennials, leaves, and other plant matter make for excellent bird nest building materials and often shelter beneficial insect babies.	Feed the birds.	Check to see if the groundhogs see their shadows.
Preparing	Prepare for spring! 	Clean out your gardening stuff. Inventory your tools, equipment, pots, and so on.	Repair broken tools, sharpen blades, and replace things you can't fix.

pring

Ahhh, spring. No other season is as welcome.

First come the snowdrops, then the crocuses,

daffodils, hyacinths, and then tulips. Soon the flowering trees and forsythia are in full bloom. Magnolias and lilacs perfume the air. The fruit trees offer their flowers to the bees for pollination and the conceiving of fruit. The grass starts to grow green and lush, drunk on abundant spring rains.

It is as if Nature is trying to convince you that winter is really over. Finally, finally, when the air is warm, the soil is warm, the rain is warm, the grass starts to grow and glow; then and only then do you truly believe that winter is over and the regeneration of the land has begun.

Breathe a sigh of relief. Get out your shorts. Pull some weeds while they are still tender. Watch the insects return. Stand amidst the windy, fragrant petals when they fall free of the trees and swirl like soft, warm snow. Yes, spring is here.

Designing

Siberian iris and peonies

Your Garden

We must turn this land from the grimy back-yard of a workshop into a garden.

—William Morris, founder of the Arts and Crafts Movement

Spring is the time to implement your design—the time to take your dreams and plans and bring them to life. Like most dreams coming to life, the reality is often more complex than you thought it would be. Making a yard into a garden requires a certain amount of will. (But where else can you exercise your will so freely and beautifully?) There are decisions to be made about materials, timing, cost, priorities, and plants. If you live with other people, their thoughts and concerns also need to be taken into consideration.

You can choose to tumble casually toward beauty or demand it quickly through hiring armies of assistants. You can scavenge all your materials from resources on hand or buy the finest. You can decide to do just one project in your yard, or you can decide to do the whole darn thing. In this section I will share with you what I learned about the different landscaping materials—their cost, their longevity, and their design statements. But it's also good to keep in mind some general principles that will help you keep your design environmentally sound and beautiful.

Leave room for surprises in your design and garden—like these self-sown Johnny jump-ups.

Principles of Environmentally Friendly Design

These eight environmentally friendly design principles will help you landscape right the first time.

Create something that will last.

1. **Think long-term.** In the States, people tend to think 10 to 20 years is long-term. What strikes me when I go to Europe is how things are *really* built and planted for the long term—100 years, a few thousand years. If you are going to spend money and effort to create something, create something that will last. Use strong materials and good workmanship. Thinking long-term will give your design a strength and beauty that will give you satisfaction for years.

2. **Think local.** With building materials, locally made and harvested materials will be less expensive to you (no expensive shipping costs added) and to the environment. Local or native plants will be more likely to thrive in your garden. I am not a strict "nativist" who believes that only flowers, trees, and shrubs native to your specific region should be planted—especially when it comes to flowers. But find out which materials are local and which plants are native before dashing off to buy something from the opposite coast or another country. You may be pleasantly surprised by what you can find literally in your own backyard. In our case, we chose locally quarried stone for our walls and walkways, but then chose one special feature—a Navajo sandstone—that was not local for our patio.

3. **Think low maintenance.** Is there going to be a lot of difficult mowing? A lot of weeding? A lot of edging? Avoid hours of unnecessary work by designing, building, and planting for low maintenance. I've found these keys to a low-maintenance yard and garden.

   - Contain grass in easy-to-mow sections and keep it to a minimum (if you must have grass at all).

This old cannonball in a yard in Ireland has probably been sitting quietly for a few hundred years.

- Edge your beds to prevent grass and weeds from intruding. My favorite edging material is stone, since wood rots and gets slippery, and brick tends to crumble and chip after a while.

- Plant thickly in layers (using trees, bushes, flowers, bulbs, and groundcovers) to minimize weeds and provide environmental diversity.

- Mulch heavily at first until things grow in, then let Nature mulch herself by letting leaves fall where they may.

- *Don't* plant trees and shrubs that need to be constantly pruned.

- Put things in convenient places so you don't waste time looking for them, getting to them, or hauling them. (This goes for tools, compost—even your vegetable garden.)

4. **Think quality.** You can buy ten tacky garden statues, or you can buy one really good one. The choice is yours. I find it extremely hard—but very worthwhile—to resist impulse buys or quick fixes that I know I'll regret later. When you go looking for furniture, statues, fences, and tools, quality materials will add long-lived beauty like nothing else. Garden materials take severe beatings from rain, snow, ice, wind, sun, plants, animals, and birds. Quality does not always mean cost, either. Decorative gravel is cheaper than brick and stone but costs the same as or less than less-desirable materials such as formed concrete or pressure-treated wood. Classic statues can be found at flea markets and auctions. Explore!

5. **Think lifetime value, not property value.** Many people seem to design their landscape and yard thinking that they can't go

Time always goes *f a s t e r* than you think it will.

In Emmaus, my cannonball came by UPS from New York City last year. In 100 years mine may look interesting; meanwhile it's quite cozy hiding behind the hosta.

overboard because they will never get their money back out of it if they sell. Or that if they get too creative or fancy, no one will want to buy their property. I was at a local nursery last spring and I had a cart full of boxwood bushes. A woman looked at them curiously and asked me what they were and whether they were hard to grow. I told her that they were a slow-growing but long-lived and lovely evergreen that was fairly hardy. She admired them but said they wouldn't add to her property value so they wouldn't be worth the money and time. Personally, I think good plants add both spiritually and financially to property values—but it may never be a straight equation. A good landscape makes a house that much more attractive and valuable. It certainly won't devalue your home! Only a yard filled with grotesquely unattractive stuff can do that.

6. **Think natural.** Part of the idea of gardening organically is questioning things—questioning how you do things and where things come from. And then caring about the impact of any of your decisions on the environment and the future. Although plastics do have an important value to society, I avoid using them in my yard and garden. Likewise for treated wood. The processes that create those durable products involve heavy usage of petrochemicals and other nasty things. They also seem to scream "compromise." No plastic border will last as long as a stone one. Treated wood products may last as long as sustainably harvested cedar or teak, but the cost to

The Renninger's Market extravaganzas in Kutztown, Pennsylvania, are a veritable feast of antique garden treasures.

the environment is much greater than just the cost to you. If you must use them, use them sparingly and only where they make the biggest difference. (I confess: I just had a fence built of cedar but had the posts pressure-treated because of both cost and the hope that they will last longer.) If cost is your main concern, read on.

7. **Think net cost, not gross cost.** When making cost-based decisions, do a long-term cost analysis. How many times will you (or anyone) need to replace it? How much maintenance will it require? What is the value of your time in maintaining and replacing—or assembling? What is the impact to the environment? Too many times we do up-front, gross cost comparisons without thinking about the true long-term cost. Often, things that seem too expensive at first end up looking like a better deal over the long term.

8. **Think antique or used.** Many of the things that were made a long time ago seem to be of better quality than things you can get today. Or maybe only the high-quality things survived the wear and tear of daily use. Of course, you can buy things made today of exceptional quality and beauty. But you will pay a small fortune for them. A few trips to antique stores and flea markets can yield amazing garden treasures. From outdoor furniture to statues, tools to garden gates, it's both fun and rewarding to find things that are beautiful, functional, and reasonably priced. Finding good antiques or used things makes me feel like a true recycler.

If you go to Renninger's, you have to stop by and visit the Rodale Institute Experimental Farm in nearby Maxatawny.

How to Negotiate (and Win) Design Arguments
with Your Family . . . or Anyone Else

You may be one of the lucky people who has complete freedom to do whatever you want in the garden.

Some of us are not so lucky (or perhaps we are just lucky in a different way). I've got all kinds of restrictions. My husband would have a backyard baseball/basketball/bocce complex if he could (surrounded by very large vegetables and flags of all the NBA teams). My daughter has excellent design ideas and spends days drawing European-style mansions and gardens. But she also hates to see change in the yard, especially when it involves a bush or tree that's a sentimental favorite. I also have the various zoning and neighbor issues that are part of any neighborhood. Ultimately, however much I would love to do whatever I want, I recognize (reluctantly) that our garden and yard should be a haven for everyone, not just me (and, my husband would like me to add, a personal canvas for my delusions of artistic grandeur).

Anyway, at some point in your lifetime you are probably going to have a garden design argument with someone, and whether or not you love them or hate them, you are going to want to win. Here are my hard-earned tips and techniques for getting your way in the garden. (Warning: Some of these tips may seem blatantly manipulative. They are.)

The Setup

Test the water. At some point, before the issue becomes emotional, casually mention that you have some ideas about changing something. Say stuff like "Gee, I was thinking it would be cool to have a . . ." or "What would you think if we did . . . ?" The more casual you are, the more you will get an honest reaction. Your goal at this point is not to get a "Wow, go ahead, honey, do it" response (although take it if you get it) but to read your opposition's level of support—or resistance.

Get their ideas and input. Casually or formally ask for their ideas. What would they do? How and why? Getting other perspectives can make the final solution much more palatable. Often, as hard as it sometimes is for me to believe, other people have great ideas, too.

Solicit their help in finding solutions. You can find a problem to justify almost anything you want to do in the yard.

The Approach

Do your homework. When you are approaching your opponent, arm yourself with pictures, drawings, facts, and figures. Leave as little to their imagination as possible. You'd be amazed how differently two people can visualize the same thing and how inadequate language can often be in describing design details.

Gather as much logic as you can find.
Justify your ideas by saying that they will serve some very logical and rational purpose. Good, solid purposes are: privacy, safety, lower maintenance, efficiency, and lower costs. And, of course, you can say that it's better for the environment.

Muster support from others. Are there friends, experts, regulations, neighbors, or handy men and women who support your plan? Can you get them to put in a good word for you? Look for articles that support your case, and don't be afraid to drop names: "I read in *Organic Gardening* magazine that . . ."

Gather cost estimates. Have alternatives.

Don't rush decisions. Give everyone time to think and adjust to your plans. This is helpful for everyone because often even you can change your mind or think of things that were forgotten. Leave the plans out on the table for a week or two.

The Attack

Find a nice quiet time when you don't mind if an argument will continue for a day or two. Avoid discussing yard issues on the way to dinner parties or events where you have to get along. Or on holidays. Also avoid discussing them when your partner is tired, hungry, or in a bad mood.

Hold the discussion on site. You could waste precious time arguing about things that aren't even there if you are not at the site. This is especially helpful for people who have a hard time visualizing.

Start out nice and flexible. Withhold the urge to say things like "That is the stupidest idea I have ever heard!" (This is often where I go wrong.)

Lay down the logic, lay out the plan.
Sprinkle your discussion with all the logical reasons why your idea is worth doing.

Put in a few emotional pleas. "I think this idea reminds me so much of what I love about your parents' yard." Or, "I've always dreamed of having one of these in my yard ever since I was a small child." My personal favorite is "I have a *desperate* need for . . ."

Try not to put your kids in the middle, unless the issue revolves specifically around a safety concern or a design change especially for them (such as a swing set or playhouse).

The Score

Best-case scenario: They love it! They say it's the greatest idea and design since Central Park. Unlimited budget is approved for all your dreams and desires.

Realistic scenario: They have lots of changes, things they hate, and reasons (stupid or otherwise) why they don't want it to happen. But you get the go-ahead, and something sort of resembling what you originally wanted gets created. All are pretty happy with the result, and you still have a happy relationship with your family.

Worst possible scenario:
They are right and you are wrong. What do you do then? Here are some options. Sulk, pout, and shed a few pitiful tears. Agree to their changes. Leave the room until you can collect yourself and the other person feels a little guilty, then resume discussions with willingness to make some concessions. Change your mind. Or try, try again.

Building and Design Materials

There are a few basic building materials that you'll turn to again and again as you build and install landscape features like walls, paths, and fences, or choose structures like trellises and benches. Which material is best for you depends on durability, availability, cost, and the look you want. Here's an overview of the different materials and what you should know about them.

Wood

Wood is a wonderful choice for many landscape features, from window boxes and planters to raised beds and fences. But, again, which wood you choose can determine how long your structure lasts. Here's a rundown of your choices.

Redwood. Redwood is the most expensive weather-resistant wood. And it comes from those giant sequoia trees that take hundreds of years to grow. It's also a key reason for the wide-scale clear-cutting of forests in the West. Design-wise it says, "I want the best, but either I don't know or don't care about the consequences." However, if you live in the West, and if you can be certain that it's harvested sustainably, then redwood qualifies as a local choice that is very durable.

Cedar. Cedar is also expensive, but it's very long-lasting. Because it's a faster-growing tree than the sequoia, a stand of cedar can regrow quickly after harvest, so using it is less traumatic to the environment. Cedar is a lightweight wood that is very good for garden fences and trellises. It weathers to a nice silvery gray if left untreated or unstained.

Teak. Teak should be purchased only if it says specifically that it was "plantation-grown" or "sustainably harvested." Otherwise, acres of rainforest were probably cut down to provide it. Because it is so expensive and comes from far away, its best use is for furniture that will last a lifetime. Like cedar, teak turns gray if left untreated.

Willow. Willow is a fabulous, underutilized wood in America. It is fairly cheap, grows back if cut to the ground, and when used properly, makes wonderful fencing, furniture, and garden structures. If willow furniture and other accessories are expensive now, it is only because they aren't being made on a wide scale. Willow is currently in the domain of craftspeople. In the olden days, willow "wattle" fencing was everywhere, and it's now making a comeback in cottage and kitchen gardens.

Bamboo. Bamboo is another potentially inexpensive "wood" that's great for the environment. (All right, I know it isn't really wood, but it's woody, so I'm including it here.) Like willow, bamboo grows back every year if cut to the ground, so each year you get a new crop of materials to use. Bamboo makes great fences, furniture, and garden structures, lending a decidedly and deliciously Asian look to your yard. I say "potentially inexpensive" because, like willow, it's underutilized in the States, so you pay for the exclusivity factor.

Cedar

Teak bench

Willow and cedar post fence

Pines and other woods. There are many other woods that you can use in your yard. Softwoods like pine and hardwoods like maple (normally reserved for furniture) are all potential yard and garden materials. However, because they don't have the natural resistance to decay that cedar, redwood, and teak have, they need to be treated with either a sealant or paint and will not last as long outdoors.

Pressure-treated wood. The scourge of outdoor woods! Pressure treating wood with chemicals makes the wood much more rot-resistant, so even cheap woods become durable materials for decking and other outdoor construction. But the processes used to make pressure-treated wood are so toxic that you need to be a specialist in hazardous waste in order to make it. Arsenic is just one of the fatal chemicals used. The worst thing about it is that Americans love it. They use it for everything from decks and fences to their kids' play equipment. *Never* use pressure-treated wood to make raised beds for growing food you will eat (that includes using old railroad ties, also) or something your kids will play on. If possible, never use it at all.

Pea gravel

Design Tip You can make a living fence by planting thorny bushes close to each other and weaving them together as they grow. Strong enough to keep cows in and strangers out, fences like these line the roads in Ireland.

Stone

Stone is an outstanding material for building in your garden. Your choice of stone will determine what design statement it will make. Certain stones can seem ostentatious and out of place. Others look as if they just grew right out of the ground (they might have). A good rule is that sticking with native stone and native colors will seem natural and elegant in an understated sort of way. Using imported or unusually colored stones makes it harder to integrate them into your landscape in a natural way. Because there are so many kinds of stone available, I'm going to discuss categories of stone and how you can use them.

Stone

Big stones. Big stones are good for walls, rock gardens, accents, steps, and borders (if you are going for that big rock look). If you get a locally quarried stone, it shouldn't be that expensive. What tends to be expensive is stone moving (both delivery and building). If you're using lots of stone or big stones, you need special trucks and help to move them. But there's nothing quite like well-used stone in a landscape to add strength, dignity, and a timeless look.

Little stones (gravel). Gravel can be the ultimate in tackiness or the ultimate in elegance, depending on how you use it and which kind you use. Personally, I would avoid using red volcanic gravel as a substitute for grass unless you live near a volcano. White granite chips may

Brick

This antique furnace grate was sandblasted, then sealed and inserted into my garden gate.

be nice for the driveway of a giant mansion, but avoid any chipped stones where someone may want to walk with bare feet. Softly colored pea gravel is lovely when used for paths, patios, or driveways. Gravel is surprisingly cheap and easy to deliver and install. It's great to use for walkways, mulch, and garden accents (like a dry pebble pool or stream). It's also good for your garden because it provides for drainage. You can even plant in it. Snow removal from an unfrozen gravel path is not very easy, however. For leaf and dirt removal, just rake occasionally.

Cut stones. Cut stones can be flat for paving and walking on or bigger for building or edging. Good stones for flat paving are slate, granite, flagstone, sandstone, limestone, and marble. Prices vary tremendously according to style and region. The benefits: Cut stones last practically forever (a thousand years) and require no maintenance (no staining, painting, or rebuilding). Square-cut stones are available in granite, limestone, and marble, among others, and are good for building smooth walls or edging. My favorite is used Belgian block for edging gardens and pathways. The soft gray color goes well with anything, and the blocks won't break apart like brick.

Metal

Metals can speak either of the industrial age, the lost art of metalsmithing, or the future modern world, depending on the style. Wrought iron was used extensively in the Victorian era and the Belle Époque in France. There are some amazing wrought-iron fences, gates, and balustrades in Europe. Local antiques dealers in Pennsylvania have waiting lists for old wrought-iron fences. Brushed aluminum, on the other hand, speaks of Smith and Hawken and modern times. Here are some good choices for your yard and garden.

Iron. Wrought iron is a classic garden material used for fencing, gates, edging, and all sorts of things. It is beautiful and long-lasting. However, it does require regular maintenance, such as painting or sanding and sealing, since it rusts when left out in the weather. Antique wrought iron is quite in demand, since you can barely afford or even find new wrought iron resembling anything close to the quality and beauty of the old stuff. There is, by the way, nothing inherently wrong with rust if you like the look and don't mind the eventual disintegration of your iron.

Copper. Copper ages beautifully into greenish verdigris when left out-of-doors. Although it is too expensive for fencing, it makes lovely arbors and accent roofs. It will also keep snails and slugs out of your garden if you use it as an edging around your raised beds. Don't expect it to stay new-penny shiny unless you seal it and maintain it.

Aluminum. Aluminum is a newer material that has a lot of potential to be a great garden tool. It doesn't rust, and it's very lightweight yet strong. Many of the aluminum garden products available today are made from recycled cans, so I support using aluminum fully. Time will tell, however, how it holds up. If unsealed, it quickly gets clouded and "salty." When sealed, it lasts longer.

Lead. I have seen lead planters available in some catalogs. They cost a fortune and weigh a ton. Here's what I think: There is enough lead in this world from pollution, so why add more to your garden?

Composites

Composite materials—the ones composed of several different substances—can be both ancient (adobe) and newfangled (plastic). Again, appropriate use for your region and style can make the difference between beautiful or over the edge. Here are some of the most available choices.

Terra-cotta. This beautiful warm orange pottery works best in warm climates because it can crack in the cold of the North. If you like the look (I do) and want to use it in colder regions, use it for planters and pots that can be brought indoors in the winter.

Quarry tile. "Quarry tile" is a generic term meaning any composite tile that can be used outdoors in all weather. There are some really good, strong, and beautiful ones that are great for tiling outdoor patios and paths. But there are also some ugly ones that can make your home look like an office building for lease.

My stone walls and steps are topped with cut sandstone. The gravel path is lined with Belgian block.

Cement. I have mixed feelings about cement. It's both natural and unnatural. I have used it quite a bit and love it for raised beds. For garden pathways it is too harsh, however. I am now in the process of figuring out how I can stain or cover my cement paths to make them look softer. What I really wanted was "brushed aggregate" walkways. That's where you mix the cement with decorative pea gravel and then brush the top layer of cement off to reveal the gravel. The expense to have it done professionally was exorbitant. But if I had wanted to mix it myself, it would have been affordable. Cement is an interesting and potentially exciting tool, but too often it ends up looking like sidewalk.

Brick. Pennsylvania is a brick-producing region. Many of the old homes are red brick. Brick can be expensive for the garden, but it adds a nice look. And it now comes in different colors. It won't last as long as stone, however. (I am constantly digging up crumbled old bricks from my garden.)

Plastic. Plastic is overused in the American landscape (and life in general). If you can avoid it, please do. Sure it lasts "forever." But outdoors it tends to get unattractively stained, cracked, and ugly.

When to Do It Yourself and When to Hire

So you have finally agreed on a plan and have an idea of the materials. Now what? Can you do it yourself or should you hire someone to do it? Many, many things factor into this decision—not the least of which is money. Here are the considerations.

Money. How much can you spend and what do you want to spend it on? Labor can be expensive, but so can botched efforts. Money usually goes toward materials and labor. Be realistic about how much you are willing and able to spend on each. There are all different sorts of labor, too. There is bartered labor (you build me a stone wall and I'll build you a fence). There is cheap and independent labor (the person who is good but can't stand working for others or can't get his or her act together to start a business). Then there is the professional crew—where you are often paying for "overhead" but in return getting reliable service.

I personally find that independent labor works best for unique jobs that require a high level of skill and creativity. If you find someone good, you can end up with astounding work for the same price—or less—than you'd pay for a professional crew.

Professional crews work best when the job is easy and requires little creativity. They tend to have higher turnover, so they're not as experienced as seasoned crews, and they go with the tried and true—services everybody wants. That is, unless you find a crew that

One of our neighbors cut down a birch tree and put it out for the trash. We found a good use for it.

you can build an ongoing relationship with, and they work well with you.

Bartering obviously works best when you have friends who know what they are doing, are willing to help, and want something or some skill that you have in return.

Skills. Honestly assess your own or your partner's skills. A homemade stone wall may be "free," but it may also fall down after a year or two. Good, strong "wet-laid" stone walls require cement footers below the frost line to keep the wall from collapsing over the winter. Do you really enjoy doing things yourself? Or do you just do it because you don't want to pay someone else to do it? How important is it to you to have a professional appearance? Sometimes it pays to have a professional do a job the first time, and use that experience to learn from them so you can do it yourself the second time around or in a different part of your yard.

Time. How patient are you? Be realistic about the time it will take versus the time you have. Are you willing to spend every weekend for two months to do a job that will take a professional only four days? Time is money. Time is life. List your priorities, and then act accordingly. A weird habit I have is working out my "hourly rate," which assumes that I would be paid to do the job at the same rate I get paid to do my job at work. If it costs more for me to do it at my hourly rate than it would cost to hire someone else, and I would probably botch it up anyway, then I hire someone.

Tools. Do you have the tools to do the job right? And if you rent the tools, do you know how to use them safely?

3 Ways to Find Good Help

If you decide that you want to hire a professional crew or an independent contractor, you'll want to get good work for your money. I've found three ways to make the process fairly painless.

1. **Ask someone you trust.** I found the most amazing stonemason by asking a contractor who had built an addition for us. This stonemason wasn't in the phone book or listed anywhere, but he returned my calls (the ones in the book never did). I am thrilled with the work he did.

2. **Ask someone who has had something done that you like.** Do you like your friend's or neighbor's fence or even a total stranger's yard? Asking them who built it is both a compliment to them and a good way to find good people to help you. It's also a good way to meet your neighbors!

3. **Attend local flower and garden shows, and check out their displays.** Some of the larger construction, landscape design, building, and maintenance services set up booths or advertise at

local garden shows. Going to see their work will give you an idea of what they can do. I found a wattle fence maker, which I had been looking for fruitlessly for years, at the Philadelphia Flower Show. Now I have my very own wattle fence. Meeting people in person at the shows also lets you find out whether or not they seem like the kind of people you want working in your yard.

Finally, in case you're wondering, I'll reveal which tasks I do and which ones I delegate.

Here's what I hire for: lawn cutting and trimming, large-scale earth moving and turf removal, stone masonry, fence building, and planting large trees that I can't lift myself.

Here's what I do myself: planting, weeding, small path and structure building, small-scale earth moving and turf removal, moving rocks for rock gardens or edging (a good strong cart or dolly works well). I work hard in my yard (there is no "gardener on staff" at my house), but I'm not afraid to recognize my limits and hire when I need it. I enjoy hiring kids in the summer. It takes a bit of time to supervise and teach them, but it makes me feel as if I might be growing future gardeners.

Our wattle fence, our cedar gate and trellis. Next year there will be climbing roses on them.

Designing Especially

Spring's Most Fragrant Plants

These plants top my list for delicious spring fragrance. There's room for at least one or two in every garden.

Akebia

Fragrant daffodils

Daphne

Honeysuckles

Hyacinths

Lavenders

Lemon balm

Lemon grass

Lilac

Lily-of-the-valley

Mints

Mock oranges

Peonies

Rosemary

Roses

Star magnolias

Sweet shrub

Viburnums

I have nothing against winter. I love it. But as far as I'm concerned, there are two special things to think about when designing especially for spring: sanity and spring fever. They are closely related. The aim is to make spring come as quickly as possible, and once it arrives, to maximize its healing power. Here's how.

Plant for early signs of life. My favorite spring flower is the earliest blooming snowdrop. Nothing warms the soul like bulbs popping up from the cold earth in February and March. Early blooming trees like willow and magnolia also are soul revivers.

Plant for bloom power. Be decadent, be vulgar. Spring-blooming bushes, flowers, and trees can be tacky and glorious at the same time. With a lack of greenery to soften it and the bright sun shining on eyes too used to the dark, spring can be absolutely psychedelic. Work with it, baby.

Plant for heady fragrance. A whiff of sweet-smelling narcissus, a breeze of sweet shrub, a cloud of hyacinth. Nothing banishes the ghosts and darkness of winter like the sweet smell of spring.

Plant for the eradication of winter. Don't just plant 1 tulip—plant 50. A field of daffodils, a drift of azaleas and dogwood, buckets full of bleeding hearts. . . . A garden filled with spring-blooming plants makes the past winter seem like a strange dream you can barely remember on waking. Good morning to you.

Fragrant white daffodils

for Spring

Tips, Tools & Techniques

In spring, the focus is on preparing and planting for that first taste of homegrown, delicious flavor from the garden and on getting ready for the "outdoor living" of summer. Nothing is more delightful than walking out your door, asking, "What's for dinner?" and finding all sorts of choices right in your garden—and then preparing and eating foods just picked and still sun-warmed and filled with life. Or try going out to your yard after a hard day's work and letting the beauty and energy of your garden restore your spirit.

Preparing your garden in spring involves cleaning up, getting your tools in order, and getting your soil ready. Planting both ornamentals and vegetables involves organizing your plan and understanding a few basic ideas that make organic gardening successful. Then you can plant away!

Spring Cleaning

On the first fine springlike day, get out there and see what happened over the winter. I am not a big fan of overcleaning or overtidying a garden. After all, that's where all the critters live in the winter. I know I'd hate to be rudely awakened from my winter nap and thrown around. Another added benefit of under-tidying a garden is that all sorts of

Kale from last winter is a nutritious gift of spring.

surprises start growing in the spring. I've gotten free pansies growing between cracks and the best spring lettuces and crisp kale. I've gotten surprise nasturtiums, snapdragons, sunflowers, and zinnias.

But still, there is a certain amount of straightening that must be done to make your garden presentable (and to help prevent plant diseases from spreading). I carry around a pruner and a basket and do a tour of the whole yard. Broken branches get picked up or pruned back and become kindling for either the last fire of the season or the first BBQ of spring.

Another thing I inspect is the state of last year's leaves. Matted leaves that I "forgot" to rake and that may prevent grass from growing get raked and put on the compost pile. However, I don't feel as if I need to rake everything. Leaves are Nature's way of replenishing the soil every year— why waste time picking them up and then feel as if you need to fertilize? The only time I ever rake is if there is a particularly large maple that literally "leaves" a very thick mat that may kill the grass. But I *never* rake leaves from garden beds. After all, it's like free mulch. And again, all sorts of beneficial creatures are being born and raised under there.

This is also a good time to make a list of things you want to do, such as fill bare spots with certain plants, move things, or redesign an area or bed. Don't be afraid to move plants. Early spring and late fall, when the plants are dormant, is the best time to shuffle plants around. I've moved certain perennial plants and shrubs as many as five times before I found the right spot for them.

Take a good look because early March reveals your garden and yard at its ugliest. My ultimate goal is to make my yard beautiful even in its ugliest moment. Kind of like wanting to wake up in the morning looking great.

Once you have done your initial spring cleaning outdoors, it's a good time to do the same indoors with your gardening tools and supplies. Spring is a time when you may feel anxious to buy new things— it makes you feel as if you are doing something in your yard before you really can. Catalogs are filled with crazy gadgets guaranteed to make your life "easier." Really, though, there are very few things you need in a good garden. A few comfortable chairs for outdoor relaxation. A table for dinners at sunset. And a few good tools.

The Only Tools You'll Ever Need

I'm not suggesting that these are the only tools I ever use. But if I could only choose ten essential tools, these would be the ones.

1. **Japanese weeding knife.** This is my favorite tool. It routs deep-rooted weeds with a single thrust and can be used to dig holes to plant small flowers or to hack off an unwanted branch. It's handy and very comfortable to hold. I use it more than any other tool. I even put one on a belt to wear while weeding so I can pretend to be a gardening cowgirl.

Leaves are Nature's way of replenishing the soil every year.

My well-used Japanese weeding knife

My special spade

2. **Trowel.** You'll need one for planting perennials and annuals. It can also be used for weeding, but it's not as good as the knife.

3. **Large pruner.** This one's necessary for cutting off large branches (dead or alive) of bushes and trees, either because they are dead or in the way.

4. **Spade.** My second-favorite tool. I can't live without the one that came with the house. It's just the right size for me (a small person), and it's sharp as an old knife at the bottom. I use mine to plant trees, shrubs, and large perennials, cut tree roots as I am digging, dig up rocks, dig up big weeds, and so on. I am helpless without it.

5. **Hose or watering can.** Plants need water. But I hate to have to water things. It seems if they can't make it in the natural climate, then they shouldn't be there. However, I make exceptions for newly planted things to give them that extra boost—*if* I remember. But I always end up waiting till the last minute, which is a sure sign that the next day it will rain.

6. **Rake.** You need a rake to rake deep leaves where you don't want them, to make big piles of leaves for jumping in, and to rake gravel paths once in a while to keep them clean. That's about it.

7. **Small pruner.** This is useful for cutting back perennial stalks, dead rosebush canes, and other small to medium stems that need to be cut. It's also good for cutting flowers.

8. **Pitchfork.** A pitchfork was the first Christmas gift I ever received from my husband—how romantic! But it took three years of marriage to learn how to use it (the pitchfork, not my husband). It is far superior to shovels when shoveling mulch or compost or even for digging. Pitchforks have a handy way of getting through barriers that shovels are too thick to penetrate. I love it now. And now he's learned to give me jewels instead of garden tools for Christmas.

9. **Hedge clippers.** I would not ever choose to have a hedge that needs to be clipped, but I have inherited some on my property that I haven't had the strength to replace yet. But if you have a trimmed hedge, you need good hedge clippers. Manual, of course. (See "Power Tools and the Problem with America" on page 114 for details.)

10. **Hoe.** Even though it is mentioned most by gardeners I respect, I hardly ever use one. But a lot of people rely on them heavily. I think that people who like to garden standing up prefer hoes, and people who like to squat and kneel (like me) prefer weeding knives. Hoes, however, are great for planting, weeding, and preparing vegetable beds.

Honorable mentions: weeding basket, garden cart, scissors, gloves for picking prickly things, and a broom for sweeping. That's about all you will ever need in the garden as far as tools go.

Good tools should last you a lifetime. They can even save you from becoming a gizmo junkie, needing to buy every latest labor-saving device or miracle tool. Most of these marvels just end up taking up space and falling all over you while you try to get to the one tool you really do need, which is that spade that is 70 years old, self-sharpened from lots of use, and who knows where the heck it came from in the first place.

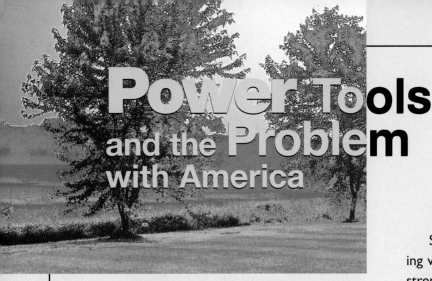

Power Tools
and the Problem
with America

I don't avoid power tools just because I am a "girl," although I have to admit I don't enjoy holding raw power in the palm of my hands that's capable of cutting off any limb in a single slip. I avoid them because they represent—to me— the vicious cycle of everything wrong with America today.

It all starts harmlessly enough. Someone mowing a lawn or trimming a hedge 50 years or so ago thinks, "There has got to be a better way to do this—and money to be made from it." So they invent "power tools" to make things easier and make some money.

But power tools cost more money, so people have to work harder to buy them. Plus, these tools use expensive fuels that pollute the environment. Before you know it, everyone has to have one, and people who do it the old way are looked at as stupid or old-fashioned. It becomes a matter of style.

Then because it's so easy to mow a lawn, people move out into the "country" (suburbia) where life is totally dependent on power tools—the lawn mower, the car—and they substitute the phone and TV for community. And where once there were farms and wilderness, now there are sterile and gardenless landscapes that are highly zoned and regulated with rules that make power tools essential.

Soon enough, however, people start gaining weight and losing muscle. (How much strength does it take to turn on a machine?) Then, because style is so important in our society, we have to get in our cars and drive to the gym, where we attempt to lose weight and "get in shape" by expending energy on totally useless activities. We go for runs and injure ourselves from repetitive motion on bones and joints that crave variety.

Next thing you know, people start feeling kind of purposeless and isolated. Families fall apart as we search for some meaning outside ourselves—some power tool for perfect love.

So we buy more things to fill an internal emptiness, get fatter and fatter on our own lack of purpose, and watch our environment fall to pieces. All this is called economic growth, which all indicators tell us is up, up, up.

I am not exempt from this cycle, either. But I've learned to enjoy the quiet and rhythm that come with using hand tools. And it's good exercise, too.

Manual hedge trimming is especially good for the back of the arms, that part that gets real flabby and hangs down when we gain too much weight and that makes us look terrible in sleeveless dresses. Gardening is one of the best all-around exercises you can do. (It involves stretching, weightlifting, and aerobics.)

Don't even get me started on leaf blowers. Imagine replacing the waist-reducing pleasant swish-swish of a broom on a walkway or the quiet rustling of a rake in fall leaves with a machine so foul that it requires earplugs and uses as much energy as about 34 cars! I refuse to allow one on my property.

Even the organic gardener's stereotypical power tool, the rotary tiller, is not exempt. You simply don't need one unless you have very large vegetable beds. If your soil is hard and unworkable, build a raised bed. (It's cheaper than buying a rotary tiller, too.) The act of tilling a garden, far from helping, can actually make things worse. Every weed seed hidden in the darkness and exposed to light in the act of tilling will become a weed. Earthworms are maimed and killed (and contrary to urban legend, a worm cut in half does not become two worms). The soil structure is ruined, so the soil becomes compacted. And nonrenewable fossil fuels are wasted just so you can have more weeds.

Just think about it. The next time you get ready to flick a switch or turn on a power tool, think of everything that it took and takes—resources, changes in society, energy, time away from family and friends, noise pollution, air pollution, and even our own health—to make a simple job "easier."

I am not against technology and "progress" at all. I am writing this on a laptop computer and listening to a CD. (I couldn't handle life without music.) But I also recognize that we have become addicts, asleep inside a hallucination that everything is fine—that for every problem, science or technology will find a solution. We are losing our own will, and the only way to get it back is to try to stay awake and make each decision and live each moment consciously. Ask yourself: Do I really need to use this tool? Is there a quieter way? How can I gain more purpose and health in my life (and my family's life) by using less and being more alive from within?

Instead of running on a treadmill (like a rat in a cage), take a walk outside and notice the nature around you (and *inside* you—you are nature, too!). Take your kids along because kids today are fatter than ever before and they probably don't get enough family time with you or enough vitamin D from being out-of-doors. (It's amazing how much kids will open up and talk to you when you are out walking and there are no distractions.)

Better yet, don't plant hedges that need trimming.

There are over 90 million gasoline-powered garden tools in use in the United States. They account for 6.8 million tons of pollution.

—Warren Schultz,
Garden Design magazine

Sweet, Sweet Soil

Nothing makes gardening easier and sweeter than having good soil. Nothing makes it harder than having bad soil. Again, most books or articles make it all seem so complicated, like you need a degree in chemistry to figure out if you have good soil or not and then how to get it if you don't. Really, it is not at all hard to understand.

Good soil is soft and fluffy, filled with vitamins, bugs, microbes, and minerals and can really be achieved only by gardening without chemicals. That's because only natural gardening techniques can replenish (with compost, mulch, and manure) what the plants take by growing.

Bad soil is hard and dense, lifeless, malnourished, and in some cases, even poisoned. Many people prefer to ignore their soil, thinking of it as mere "dirt." Then, if they have bad soil, they get frustrated with gardening or planting anything and give up.

If you've got tough soil that makes it hard to plant, here are four things you can do.

1. **If you only need a little help:** Add a lot of compost. (See "Compost: The Secret Ingredient of Great Gardens" on page 121 to learn how to make it.) Or buy bags of organic compost and topsoil from a local garden center.

2. **If you need a lot of help:** Have a load or two of mushroom soil or any local high-grade topsoil brought in. Mushroom soil mix is part poultry manure, part topsoil, and part sand, and it's fabulous for growing. Since I live in the mushroom-growing capital of the world, it's easy for me to get. In other areas, you may have to either make your own mix or get something similar locally. If you are just going to get "topsoil" in bulk (by the truckload, for instance), check the quality first. Much of what is called topsoil is really junk, and who knows where it came from (some farmer's poisoned field, for instance). You may be better off getting large quantities of compost. But even then, you have to be careful to make sure the compost is "clean" and organic. Asking around is usually the best way to find the best organic sources.

3. **If you only want to do a part of your yard:** Build raised beds right on top of your bad soil, and then fill them with purchased organic topsoil mixed with compost. If you don't even want to dig out the grass, you can put down several layers of newspaper, *then* add your topsoil and compost. It's an instant weed-free bed.

4. **If you don't want to pay for topsoil and have a lot of patience:** Plant daikon radishes and let them grow for a year and then rot in the ground. These deep-growing radishes both soften and fertilize the ground.

Good soil can only be achieved by gardening without chemicals.

Borage and lettuces

Double-Digging:
What Is It? And Should You Do It in Your Yard?

I pretended for years that I knew what double-digging was every time some gardener would mention it. I figured it was just as it sounded . . . digging something double. Well, it is, and it isn't.

Double-digging is a process of digging up and removing the first foot of soil, loosening up the next foot of soil, adding compost, and then putting the first foot of soil back on top again. What it does is loosen and fortify 2 feet of soil to make an amazingly fluffy and potent garden bed.

Here's what double-digging is good for: a new vegetable or flowerbed where the soil is hard and needs more compost. Here's what it's not as good for: an established bed that seems to be producing just fine as it is. Unfortunately, the act of double-digging exposes long-dormant weed seeds to light, therefore waking them from their long sleep. But a good dose of mulch on top after double-digging should keep the weeds from taking over.

A rotary tiller sort of does the same thing, but only to the first foot of soil, so it's not double-dug. And you can do a whole bed with a spading fork in the time it takes you to get the rotary tiller out of the garage and fire it up.

Potatoes love to grow in double-dug soil.

You can't *really* tell what is in your soil until you have it tested. As I mentioned in the beginning of this book, we gardened organically for years with soil that seemed fine (although filled with an astounding amount of historical materials, such as pottery, bottles, and bricks). But when we had it tested, we found that it was contaminated with lead. These days, there are so many foul and invisible chemicals that it is very prudent to test your soil. Here's how to do it.

Call your local county or state agricultural extension office (listed in your phone book) and ask for a soil test kit for a home garden. Get a special bag from them. Fill it out and follow directions on the bag. Send the soil sample to the address listed on the bag. In a week or two you will get a full report on more than everything you ever could imagine knowing about your soil . . . except where that lead might have come from.

Don't be surprised, however, if you get a recommendation to add large quantities of chemical soil amendments. Extension agencies exist mostly to serve large-scale commercial farmers. Ask for the recommendations to be supplied with organic amendments only, and hope that they give it to you. If you want a more expensive, comprehensive analysis, try a company like Peaceful Valley Farm Supply (916-272-4769).

The most important thing for you to remember, however, is that almost all soil problems and deficiencies can be corrected, and even good soil can be improved with an annual dose of organic compost.

Secrets of the Soil

For all of you who slept through science in junior high school, here is all the science you'll need to know to understand what's in your soil.

Calcium. Low calcium causes spindly plants and blossom-end rot in tomatoes. It's most often low in coastal soils. You can add limestone to boost soil calcium.

Magnesium. Magnesium is an essential component of chlorophyll. A magnesium-deficient plant will turn brown from the bottom up. It's also most commonly deficient in coastal areas, and it can be increased by adding magnesium-rich dolomitic limestone.

Nitrogen. Gardeners are overly fixated on nitrogen. To make sure your soil has plenty, the best thing to do is add lots of organic matter like compost and manure to your soil. You can have too much nitrogen—for instance, if you notice lots of leafy green growth but not a lot of fruiting, you may have too much. An inch of compost a year is usually enough to provide more than enough nitrogen to your garden. (If you live in the South, you can add more.)

Phosphorus. Phosphorus is an important element in soil, especially for seedlings and shallow-rooted plants. Lack of phosphorus will cause stunted growth and a purplish cast to the foliage, but you can't be sure a phosphorus deficiency is causing this until you test. You can add rock phosphate or bonemeal. For a tempoary quick fix, spray fish emulsion on the soil around your seedlings in spring.

Gardeners are overly **fixated** on **nitrogen.**

Potassium (or potash). Potassium keeps plants healthy (especially beans). If your soil is low in potassium, add granite powder or seaweed.

pH. This is the measurement of your soil's acidity or alkalinity. The pH scale runs from -14 to 14. Numbers higher than 7.0 mean your soil is alkaline (the higher the number, the more alkaline the soil is). Lower than 7.0 means your soil is acidic. Neutral is 7.0. It's better to be slightly acid than slightly alkaline. The reason pH is so important in gardening is that the further out of the neutral range your soil is, the more the nutrients in the soil are just not available to plants. They refuse to be used.

Too much wood ash, chicken manure, or lime applied to your garden (all common organic soil amendments) can cause high pH levels (high alkalinity). And that's bad for growing anything. Don't add lime or wood ash if your soil's pH is above neutral, and go light on the super-concentrated chicken manure.

Heavy metals and other toxins. Lead, mercury, and arsenic are all poisons that are often found in urban and industrialized soils. Pay extra to get your soil tested for these toxins if you live anywhere near town, traffic, gas stations, or factories. If you test high, you may need to remove your soil or stop growing edible things in it. Chemical runoff from farms and factories is also a hazard.

Salts. If you live in a dry area, you may have to worry about salty soil. Rain washes natural salts out of the soil. (Too much irrigation, however, brings them back up.) Too much salt takes water away from your plants and injures the plant roots. Even the manure out West may contribute to too much salt in the soil because of how much salt the cattle consume (and then excrete). If your test shows too much salt, add gypsum to your soil.

Sulfur. The soil needs sulfur to use the nitrogen in it. Manure adds sulfur.

Although lots of magazine articles and books tell you to add lime or other things to correct your soil, don't add anything other than compost unless you have had your soil tested and you know you need it. It is entirely possible to ruin your soil by trying to care for it too much. (This is a recurring theme of mine—we love to complicate things, when really they are all so simple.)

The whole point of fertilizers is to make up deficiencies in your soil in order to give plants the nutrients they need to grow into healthy adults. But adding nutrients in chemical form is not only inefficient but also harmful—most fertilizer gets washed away and ends up in our groundwater, where it causes environmental and health problems. A regular dose of compost (applied once or twice a year in spring and fall) will not only provide your soil with all the nutrients it needs but also will add to its workability (softness) and microbial life.

As far as acidic and alkaline soils go, your best bet is to work with what you have. No amount of chemicals will fundamentally change a highly acid soil—so plant acid-loving plants like rhodendrons, azaleas,

It is entirely possible to ruin your soil by trying to care for it too much.

and blueberries. (And the same goes for alkaline soils.)

We often tend to think of things like microbes, worms, ants, and other bugs as "yucky," but in truth we couldn't live without them. When everything is working together and cooperating in your garden, there should be no need to fear the bugs—they won't grow to giant sizes and take over Manhattan. In fact, that's more likely to happen because of pesticide use, since the bugs develop resistance to pesticides startlingly fast.

> *The insect is the sensor of nature to destroy unwanted vegetation. When something is wrong with a plant, then comes the insect. The insect has a distinctive taste, a perverted taste for sick tissue.*
>
> —J. I. Rodale

Compost: The Secret Ingredient of Great Gardens

All this talk about compost. More than any other thing, compost is identified with organic gardening—and it's partly responsible for giving organic gardening its questionable and "icky" reputation. But that's a fairly new reputation. Before the advent of chemicals, compost was revered by every homeowner and farmer as a key ingredient in creating beautiful gardens.

My mother was a composter in the '50s.

Gardeners well know the value of manure, and especially of liquid manure. They spare no pains or price to get all they can, and often apply from 20 to 40 loads of compost or decomposed manure per acre annually. It is what makes or mars the profit in gardening.

—F. M. Lupton, *The Farm and Household Encyclopedia* (1886)

Compost is not only essential to provide your soil with great nutrients, but it is also practical, easy, and efficient. Think of composting as your home waste disposal system, which results in a product that is 100 percent recycled and 100 percent valuable in your garden. Here again, people like to "get creative" with their compost and come up with all sorts of fancy gourmet recipes. But there is absolutely no need. Just throw stuff on the pile. What kind of stuff, you ask?

Typically, compost is made up of three things.

1. **Carbon:** dry leaves, chipped wood, sticks, straw, paper

2. **Nitrogen:** grass clippings, weeds, garden trimmings, kitchen scraps

3. **Soil:** the soil on plant roots is enough to bring the microbes that will cause the other materials to break down and form compost

Horse manure (or any animal manure) is great to add to your compost pile *only* if you're sure it comes from an organic and healthy source.

Studies have shown that home composting of food wastes can cut curbside waste by 30 percent. Composting your kitchen scraps prevents serious environmental pollution and expense while creating *free* fertilizer for your garden. And it's practically the easiest thing you can do.

You can compost simply (and that's how I do it). Find a good place for a pile in a part of your yard that is hidden from view (and not right next to your neighbors), and dump there. Dump it all—sticks, weeds, kitchen waste, and garden waste. If you can get cow, horse, or other farm-animal manure (from a source that you know is organic, hormone-free, and healthy), great. Use it. If you can't, no big deal.

Here are the six things you shouldn't put on your pile.

1. Meats or animal products

2. Grains, breads, oils, and fats (all of these attract rodents)

3. Anything toxic, nonbiodegradable, or poisonous (like poison ivy or Drano)

4. Dog or cat waste (too many potential parasites)

5. Weeds that have either gone to seed or have strong root systems

6. Diseased plants

There's really not much else you need to do, except occasionally dig out the stuff at the bottom of the pile that has been miraculously turned into "black gold," and spread it on your garden. I don't turn my pile or water it or anything else except use it.

If you prefer the tidiness of a compost bin, there are lots of good ones available at garden stores and through catalogs. But if you have a big garden, those may be too small. One option is to make a row of neat-looking bins out of pallets. (The world currently has far too many pallets sitting idle, anyway.) The bins can be as long as you need them to be.

Troubleshooting Compost

An active compost pile smells fresh and cooks along as the microbes decompose the stuff you've put in it (slowly if you leave it alone, faster if you water and turn it). If your pile is turning into a problem—or isn't turning into anything at all—here's what to do.

If nothing is happening to your compost, two things may be wrong. First, the pile may be too small. Make it bigger. Small piles don't have enough volume to get the action going. Second, if you haven't had any rain in a long time, the pile may be too dry. Add enough water to make the pile damp (*not* wet), and things should heat up. Turning a slow pile also mixes the ingredients, adds air, and tends to speed up the "cooking" time.

If your pile starts to smell (which it shouldn't), it probably either needs more air or has too many high-nitrogen ingredients, like fresh grass clippings or gooey kitchen scraps, which have matted down and are rotting. Turning the pile and mixing in some bigger materials like big stalks (sunflower stems, for example) or sticks will let in air and keep the pile from packing down. You can also add more carbon. Mix in shredded newspaper. Or cover up the pile with leaves or straw. That will both suppress the smell and add the carbon necessary to balance the pile. It also covers up unsightly freshly dumped kitchen waste, if you are concerned about that.

> *In the soft, warm bosom of a decaying compost heap, a transformation from life to death and back again is taking place.*
>
> —J. I. Rodale

Compost Facts

Still need convincing? Here are four more reasons to use compost in your garden.

1. Compost has been proven to increase yields and repair worn-out soils.

2. Compost in orchards and around fruit trees keep trees healthy and productive.

3. Compost increases the earthworm activity in the soil.

4. Compost can suppress plant diseases by up to 80 percent—tests done on onions, strawberries, cabbages, and flowers have proven it.

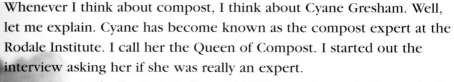

with Cyane Gresham

Whenever I think about compost, I think about Cyane Gresham. Well, let me explain. Cyane has become known as the compost expert at the Rodale Institute. I call her the Queen of Compost. I started out the interview asking her if she was really an expert.

"I came to the Institute in June of 1988 as an intern in the garden," Cyane said. "Eileen Weinsteiger, the head gardener, asked me to run the compost program. And for better or worse, I have been running the garden-scale compost program since 1988.

"I studied geology in school, and for some reason I made the jump to being interested in plants and gardening. For ten years here I have had the chance to expand, to learn, to drift in that stream with all this knowledge and stuff going by."

But unbeknownst to me, Cyane is also fast becoming an expert in native plants and their role in the home garden and the environment. So after we talk about compost, you'll get some interesting insights into native plants as well. So, let's talk compost!

From your perspective, what is the best way to look at compost?

The best way to look at compost—with all due respect to J. I. Rodale—has changed. I think the world has changed so that most people are worried about lack of time more than lack of soil fertility. So, given that, compost to me is a system of recycling organic materials. And the reason people would be drawn to composting is that they have this waste and they need to get rid of it.

Of the people that I meet here, there are a lot of older people who have a lot of time, and those are the people who are the best composters. They are the ones who compost because they love the process and want to produce beautiful compost.

But there are a huge number of people who come in who have kids, live in the suburbs, and don't have a lot of time. They need to have a way to compost as well.

My point of view is that composting is a system of recycling that should fit the goals of the gardener. So what are the possible goals of the gardener: to recycle organic materials with as little work as possible, to get physical exercise, to educate their kids, or to produce healthy soil?

Decomposition happens. Everything living—or once living—breaks down. Composting is a way of accelerating that natural decomposition. Like all human activities, composting entails a trade-off: work for faster decomposition. And the quality of the product figures in there, too. Composting involves a set of choices about what your goals are.

What if all those goals are mixed together and you have no time?

You make a pile in an out-of-the-way place under a tree that nobody sees. You dump only food scraps and cover it with dirt. Maybe you put some good weeds in there, but not bad weeds. Good weeds would be things like chickweed—soft green weeds that have not gone to seed and do not have strong root systems.

Bad weeds are invasive plants, ones with root systems that you know will survive the compost process (quackgrass, mugwort, bindweed), or plants that have gone to seed. Poison ivy. Things with thorns. These types of weeds should not go in a compost mixture.

What do you do with the bad weeds?

Put them in the trash or burn them (but never burn poison ivy or poison oak).

If someone had a lot of time and wanted to make really beautiful compost, what should they do?

They should probably buy a chipper shredder. That's the big investment right there. Chopping raw materials speeds decomposition. Then build a big pile, layer in soil, and make sure it's moist.

What do you do if you're in between?

If you just heap stuff in a pile, it will probably break down, but it will take a year.

What's the best way to get a hot pile?

The key in composting is to have a big enough pile. If your pile is less than 3 feet high, it's not going to heat up.

Make sure you have a pile at least 4 feet high, and make sure that it is turned. Once you get larger than 4 feet, it's not much fun to turn it by hand. Decomposition is natural, but composting is human. To do it on any large scale at all, you need machinery. So, the ideal height for a home composting pile is 3 to 4 feet.

What about those home composting bins?

They are good for aesthetics—they look nice. Tumblers are good for keeping pests out. But they are not good for decomposing large amounts of materials. Most bins don't get any bigger than 27 cubic feet, but I feel that is the minimum size for hot composting.

How often should compost be applied?

There is no one answer to that. It depends on what you are growing and your natural soil conditions. You might never have to put compost on trees or shrubs. In the Rodale Institute garden, for instance, we have rich soil.

After 20 years of composting, I only apply compost here if the soil is low, if there is a hole, or if the soil is cracking and appears to be low in organic matter.

So if you want fluffy soil, put compost on it?

Right. That's my approach.

What is your viewpoint on animal manure?

You have to be careful about introducing weed seeds with horse manure in particular. Chicken manure that I've seen doesn't have any weed seeds in it but is so high in nitrogen that it's almost a problem.

What about the antibiotics and growth hormones that they feed animals these days? Do we have to worry about that in our compost if we use manure?

Yes, you have to be careful. When I tested chicken manure in 1990, it was really high in cadmium. Sometimes you bring horse manure in and there are syringes from the racetracks and trash. With compost there really is a quality concern. You have to be careful about what goes in it, especially in municipal compost.

So that's another reason for someone to compost at home rather than get municipal compost.

Municipal compost is great, but, in my view, as much as possible should be composted at the source.

What else should people not do?

The reason people don't put meat in compost is because it attracts pests. But everything breaks down. If you comb your dog and put the hair in, it will break down.

The best things are food scraps without meat or fat. Coffee grounds are ideal; tea is good. Good weeds are fine, too, like chickweed, which is a spring weed. Other good weeds are pigweed, lamb's-quarters, and galinsoga.

What about worm composting?

It certainly has become popular. It has its good points and bad points. It's not a panacea (nothing is). It's really not composting in a technical sense. What it is is a waste disposal system, using worms to process food scraps. The good part is that it's for food scraps and people can do it even if they live in an apartment. The bad side is that worms only operate at temperatures between 60° and 90°F, so you cannot leave them outside all winter. Also, it tends to be a little goopy and can attract some fruit flies. But kids love worms.

If you do have worms, you have to put them in a heated garage or basement. The bedding has to be completely changed twice a year. For people who want to do that, it's a useful thing. It's probably more useful in urban areas.

What are the most common misconceptions about compost?

The people I come in contact with are fairly knowledgeable about compost—so maybe 50 years of *Organic Gardening* magazine has paid off. But there is a misconception that you can get something for nothing. Or that you can get a high-quality product with no input. In my mind at least, it's a fairly simple trade-off: The more work, the faster it happens, and the better the product is. I don't think there is a free lunch, even with compost. You will get a decomposed product, but it will have weed seeds and be lumpy.

The other thing I don't think people know is that in order to get a hot composting process going, the pile has to be at least 27 cubic feet. And I don't think people realize that there is a minimum for hot composting.

What are your other gardening passions?

I've become convinced that there is a whole revolutionary way of looking at gardening that is encompassed in native plants. I'm personally obsessed with how people create their home yards and gardens and how that relates to the environment.

For me, native plants are a powerfully leveraged way of looking at my garden as part of the earth. But I have to acknowledge that different people care about different things.

What do you think are the three most important things you could do to impact the earth in your own yard?

Well, as a preface, although it may not seem important what you do in your yard and what I do in my yard, in aggregate, it's very important. All the yards added up really create a new ecosystem. I believe that the decisions you make really are important.

The first thing would be to *learn*. Most of us are walking around essentially blind. We do not know what's going on in the natural

> Although it may not seem important **what you do in your yard** and what I do in my yard, in aggregate, it's very important. All the yards added up really create a **new ecosystem.**

world. At best we understand our gardens. But we don't understand what's going on in the landscape outside us. And what's happening is not very healthy; there's a huge degradation. Learn to identify plants; get familiar with plants. Insects, if you care to. Birds, if you care to. Learn something about your environment.

The second thing would be not to plant invasive plants. One of the things people worry about is loss of biodiversity. The biggest cause of biodiversity loss is loss of habitat. A rare plant grew in a wetland, and now it's a parking lot. The second biggest cause is habitat displacement by either disease, competitors, or other plants. So we gardeners leave a legacy of dangerous plants that we have introduced. Because we think it's sexy and cool to bring in a plant from China, we bring in something that later may cause environmental havoc.

An example of that is the Norway maple. Norway maple is still one of the most widely planted street trees, brought in from northern Europe. It's rugged and tough, so it does well in urban situations. It's now spreading through Pennsylvania forests, displacing the native trees that grew there before. It has a shallow root system and allelopathic tendencies—that means it poisons other plants around it. So nothing grows underneath it. Some of our native maples are the silver maple, red maple, and sugar maple. Nonnative maples include Norway maple and sycamore maple, which to me aren't nearly as attractive as the natives. Why not plant native maples?

One thing about invasive plants, however, is that there is not one answer for around the country. The invasive plants here aren't the same as the invasive plants in California. So, once again, we come back to learning about our environment.

The third thing is be careful not to use herbicides, pesticides, and chemical fertilizers.

I am going to launch now into the topic of soil fertility to try to illustrate some of this. The traditional organic gardener's cry is "compost, compost, compost." Gardeners who use chemicals would say, "OK, figure out how much nitrogen you need and pour it on; no problem." Each side has this answer: You need lots of soil fertility. And we have all believed for a long time that lots of soil fertility is good.

But what I am starting to find is that there is some evidence that we are awash in nutrients. That there are too many nutrients. Many native plants grow in an environment where nutrients are limited or scarce. They don't do well in environments that are high in nitrogen. You are starting to see research that high nitrogen levels are killing off native plants that have evolved to be very efficient nitrogen users.

Shooting stars

On the other hand, a lot of our garden plants are very greedy nitrogen users, which is also true of a lot of our weeds. So we are actually, organic and nonorganic gardener alike, creating an environment that's conducive to garden plants as well as weeds. We are helping to displace native plants with weedy plants because there are so many nutrients.

Soil fertility is a lot more complicated than it appears. You have to be careful about what your objectives are and not just aim for higher soil fertility. If you want to grow cabbages or celery, high soil fertility is good. But if you want to grow a meadow in this region, it's no good. It's actually harmful. It will get too weedy. To me, that's fascinating.

So a meadow would be a good thing for someone to grow in their yard if they have really bad soil?

Exactly.

What do you think are the major challenges that gardeners face as we try to become more aware?

There are a lot of challenges. One thing that I wish is that we understood the landscape enough to do *what's* appropriate, *where* it is appropriate. It seems that it is appropriate to have carefully manicured and maintained areas that are weed-free right around your house, but as you go out from your house, the landscape doesn't have to have that high an input.

I recognize that not everybody has the ability to choose for themselves—some people live in housing developments where, believe it or not, they are told how they have to landscape. And in some housing developments they probably wouldn't even want you to have compost piles. But in more natural areas, you have a little more latitude. You can make brush piles. You don't have to pick up the leaves.

In our arsenal, we should have an array of choices. Compost should be one of them, mulching should be another, letting it go should be another. If you're trying to immaculately maintain everything, you are just going to drive yourself crazy and probably destroy the environment doing it.

If you could have only one tool, what would it be?

A shovel. Because you can plant trees, you can rip out trees or other plants, you can take stalks and (with a great deal of patience) cut them up, and you can even weed. It's a pretty useful tool.

Magnolia

Pruning

I could have filled this book with pictures of the horribly maimed plants I see in my town—plants that have been pruned beyond reason. Forsythia bushes are pruned to be 2-foot-high gum balls (when they should really be 10-foot-high sprawlers). Azaleas are pruned into square shapes. Giant trees are "topped" into what I call the Pennsylvania cactus—when a tree like a maple is cut back every spring to its main branches only. I didn't put those pictures in here, however, because this is a book about *beautiful* gardening.

I am not opposed to pruning. It is a vital tool for gardening. But people take it to excess for some reason. Maybe it's a control-versus-nature thing. My general belief is that bushes and trees should look natural, not as if they are being sent off to war.

Here's when you should prune.

- When a tree or shrub is blocking access to something

- When branches are dead and could fall and hurt someone or enable disease to enter

- When you want to increase production of certain fruits and flowers

- When topiary or bonsai is a hobby that you enjoy

Here's when you shouldn't prune.

- When you have planted the wrong plant in the wrong place to begin with and you are trying to make up for it. (Instead, cut it down, or move it and plant something more appropriate.)

- Just because you think everything ought to be pruned

You don't have to prune fruit trees if you don't want to. This unpruned apple tree bore beautiful fruit for over 70 years.

Interview

with Reds Bailey

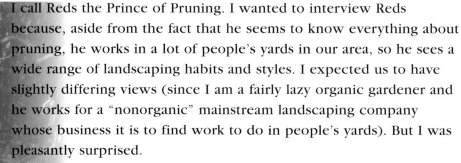

I call Reds the Prince of Pruning. I wanted to interview Reds because, aside from the fact that he seems to know everything about pruning, he works in a lot of people's yards in our area, so he sees a wide range of landscaping habits and styles. I expected us to have slightly differing views (since I am a fairly lazy organic gardener and he works for a "nonorganic" mainstream landscaping company whose business it is to find work to do in people's yards). But I was pleasantly surprised.

Reds Bailey started out thinking he was going to live a "normal" working life. He got an economics degree and a job. But he hated being indoors and felt he wasn't cut out for it. So he "picked up stakes" and took a trip around the country for a few months with his wife. When he returned, he went to the New York State Ranger School's Forestry Program, but, he says, "It didn't take me long to realize that was just another kind of business—treating nature or the woods as another marketable resource."

So he got a job with Gary's Tree and Shrubbery Service 19 years ago and has been working outdoors ever since, continually expanding his knowledge and expertise of trees and landscaping.

When should trees be pruned?

Different trees should be pruned in different ways at different times of the year for different reasons—and always for a reason—but not for the reasons you hear around here, like it's "getting kinda big nah." (In case you don't recognize the accent, we live in Pennsylvania Dutch country.)

It's so critical to prune early. Waiting is the biggest mistake people make. If you don't think about it when the tree or shrub is small, when it's so much cheaper to prune right, you—and your plant—will pay for it later. Nurserymen are under more and more pressure to get things done, and they are not doting over plants the way they used to. This is high-scale, high-volume production we are talking about, and they may not have time to do corrective pruning. In addition, the energy required of a young tree to recover from pruning wounds is so much less than on an older tree—it's like older people. They just don't heal as fast.

If you had to simplify it, what are the basic things someone should know about pruning?

Always prune for a reason and for a reason that makes sense, such as for health (deadwood removal) and for proper branch formation, avoiding crossing branches and weight stress on the ends of branches. Be aware that any pruning cut is a wound to the plant, and it requires energy to wall over or heal.

People have to realize, too, that trees do a really good job of shaping themselves without any help. Even if they are not well-shaped, one has to keep in mind that things in nature aren't perfectly symmetrical anyway.

The need for pruning can be often overemphasized. There are probably many more healthy trees in existence that have been left alone than there are trees that are healthy because someone has pruned them.

There are a lot of pruning techniques that should or could be done to trees to make them healthier, but in general, people don't do them or don't do them properly.

What are some good reasons for pruning?

Deadwood pruning is one of the most important reasons. Deadwood is like tooth decay. It just sits there attracting infection, and it inhibits the wound from healing.

Another good reason to prune is if a branch is in the way or is a safety problem. For example, is somebody going to poke their eye out on a branch?

What are some bad reasons for pruning?

Controlling size and proportion. People often have a peculiar notion of a plant's proper proportion. Instead, I really feel that people should look at what they really like about natural habitats when they go out to wild places, then try to duplicate that as closely as they can. That's what makes them feel good, and that's the natural thing.

One of the most difficult things to do is to try to control the size of a tree—especially a large, mature tree.

What about thinning?

Some people think that thinning is removing branches to let in more light—to make the tree 'thinner'—so you can grow grass under it. When you do that, you're fighting nature. Overthinning a tree causes the tree to overreact and try to gain what it lost. You are taking away a major source of food production and also causing a wound. Stripping all the inner branches out causes the ends to get heavier, and then they may break.

Overthinning flowering trees causes more vegetative growth and less flowering. For example, the worst thing you could do to a crabapple tree is to strip out the branches.

In general, there should be less drastic pruning and more cabling, and in some cases, lightning protection. Instead of having a tree thinned out and topped every year, have it done once every five to ten years—everyone, especially trees, would be better off.

What other things do people do to their trees that they shouldn't do?

They shouldn't use pruning sealer. Experts are finally putting that to rest. It not only doesn't work but also actually inhibits the healing process in some cases.

Not sterilizing pruning equipment passes diseases from tree to tree. Sterilizing is simple. I just use a spray bottle of rubbing alcohol.

Guying and staking the trees are frequently unnecessary. The theory is that the tree needs to be steadied and kept from blowing over. It's ridiculous. If you plant a healthy tree, the size of the rootball far outweighs the crown, so there is very little reason to stake it. An evergreen is a little bit of an exception because many times the bulk of its canopy will outweigh the roots or at least create enough of a sail effect to knock it over.

Tamping is another notion that is often carried to extremes. People tamp the daylights out of the soil to keep air pockets away from the roots. You want the tree to have oxygen; you just don't want so many air pockets that the rootball isn't secure. You want to tamp the soil to the degree that you've gotten rid of pockets that may allow the tree to list from one side to another. But that's about it.

Soil amendments for tree planting are also on the way out. Amending the soil in the planting hole is not recommended. It creates a different soil texture, which causes water to fill up the hole and rot the roots.

If you have a large area under a mature tree that you are trying to grow grass on, you are going to be fighting a losing battle. If the grass is already there and you don't mind raking, fine. If you want to do the best thing for the tree, however, you'll take the grass out and mulch instead.

A lot of people I talk to want a fast-growing tree to plant next to their house, but one that lives a long time and won't fall down on their house. What kinds of trees do you think people should plant next to their houses?

People have unrealistic expectations—they want the best of both worlds. Scientists are working on growth inhibitors, messing around with plant physiology and root zone inhibitors. Personally I have my doubts about how practical they are.

There is nothing that is going to grow really fast and still be safe to put next to your house—there just isn't. You are not going to get the wood density that you want. Fast-growing trees like tulip poplars and silver maples are brittle. You can plant trees that grow *relatively* quickly, to get shade, like river birch and red maple.

If you plant the wrong tree in the wrong place, you'll end up having to cut it back or cut it down and then plant something else there.

You see a lot of trees. Which are your favorites?

White and red oaks, copper beech or beech trees in general, sugar maples, and red maples.

How do you feel about tree topping?

I find the stark look of a topped tree offensive, unnatural, and often simply ridiculous, especially as the branches grow back resembling a Don King hairdo. The damage that topping does to a mature tree that has taken years to attain its majestic appearance is usually irreversible.

Let's switch topics here. You go into a lot of people's yards and get involved in helping them design their landscapes. What are the biggest mistakes people make in their home landscapes?

They tend to overplant. They tend not to keep their landscapes to a single theme. They need to have balance and diversity. Big trees provide shade for other smaller trees, for example. A variety of plantings invites wildlife and natural insect predators.

Most people just want plantings around the foundation of their house. I say to them—wouldn't it be nice if there were some large shade trees here?

You have to pay attention to the things that you want to get big first. You've got to get them started. Those big trees create passive solar effects, suck up a lot of dust and air and noise pollution, and provide screening. Those are the things people all too often don't pay attention to. I guess they are intimidated by the size of a big tree or where to actually put it.

What are other common mistakes?

People spend a lot of money on the landscaping around their house without getting professional consultation. Most people wouldn't think of building their own house without some sort of architectural advice.

> If you plant the **wrong tree** in the **wrong place,** you'll end up having to cut it back or cut it down.

Another mistake is paying too much attention to fancy little doodad plants around the foundation and planting them too close together.

And using landscape fabric. Oh, deliver me from landscape fabric! These things that people devise that don't work are the plague of people who really take it seriously. If people spent half the time and energy reconditioning the soil in the planting beds rather than putting down these weed barriers, they'd have great-looking landscapes. Instead, they put down landscape fabrics that break down in a couple of years, don't work, choke out the plants, and actually restrict water.

Mulching is a wonderful, wonderful thing, but people assume that because some mulch is good, more mulch is better. The reality is that too much mulch against the bark causes rotting and encourages the formation of girdling roots. It can actually keep water from reaching the roots when it crusts over.

People need to realize that there is no such thing as no maintenance—even low maintenance—if you want to have anything extensive. That's because a landscape is such a dynamic thing, it's not standing still, it's always changing. Something is always happening. It's like the chaos theory.

I also see a lot of improper planting techniques. A surprising number of shrubs and trees are planted too deeply. People think they are being generous or something, but they're really suffocating the roots. Frequently you'll find that the soil level of the rootball of a tree or shrub is already too high on the trunk straight from the nursery.

What do you think are the barriers to people being organic?

Paranoia. Impatience. Ignorance may be too strong a word, but people are not educated about how the natural system works. They don't take nature and landscapes seriously. They just want quick fixes to problems because they don't want to be bothered. I hear things like 'Just fix it; I don't want to wait; I want it done now.' It's just the nature of people today. They are not patient and they want immediate results, and yet they don't want to pay people to do it properly.

Do you have any other advice for people?

Start out simple. Plant your big trees right away, then gradually develop planting beds.

It's a wonderful world out there, and gardening is a great way to get in touch with yourself and get an appreciation for nature. There is so much to it—simplicity and yet complexity at the same time.

Finally, I'd advise people to live with nature and not try to conquer it.

If you could have only one tool, what would it be?

I would need two: bypass-type hand pruners (they work like scissors). They enable you to get a clean cut, whereas the other type (anvil) tends to crush the branch. You can use bypass pruners as a hammer, chisel, or even wire cutters. Felco is my brand of choice—I wear them on my belt.

My second essential tool is a good, strong nursery spade (steel reinforced or all steel). It can be used to transplant, strip sod, and prune roots.

And if I could have three things, the last would be Michael Dirr's *Manual of Woody Landscape Plants*. Because, after all, isn't knowledge one of the best tools of all?

Even though dogwoods are beautiful, they tend to be susceptible to diseases. Reds says to be sure to rake up the leaves in the fall to keep them healthy.

Planting

Spring is the time to plant; there's simply no getting around it if you want to garden. There are other times to plant, too, but spring is the main season. The spring planting season goes like this: First, plant trees and shrubs while they are still dormant (while it's still cold and before the leaves have sprouted, but after the soil has thawed). Then plant cold-season vegetables and perennial herbs and flowers. Then, finally, plant the warm-season vegetables and annual or tender perennial herbs and flowers after all danger of frost has passed.

Planting is easy, fun, and good exercise—especially if you are a "plant pig" (as my husband calls me). I buy so many plants sometimes that I end up planting for a few hours a day. The main thing is not to be afraid. Some plants will make it. Some plants won't. That's life (and death). If you put it in the wrong place, you can always move it later. Basically, dig in.

Landscape Planting

Most of the time, when we think of landscaping with plants, we think in terms of separation. Trees get planted in the "yard," flowers get planted in "beds," and bushes get planted around the "foundation." For the creative landscaper, you could go the next step and plant ground-covers under trees or bushes among the flowers. But the ideal situation is what are referred to in Permaculture as *guilds*.

If you look at how Nature plants herself, there is a distinct system that works together to make a continuously regenerating grouping of plants (and animals). You can see it while driving by any woods along the road. First there are the big trees, then the smaller understory trees, then the small bushes, then flowers, herbs, and "weeds." Then there are the groundcovers.

All the animals and organisms serve roles. The fungi and worms clean up the mess. The insects eat the weak things and pollinate and plant seeds. The birds and animals eat the plants, bugs, and berries, then fertilize the soil with their compost, planting seeds that have passed through their systems and depositing them in convenient "compost pellets" (otherwise known as scat).

The closer you try to duplicate nature's guild system in your landscape, the happier everything in your landscape will be. That does not mean your yard should look like "the woods" by any means. It just means that if you think in terms of layers (and habitat for wildlife), you will have less work and more success in your plantings. Integration is the key—big trees, small trees, shrubs, flowers, groundcovers, and any living thing that comes to visit.

(The other day my neighbor leaned over the fence and told me with grave concern that he saw an opossum going into my yard. By the tone of his voice, I could tell he thought "something oughtta be

A sign of spring: sprouting peonies

A sign of summer: blooming peonies

done about it." I tried to suppress my glee. An opossum! On Main Street! It's working!)

An example of a common guild found in the woods around me would be: a tall maple, a small dogwood, a rhododendron bush, ferns, and moss (and other assorted small plants and bushes). Ironically, many people plant those plants in their yards around here, too—they are just planted in separate areas of the yard instead of mingled together.

How to Plant a Tree (or Shrub)

So many garden and landscape books are filled with detailed step-by-step instructions on how to plant trees. Even I feel intimidated by them. But I have planted over 30 trees in my little yard, and I can tell you with certainty that there are only three real steps.

1. Dig a hole large enough for the tree's root system.

2. Plunk the tree in the hole (without any of the burlap or plastic wrapping—some of the burlap bags are dipped in chemicals that will inhibit the growth of the plant if you leave them on, and others only look like burlap but are really plastic).

3. Cover it up with dirt.

If you time your planting before a good rain or when the ground is already wet, you just need to water to settle the soil around the roots.

Sound scandalously easy? It is. I was just trying to remember if I have lost any trees that way. The only ones have been catalog trees. But they are a tender lot to begin with. How would you feel if you were

Nature does nothing uselessly.

—Aristotle

Japanese maple

knocked unconscious, wrapped in plastic, stuffed in a cardboard box, and shipped halfway across the country, only to arrive when the person who was planning on bringing you back to life has gone on a vacation? Most catalog companies will replace trees that don't make it. But in general, they are much smaller than local nursery-bought trees and therefore more sensitive when they arrive.

Once, I ordered a franklinia tree from a catalog. When it arrived, it was about 2 feet tall. First the dog accidentally broke it when she tripped over it playing fetch. Then a nephew who shall go unnamed rode his bike over it or something. Still, it grew for two years. What finally did it in was the dog biting it off to use it as a stick for fetch. All this from a tree that is now extinct in the wild. (I guess I planted it in the wrong place, too.)

Then there was the maple tree. My sister planted a silver maple right next to the patio before she moved out. As soon as she moved out, I knew I wanted to move it because it would spill too many leaves and whirly-seeds, not to mention the invading roots so close to the house. It was from a nursery, so it was already about 8 feet tall when I decided to move it. I hacked at the roots and made the ball as little as I could. It still took every ounce of energy to move it to the far side of the yard. Eight years later, that tree is now 50 feet tall. I sure am glad I moved it when I did! And it didn't seem to suffer from such abuse.

Spring maple

But please let me clarify. My rough treatment during tree planting doesn't mean I am not nice to trees. I love trees and like to get to know them personally. I can spend three times as much time deciding where to plant one as actually planting it. I just don't think they are as sensitive as people make them out to be. I've never staked one, wrapped those silly things around their trunks, or held them up with those trusses or whatever they are. I have never added peat moss, and I have certainly never fed them. They feed me . . . fruit, nuts, mulch, shade, kindling, wood, oxygen.

There are a few exceptions, when trees are deserving of special attention. Trees should only be planted in spring or fall, when they are dormant. Sometimes it is necessary to plant them in the middle of summer—like the river birch I rescued from execution this summer. The landscaper was going to get rid of it because it was too big and too gawky—a Charlie Brown among river birches. Well, I took it and I actually did water it consistently for a few weeks.

But remember, trees are living things. It is their instinct to find water. If you plant one and don't water it too much, its roots will go in search of water. Planting a tree when it is in full leaf, however, will send it into shock—especially if it's balled-and-burlapped or bare-root rather than container-grown—and it will need some nursing for a while. But give it the winter to recover and before you know it, it will be back full strength.

Some trees in my yard have even planted themselves. I had a 30-foot walnut tree that started because of some squirrel. When it was smaller, the kids loved jumping on its bouncy branches. Then the branches—and the kids—got too big to bounce, but those branches were perfect for sitting on. We noticed that the rope the kids had tied around one of the branches for swinging and climbing had actually been consumed by the tree and stuck out of the middle of a branch.

But then I found out that walnuts are toxic to other trees and smaller plants (especially apples) and it was growing right next to my 80-year-old apple tree and my compost pile. So now I've cut it down and have wood for fires. More important, I've got a giant stump to make an outdoor table and chairs for my newborn daughter to hold tea parties at next year . . . and that's the story of the short but happy life of a walnut tree.

The self-planted tree that spewed hard little black berries onto my patio every summer also had to go, since I hate wearing shoes between May and September. I now have a nice little woodpile to show for it.

If I stopped doing anything in my yard today, within three years I would have a little forest of walnut, mimosa, maple, and goodness knows what else. Tree seedlings sometimes seem to be my greatest weed problem. That thought can be both reassuring and frightening. It's reassuring because it reminds me that the earth has a huge potential to heal itself no matter what kind of damage we do to it. (It will

If you want to get an idea of the natural fertility of the earth, take a walk to the wild mountainside sometime and look at the giant trees that grow without fertilizer and without cultivation. The fertility of nature, as it is, is beyond reach of the imagination.

—Masanobu Fukuoka,
The One-Straw Revolution

survive long after we are gone.) But then again, it's frightening to know that something you put so much love and attention into can be so impermanent . . . which is all the more reason not to fuss too much over it.

Here are some tips for planting trees.

For cleaner air and cooler summers, plant trees.

- Planting trees in urban areas can reduce the amount of ozone in the air (smog) *and* absorb heat, therefore cooling down those sweltering summers in the city. The bigger the trees (and the more of them), the better.

- Many of the most-used and most-loved landscape trees are highly susceptible to diseases and pests, much like overbred dogs that suffer from genetic problems. Avoid the problem trees (flowering dogwood, crabapple, white birch, Canadian hemlock). Many of these trees have varieties that are disease-resistant. Spending the time to seek them out will reward you with many, many maintenance-free years of enjoyment.

- Many fruit trees can also be notoriously finicky. Often, varieties sold in local nurseries are not very disease-resistant. Trees ordered from catalogs can arrive small and vulnerable. Your best bet is to research varieties that will do well organically in your area, and either find them in a local nursery or nurse mail-order plants into fruition.

- Don't plant trees too deeply. The rootball should be close to the soil surface.

- If you prune a tree for any reason, *don't* use any sort of limb sealer. It can actually prevent the healing of the tree.

- When planting a tree, there is almost *no reason* to stake the tree. The only reason would be if the top part of the tree is significantly heavier than the rootball—for instance, in the case of a large pine tree.

- Don't add all sorts of stuff to the hole when you dig it to "coddle" the tree (examples would be peat moss, lots of compost, or fluffy topsoil). What happens when you do that is it creates a sort of "bucket of water" effect that can rot the roots and prevent the tree or bush from getting a good start. It can also trap the roots in the original planting hole.

Planting Flowers, Herbs, Groundcovers, and Other Plants

This is also not a difficult thing. Squat, dig a small hole, stick the plant in, cover with soil, and water. You're done!

Giant allium extravaganza

The Right Plant in the Right Place Makes Your Garden Happy

Seriously, the most important thing to consider when planting *any-thing* is to plant it in a place where it will have the conditions it likes. Don't put a shade-loving plant in full sun, a big plant in a small space, or a wetland plant on a droughty slope. A happy plant is one that's growing where its needs are met.

Sun and Shade

If you plant a shade-loving plant in full sun, no amount of care, chemicals, or compost will make it do well. It won't grow, it will probably look burned, and it will quickly succumb to disease or pests and then die. Nurseries and catalogs will tell you the planting requirements for each plant (so will a basic plant identification guide). Occasionally you can get away with ignoring the plant's requirements, but the plant will show signs of being out of place (usually by looking small, pathetic, and sickly).

Bleeding heart

Shade-Loving Plants

Ajugas

Azaleas

Bleeding hearts

Ferns

Hellebores

Hostas

Lamium

Periwinkles (vincas)

Primroses

Pulmonarias

Rhododendrons

Size Is Everything

If you plant a large tree or plant in a small space, eventually you will have to move it or pay the consequences. It may be very tiny when you first plant it, but as it grows, it can uproot and consume other plants, sidewalks, and anything else in its way, including small animals and toys. It can also block the light from your windows, plunging your house into darkness, or converge on the door, forcing you into using daring tactics every time you need to get in or out.

A small plant will never get bigger than it's meant to be. So if you plant a small plant to fill a large space, no amount of fertilizer will help. Better to plant a tree that will grow to the size you want rather than constantly pruning it back or wishing it were bigger than it can ever be. Here's one case where it really pays to do your homework: Find out the plant's mature size *before* you buy.

Tulips like the sun . . . and the shade.

Sizing Up Trees

It may look small in the nursery—and even smaller planted in your yard. But that 6-foot, scrawny sugar maple sapling can eventually turn into a 100-foot tree with a 50-foot-wide canopy. The cute little living Christmas tree you planted out by the back door can grow into a hulking giant that threatens to topple the porch roof. It makes sense to choose trees by their eventual size, not by their present appearance.

Big Trees

Beeches

Buckeyes and horse chestnut

Red, silver, and sugar maples

Oaks

Spruces

Sweet gum

Sycamores

Tulip tree

Walnuts

Medium Trees

Birches

Carolina silverbell

Cherries

Golden-rain tree

Hemlocks

Magnolias (most)

Japanese maples

Pines

Red cedar

Small Trees

Crabapples

Dogwoods

Japanese maples

Redbuds

Stewartias

Witch hazels

Bearded iris

Wet and Dry

Wet and dry soils present their own challenges. Picture what a moisture-loving plant looks like in a dry location: shriveled. Or what a plant that hates wet soil looks like in a damp location: moldy, fungusy, and limp. Luckily, there are plants that are unusually well adapted to wet or dry conditions.

Honeysuckle

Plants for Wet and Dry Sites

If you have a boggy site or a dry, exposed slope, choose plants that thrive in these conditions. Here are some good choices.

Moisture-Loving Plants

Cardinal flower

Cranberry

Daylilies

Elderberry

Ferns

Forget-me-nots

Hibiscus and rose mallow

Horsetail

Irises (except bearded iris)

Jacob's-ladder

Joe-Pye weed

Summersweet

Viburnums

Winterberry holly

Drought-Tolerant Plants

Asters

Butterfly weed

Coreopsis

Daylilies

Ornamental grasses

Honeysuckles

Bearded iris

Lavenders

Cheddar pink

Pomegranate

Prickly pear

Rosemary

Sedums

Trumpet vine

Verbenas

Soil pH Makes a Difference

Planting a plant that loves alkaline conditions in an acid soil is a lot like planting a sun-loving plant in the shade. It may grow, but it just won't do as well. You can change pH slightly by adding stuff to it, but as I said before, your best bet is to go with your natural system—don't fight it. However, if you insist on fighting, here's what you can do.

- **To make an acid soil more alkaline:** Add lime or wood ash

- **To make an alkaline soil more acidic:** Add elemental sulfur, pine needles, or coffee grounds. I heard about one lady who waters her azaleas and rhododendrons with leftover coffee. I don't know if it helps, but it sounds like a good idea.

- **To bring either an acid or alkaline soil closer to neutral:** Add compost. It sounds too good to be true, but compost will help to neutralize both acid and alkaline soils.

By now, you may be feeling overwhelmed with all these conditions. But don't worry. Remember, if you plant something in the wrong place, just move it.

Clematis and
lavender

Rhododendron

Plants for Acid and Alkaline Soils

Lucky for us, there are plants well adapted to growing in either acid or alkaline soils. So I say, why fight it? If you have either pH extreme on your property, grow your veggies in trucked-in topsoil in containers or raised beds, but plant your landscape with plants that thrive in the soil you've got.

Plants That Grow Well in Acid Soil

Azaleas	Lilies
Beeches	Lily-of-the-valley
Blueberries	Mountain laurel
Cranberry	Pieris
Ferns	Pines
Heathers	Rhododendrons
Heaths	Sourwood
Hemlocks	Woodland wildflowers
Hydrangeas	

Plants That Grow Well in Alkaline Soil

Boston ivy	Prairie wildflowers
Catalpa	Rosemary
Clematis	Snapdragons
Euonymus	Sycamores
Hackberry	Virginia creeper
Hawthorns	Zinnias
Honey locust	
Lavenders	
Pinks	

Planning and Planting Your Delicious Organic Garden

It's spring—time to plant. But first, take a time-out and plan your garden. I know it's hard to resist the urge to get your fingers in the ground, but you and your family will enjoy your garden more if you think about what you want to do. To steal a phrase, think twice, plant once.

Planning Your Vegetable Garden

If you are going to grow vegetables and herbs, there are many ways you can go about it, but there are three basic styles: extremely organized, totally disorganized, and somewhere in between. All three styles are completely acceptable because basically you can do whatever you want, however you want, in your own vegetable patch. There is no inherently wrong way to do anything. Of course, there are ways to do things that will make you more likely to succeed and reap the juicy benefits of your efforts. But first, I have a special message.

Lettuce is one of the easiest and most delicious vegetables to grow.

A Special Message for People Who Have Never Grown Vegetables

When I mention that I am writing a gardening book including vegetable and fruit growing, people often confess their gardening fears to me. A common confession is "I'm afraid to grow vegetables." Or "I have no idea how to begin growing vegetables!" Or "Vegetable gardens are so ugly! If you can show me how to make a vegetable garden look nice, then I'll consider growing them."

Vegetable growing is extremely easy. If you've never done it before, here's how.

1. Get some good soil (with lots of compost).

2. Stick in some seeds.

3. Water.

4. Watch it grow.

5. Eat it.

I'm really not joking. It's that easy. There are an endless amount of other tips, techniques, and secrets, but the most important thing is to get in and try it and learn by doing.

Choosing a Site

When you start thinking about your garden, the most important thing to begin with is choosing a good site. Here's what to look for.

- Good soil (either build raised beds or bring in new soil if you don't have it, especially in urban and suburban areas)

- Good drainage and water flow

- Good light (most vegetables and herbs need 8 to 12 hours of full sunshine daily)

- A beautiful location integrated into the rest of your landscape

Organizing Your Plantings

This is where the best intentions often break down. What works best for me is to plan my garden on paper as I'm reading and picking out my seeds from the mail-order catalogs in the spring. That way, after the seeds arrive, all I have to do is plant them in the spot where I was thinking they should go. (Before you rush ahead and do that, however, read the upcoming sections on rotation and companion planting for best results.)

But I have been known to just go out there and start putting seeds in willy-nilly. The more you are concerned about beauty, however, the more it pays to plan.

How to Make Your Garden Beautiful

There are two effective ways of making a vegetable garden beautiful. First is how you build and design your vegetable beds. Second is how you decide to plant. A beautiful vegetable bed has the following characteristics: a prime location, a pleasing layout, and quality building materials. Let's look at how each part works.

Prime location means that your garden isn't stuffed in some unwanted corner or plunked right in the middle of an odd space, but is integrated into the overall design of your yard so it not only fits in but also adds beauty.

The most important thing is to get in and try it and learn by doing.

Pleasing layout doesn't necessarily mean the proverbial square or rectangular patch, but a shape that, again, fits into your overall design. It could be circular or curvy, it could be long and line your patio, or it could be integrated into your flowerbeds. It could be a classic shape, like the four square beds popularized by the kitchen garden style. Or it could be modernist and angular. The only limits are your imagination and energy.

Once you have picked your prime location and designed your pleasing layout, you will want to edge your beds with **quality materials.** You could go naked and not edge with anything—whatever your pleasure. But if you do choose to edge your garden or build a raised bed and are concerned about beauty, don't use things that are ugly to edge it. (Usually things made of plastics or composites tend to be ugliest.) Please also avoid sloppy construction. Wood, stone, cement, and brick are all attractive and effective.

Beautiful Plantings

Perhaps you have seen the pictures in magazines of beautifully designed vegetable gardens—they look like quilts, or works of art. If

You can use any old sticks stuck in the mud as trellises for spring peas. I like using curly willow.

you have the patience and the energy to do that in your vegetable garden, go ahead. It truly is beautiful. But I find if I get too fussy about beautiful plantings, it's so pretty that I can't bear to pick anything because it ruins the whole look. And eating vegetables is why you have a garden in the first place. However, that doesn't mean my vegetable garden is ugly. Here are a few tips for keeping your vegetable garden beautiful (and delicious!).

- You don't need to plant in rows. Plant in squares, zigzags, circles, or other patterns. In fact, planting in masses as opposed to rows is usually more productive . . . although planting too much too close together can reduce yields.

- Don't use ugly stuff to do practical things. If you are going to use a trellis, buy or make a nice one that you will be proud to show off. (I bought one of those flimsy trellises sold at local garden and hardware stores—twice. Neither of them lasted a season.)

- If you are going to scare away birds and rabbits, do it tastefully, not with garish devices. (See the "Summer" section on birds and rabbits for advice.)

Rotation

Garden beds can be permanent, but the way you design your vegetable plantings each year should not be permanent. One of the most important tools of good organic gardening is rotating your plants every year. Rotation means that you don't plant tomatoes (or any other vegetable) in the same place every year—or even every other year.

Keeping vegetables in the same place year after year allows insect pests (many of which need a few years of reproduction to get established) and diseases to do major damage. By moving your vegetables around, you are, in effect, starving and tricking the pests.

There is no real trick to crop rotation other than vaguely remembering where you planted things the year before and the year before that (a good reason to keep a garden journal). Then, plant them somewhere else. If you can keep things out of the same bed for three to five years, you should greatly reduce, if not eliminate, your chances of insect and disease problems.

Companion Planting

Companion planting is one of those things that has been around forever, but much of its wisdom has not necessarily been scientifically "proven." Some things seem to grow really well together, and others don't. The main justifications for companion planting are the plant diversity that results (mixing plantings make it harder for pests to find their target plants), the substances released by the plants themselves, and the cooperation (or lack thereof) between plants regarding insect and disease problems.

Don't plant broccoli near your tomatoes.

Some plants help keep each other healthy, and others can make each other sick. Take, for instance, the black walnut tree. Black walnut trees are known to produce substances called juglones that are toxic to many plants near them, including fruits, vegetables, and other plants. On the other hand, growing dill with your vegetables will attract beneficial insects.

Another example of companion planting that is a fascinating use of space in the garden is the "three sisters" planting scheme of the Native Americans. The three sisters are corn, beans, and squash. It just so happens that if you plant them together, they work in beautiful harmony. The corn provides trellising for the beans (pole beans, which are climbers) and the squash acts as a groundcover amidst the corn. Planting the three together not only saves lots of space but provides a better growing environment for each. Now *that's* companion planting.

Here are some popular companions.

Garlic and roses

Garlic and tomatoes or eggplant

Marigolds and tomatoes

Strawberries and peaches

Tomatoes and basil

Keep your potatoes away from your melons.

Here are some combinations to avoid.

Apples and potatoes

Broccoli (and other cabbages) and tomatoes

Corn and quackgrass

Garlic and onions next to peas and beans

Grapes and cabbages

Marigolds with beans and cabbages

Peppers and beans

Potatoes and melons

Pumpkins and potatoes

Succession Planting

Unlike companion planting, succession planting doesn't need to be proven or disproven—it's just common sense. Basically, succession planting comes down to this: If you want to get more out of your garden, think of your garden beds as a continual planting ground over the growing season. When the peas are done in the spring, plant green beans. When the green beans are done in midsummer, plant another crop of peas for fall harvesting.

Certain plants, like melons or peppers, have a long growing season and will stay comfortably in their places the whole summer. Others, like lettuces and other cool-weather vegetables, grow quickly and are harvested well before the season ends. For a second crop from some of those quick-growing plants, plant them again in early August for a fall harvest. Vegetables that do well when succession-planted for fall include lettuces, cabbages, beans, peas, beets, and carrots, to name a few.

Planting Herbs

Few plants are as satisfying and easy to grow as herbs. They look nice and smell great. You get powerful fresh flavor for cooking right outside your door. Herbs are practically carefree . . . except a few you should know about. Certain herbs are, shall we say, a bit overeager to grow—some by roots, some by seed, some by any other means.

Take mint, for example. Mint would, if allowed, take over the world. But nothing is as naturally sweet and delightful as a glass of chilled fresh mint iced tea in the summertime. (And nothing could be easier to make: Cut a few stalks of mint before it flowers, rinse, and put in a heat- and cold-proof container. Pour boiling water over it. Let it steep for a half hour or so. Refrigerate until cold. Drink.)

There are three ways to grow and control mint.

1. Plant mint in a container that will keep its roots and stems from spreading, and bury the container in the ground (for example, a plastic pot with the bottom cut out, a can with both ends cut off, or a ceramic frostproof pot).

2. Plant it in a shady out-of-the-way area where it can spread naturally but is somewhat controlled by the shade.

3. Constantly hack it back.

Mint's a spreader, so you have to keep it under control. But it's worth it!

Some herbs reseed themselves every year, which can be good or it can be nightmarish. Consider feverfew, for instance. I let one plant go to seed in my herb garden last year (it had such pretty flowers!). This year I spent quite a bit of time (not thyme) digging it up. Lesson from the herb garden: Don't let your herbs go to seed unless you want them to reseed prolifically. (But I always intentionally let parsley reseed.)

Many herbs, however, pose no problems at all and are the true gems of the culinary garden (the biggest bang for your work). Grow them as close to your kitchen as possible so that you can forage for them while you are cooking. I always put fresh herbs in salad. Here are some favorites.

Annual herbs: basil, cilantro, lemon verbena (a tender perennial grown as an annual), and parsley (a biennial grown as an annual)

Perennial herbs: bay leaf (a tender perennial), chamomile, chives, lavender, mint, oregano, rosemary, sage, and thyme

Thyme is very well behaved.

Mint as it was meant to be

A pear tree makes a beautiful landscape plant (although fall can be a bit messy if you don't eat the fruit).

Planting Fruit

Many people, even good gardeners, fear fruit. Growing it, that is. Fruit has the reputation of being buggy, diseased, and just plain difficult. Some books make it seem as if you have to have a master's degree in pruning to have even one fruit tree in your yard. But it doesn't have to be that way.

When I moved into my house, there were three fruit trees in the yard: a 65-foot ancient black cherry tree that died the moment I looked at it; an 80-year-old, 50-foot-tall apple tree that looked as if it had never been pruned; and a beautifully shaped unpruned pear tree about 25 feet tall and also well aged.

The first year, I had beautiful 'Golden Delicious' apples. An apple just picked from an autumn tree has a taste like no other—very spiritual and primordial (something about the garden of Eden thing . . .). The second year, however, there was hardly any fruit. So, thinking the tree needed to be pruned, I had a pruner come in and chainsaw it back. I don't think the tree has ever fully recovered. I have also since found out that some varieties of apple (and other fruits) often are biennial bearers—which means they only fruit heavily every other year.

The pear tree has been beautiful left unpruned. Although its production has decreased with age, the pears are truly beautiful and delicious. And even if it didn't bear fruit, just the blooming and the beautiful shape of it are enough to make me want it.

I've had a little less luck with planting new fruit trees. But even so, I have growing in my yard in varying ages and stages quince bushes, persimmon trees, pawpaw trees, raspberries, elderberry bushes, Alpine strawberries, grapevines, apple trees, hardy kiwi vines, blackberries, sour cherry trees, cranberries, and peach trees. (The blueberries I planted last year got eaten by my pumpkins.) I also have lemon and olive trees growing in pots.

My advice is to try a few fruits, and see which ones work for you. If the aphids or other bugs come, deal with them by spraying soapy water on them or picking them off. Just don't let the pests freak you out because that doesn't help anything or anybody. Rarely do they kill the tree, and sometimes it's just a phase—like kids getting chicken pox.

Prune the trees or bushes slightly when you first get them to shape the plants (cut back dead branches and branches that are rubbing against each other). If you are so inclined, thin the fruit on trees like apples so that most of the energy goes into the nicest fruit. Most important, buy disease-free varieties to begin with, although even that won't be a guarantee. Old heirloom varieties are probably your best bet if you can find them for your area.

If deer are your problem, I just read that "free-range" dogs are your best bet for keeping deer out of orchards and gardens, according to a study done at Cornell University. Letting your dog roam the orchards

will be both your alarm system and your removal system. Otherwise, high fencing is the most reliable way to keep out deer.

Last, but not least, if you want your fruit all to yourself, you may need to protect it from birds by using netting. But if you don't mind sharing, there is usually enough for everyone—unless you're growing blueberries. Birds love blueberries!

Quince trees are both small and beautiful, and they produce fruit that is delicious when it is cooked and sweetened.

These beautiful blueberries were grown organically by a neighbor who has an organic vegetable and fruit delivery service.

An Organic Family Tree of Philosophies
(and Which One Is Best for Your Personality Type)

Organic gardening has its share of snobbery and name-dropping. For the beginner (as in any hobby), it can be intimidating to hear more experienced people throwing around terms and names and not to have a clue what they mean or who they are (Fuko-*who?*).

Sir Albert Howard

There are actually five distinct methods of organic gardening based on the different styles of their proponents. The reason I am going to all this trouble is not to force you to pick a style but to clear away the flotsam and jetsam that surround organic gardening's history and to clarify it once and for all (for both your sake and mine—I learned a lot putting this together).

Many of the people cited here would also credit Rachel Carson (not a gardener, but an ecologist) with bringing to the attention of the public the negative effects of chemicals on nature and wildlife in her groundbreaking book *Silent Spring*. I have also listed famous organic gardeners in the approximate style I would categorize them in, which is by no means the way they may categorize themselves. The following methods are in order of the age of their development.

Rodale Organic Method

This method was inspired by the work of Sir Albert Howard, an early twentieth-century British agronomist who developed the Indore method of composting in India and was the author of *An Agricultural Testament*; Lady Eve Balfour, author of *The Living Soil*; and F. King, who looked at thousands of years of continual, productive, and natural farming in Asia in his book *Farmers of Forty Centuries*.

J. I. Rodale brought their theories to America in the early 1940s. **He connected the idea of organic gardening to human health** at a time when the chemical fertilizer industry had convinced farmers that all they needed to do was supply nutrients in powdered form for infinite fertility. He started publishing *Organic Gardening and Farming Magazine* in 1942. His son, my father, Robert Rodale, continued the organic mission. He did the first scientific studies at the Rodale Institute in the 1970s and 1980s to prove that organic and sustainable agriculture was equal or superior to chemical agriculture.

The most traditional gardening method, the Rodale Organic Method is adaptable to

Photo by Rodale Images

J. I. Rodale

many styles of garden design but is most committed to the use of **compost, compost, compost.** This style is best for people who are concerned about their health and want their yards and gardens to thrive and provide lots of healthy food as well as a safe environment for people and for wildlife.

Biodynamic Method

Rudolph Steiner, the founder of anthroposophy and the Waldorf schools, developed this method in Germany in the 1920s. His basic theory was that **nature is a mystical, spiri-** **tual thing,** and to garden it well, one must treat it as a whole entity and system, both physical and spiritual. Plantings and harvesting are done based on lunar and planetary phases.

Although much of what is known as biodynamic gardening and farming is considered "New Age," some of Steiner's holistic ways of looking at soil, plants, and nature have been integrated into more conventional methods. However, his method is best for you if the thought of administering strange mystical brews to your garden by the light of the moon while you are naked and chanting appeals to you.

Masanobu Fukuoka

Fukuoka Method

Masanobu Fukuoka is a Japanese farmer (and former scientist) who has developed a unique and natural system for farming and living that maximizes nature's benefits and minimizes human work and effort. Rather than ask what you need to do, he asks what you *don't* need to do. His major book was *One-Straw Revolution,* published in the United States in 1978. He has five basic beliefs as they relate to gardening and farming.

1. **No cultivation.** Let nature work the soil with roots, animals, worms, and microorganisms. Fukuoka does not till the soil.

2. **No chemical fertilizer or prepared compost.** Let the soil find its natural balance. Fukuoka does compost kitchen wastes and feeds them to animals and chickens. On his fields, however, he only mulches with the waste from the crops that were grown there.

3. **No weeding by tillage or herbicides.** Control weeds with straw mulch or white clover. Don't try to eliminate them. The more you till, the more weeds you will have.

4. **No chemicals.** Create a healthy environment! The more bugs, the more balance.

5. **Sow the seeds on top of the soil.** Fukuoka has developed a method of coating seeds in clay and then just sprinkling them in the fields. That way, he doesn't do *any* tilling and disturbing of the soil.

His method is best for you if you don't mind a bit of chaos in your yard and want a very natural, integrated look with vegetables reseeding themselves and plants mulching themselves with their own stalks. It's also excellent if you want to grow rice.

During the past few years the number of people interested in natural farming has grown considerably. It seems that the limit of scientific development has been reached, misgivings have begun to be felt, and the time for reappraisal has arrived. That which was viewed as primitive and backward is now unexpectedly seen to be far ahead of modern science. This may seem strange at first, but I do not find it strange at all.

—Masanobu Fukuoka, *The One-Straw Revolution*

John Jeavons Biointensive Method and the John Seymour Self-Sufficiency Method

These methods were developed in the early 1970s, with the goals being high-yield, small-scale garden farming and self-sufficiency.

John Jeavons wrote the book *How to Grow More Vegetables Than You Ever Thought Possible on Less Land Than You Can Imagine* (1974), based on the hybridization of the Biodynamic and French Intensive methods developed by Alan Chadwick (from England). The French Intensive Method involves creating deep beds (18 inches) of very fertile, aerated soil made by "double-digging," raising the beds up and not walking on them, and then planting things very close together.

John Seymour was inspired by Alan Chadwick as well but also by his years spent in Africa and his studies of the way of life of rural people. He wrote *The Complete Book of Self-Sufficiency* (1975) and *The Self-Sufficient Gardener* (1979). His approach involves the whole life as a means of creating self-sufficiency and *more joy*. **He brings domestic animals into the whole cycle of nature, animals, people, and gardening with a unique perspective that by losing the old way of life, we are also losing a form of happiness that is as essential to humans as good soil is to growing good food.**

Both of these methods are good for you if you are not afraid of hard work (double-digging, raising animals, preserving your own food) and are looking for an intensive, total way of living that is in harmony with the earth. As Angela Ashe (the woman who lives with John Seymour and does most of the preserving) says, you need "common sense, responsibility, and organization."

In the basement of the great concrete building, powerful generators supplied air and warmth; there was no sign of design for energy conservation. I invited my audience to look out the windows at the smog, the constant process of demolition, the traffic. How could they, traveling more than 80km to work daily (and then home), and living in inefficient houses, in all conscience go to Africa to help build grass huts? How can we help people if we can't help ourselves?

If we recommend mud, let us live in mud. Congruence in lifestyle and work, if we think about it, is essential to our ability to teach. Nobody can be perfect, but we should be on the way to greater congruence.

—Bill Mollison, *Travels in Dreams*

Bill Mollison Permaculture Method

Permaculture (a combination of the words permanent and agriculture), although rooted in older techniques, is the newest branch of gardening to sprout from the continent of Australia. As Tasmanian Bill Mollison, author of *Introduction to Permaculture* and other books, says, "Organic isn't enough." You have to look at the whole landscape and how we live and integrate everything into it—from our homes, energy usage, water usage, and all the waste streams to how we grow, raise, and consume our food. The philosophy has three main tenets.

1. **Care of the earth**

2. **Care of all species (including people)**

3. **Contribution of surplus time, money, and energy to achieve the aims of earth and people/species care**

Although Mollison's approach may seem "hard line," there are many aspects of his method that are applicable to the home gardener, some of which are in this book. His style is best for you if you are really earnest about changing the world and want to make a big difference . . . starting in your own backyard.

All of these different families in the organic philosophy tree have aspects of value to the home gardener. Although many of the men mentioned above would disagree with me when I say this, feel free to pick and choose from the different techniques and ideas and integrate them into your own personal style.

Bill Mollison

14 reasons why you should never, ever, ever use chemicals again

If by now you still aren't convinced that totally organic is the way to go, here are 14 good reasons why you should never, and I mean never, use chemical fertilizers and pesticides on your property or anywhere else.

Admit it, the first sight of an ugly bug and you just want to get something to kill it and kill it fast. Or maybe your plants look scrawny and you don't want to bother with figuring out why and a dose of Miracle-Gro seems like the quickest way to get results.

You may think that a little bit of chemicals here and there won't hurt you or anybody else. What's so bad about a little Miracle-Gro here and a little Roundup there?

It all adds up, that's what. According to the Environmental Protection Agency, in 1995 homeowners spent more than $1.9 billion dollars on pesticides for the home and garden. Ironically, it's not even necessary.

If you ever needed a reason not to use chemicals in your yard, here are 14 of them.

1. They smell really bad. I mean it. The smell of fertilizers and pesticides practically ruins the spring nursery-shopping experience. The places are full of it and it stinks . . . and people complain about compost. Ha!

2. They can make you and your family and your pets and the wildlife sick. S-I-C-K. Nausea, vomiting, skin rashes, leukemia and other cancers, weakened immune systems—lovely, have some more, dear! They can also potentially make us infertile as a species.

3. They leach into the groundwater and pollute our drinking water, making people, animals, fish, and birds sick. S-I-C-K. (See above.)

4. Pesticides kill the bad bugs and the good bugs and the birds. Then the bad bugs get resistant, and the birds have less to eat, and what they eat makes them sick. Pesticides also kill bees. And many plants depend on bees for pollination. Without bee pollination, there would be fewer fruits and vegetables. Not to mention honey.

5. Chemical fertilizers add nutrients to the soil, but they don't add anything else. Before you know it, the soil structure is so weak that it can't hold itself together, and it starts to erode and collapse. Once it starts eroding, it clogs up the rivers and streams, and it goes all the way out to sea and kills the coral reefs. No kidding. Erosion is the number one cause of damage to coral reefs.

6. The more you use, the more you need to use. Just like a junkie.

7. Wouldn't you rather spend your money on some great new plants?

8. Buying chemical fertilizers and pesticides supports huge corporations who spend millions and billions of dollars lobbying to try to suppress research that shows just how bad the stuff really is. And then they go and sell billions of dollars' worth of DDT to Third World countries where it is still legal.

9. Did you know chemical herbicides were developed by the Pentagon as defoliants in the Vietnam War? People make bombs with chemical fertilizers. Find another way to be patriotic.

10. Using chemical fertilizers is a substitute for thinking. If you don't want to think, fine. Just don't ruin it for the rest of us.

11. Pesticides travel and have contaminated even the most remote regions of the world. From the rain forests of South America to the polar caps, high concentrations of pesticides can be found, even though none of the chemicals were ever made or used there.

12. Even using pesticides *inside* the home can contaminate water supplies. Believe it or not, many people dump excess home pesticides down sinks, toilets, sewers, and storm drains. It all comes back to your drinking water. Don't do it. *Don't* buy them in the first place.

13. Studies have shown that pesticides are strangely attracted to children's toys—most of which end up in their mouths.

14. Up to 20 percent of the chemicals you buy legally include heavy metals—toxic wastes, which include lead, dioxin, and arsenic, that would otherwise be subject to rigorous hazardous waste disposal laws—as fillers. I guess the government figures if you're willing to put chemical fertilizers and pesticides in your own backyard, you'd be willing to do your part to get rid of all the toxic waste in the world. Not in my yard!

Nature Needs a Skin:
Groundcovers, Mulches, and Lawns

If you care to notice, Nature heals herself constantly. Anytime we remove her skin—whether it's to build, to plant, or by accident—she will do her best to replace her skin with plants, mulch (leaves), or trees. That's regeneration. When Mount St. Helens erupted, the landscape looked as barren as the moon. Now, it is covered with trees, smaller plants, and animals, all put there without our help.

Understanding the principle of regeneration in your home landscape is the key to making it more maintenance-free. As long as you leave the earth exposed, you will be fighting a losing battle. Nature wants her skin to heal, and she will make it happen. Think about having a wound on your skin. The only way you can stop it from healing is to constantly pick at it and re-wound it. Ouch.

That's why groundcovers, mulches, and grasses are so important. With them, you can put the "skin" of your choice on your patch of Nature.

Groundcovers

Groundcovers are perennial plants that spread across the ground to cover it with a living mulch. From the typical choices such as pachysandra and periwinkle to more unusual plants like lamium and ajuga, there are a host of selections that can, after they're established, provide a strong skin. See the section in "Fall" on groundcovers for a few of my favorites.

Mulches

Mulches are dead matter (leaves, bark, stone) that cover the ground like a bandage. Except for solid stone, they won't permanently keep other plants from growing, but they will provide a protective barrier while they decompose. Mulches mimic nature's own cover of falling leaves and branches, which both suppresses competitive plants and provides a continuous supply of new soil as the leaves and branches decompose.

Here are the benefits of mulching.

- Mulch suppresses weeds.

- It keeps moisture in the soil.

- Mulch can increase yields.

- Plants stay cleaner and healthier.

The most popular and best mulches are compost, grass clippings, bark mulch and other wood mulches, straw, and chopped leaves. There are some other unusual mulches, like cocoa hulls, which will make your yard smell like chocolate. The best thing to do is to use mulches

that are close by, locally made, and organic or as natural as possible. Here are the facts about each type.

Compost. An inch or two of straight compost makes a good mulch for increasing soil nutrition, as long as you didn't put a lot of seedy weeds into it. Best for vegetable beds and flowerbeds.

Grass. Best used in northern climates (compost it instead in the South), grass clippings work really well as mulch as long as they don't contain grass seed, they are organic, and they do not include Bermuda or Zoysia grass. Best for vegetable beds and flowerbeds.

Bark and wood chips. Wood mulches are the slowest to decompose, and they keep the soil especially cool (so they're better for the South than grass clippings). Try to look for high-quality organic wood mulches. You wouldn't want to put mulch made from pressure-treated wood, for instance, on your garden. Bark and untreated wood chips are best for flowerbeds, landscape beds, and pathways.

Straw. Straw is an ideal mulch for vegetable beds. Studies have proven that it prevents diseases, increases yields, and even makes things taste better. Best for vegetables and fruits (like, say, strawberries).

Leaves. Put leaves on flowerbeds and vegetable beds in the fall to slightly decompose over the winter, while protecting your plants and soil from winter winds and erosion. Leaves are great for mulching flowerbeds in the summer, since they have a cooling effect, so keep them off heat-loving vegetables in the early spring. Best for flowerbeds.

Pine needles. Pine needles and boughs can be used as mulch without making the soil acidic. Best for flowerbeds.

Newspapers. Sorry, newspapers don't qualify as "beautiful," so I really wouldn't recommend them. But really, newspapers are safe and

This beautiful lawn has never seen a chemical fertilizer or pesticide.

effective when layered on 6 to 8 inches deep (which is pretty deep). Interestingly enough, Kraft brown paper and cardboard also make excellent mulches (even better than newspapers, studies show). They're all great for suppressing weeds. So if you can find a way to use them without detracting from the beauty of your yard, they make a great mulch. Hint: Cover them with wood chips to disguise them. Best for vegetable beds and flowerbeds and killing off sod and weeds for new beds.

Natural Lawn Care

By now you may think I am totally against lawns. I am not. There is nothing quite like the silky softness of moist warm grass beneath your feet in the summer. The smell of fresh-mown grass is intoxicating to me. There is no better surface for playing, picnicking, and just lolling about on a warm summer evening.

The key to a successful, nonwasteful lawn is to plant a mix of seed varieties and then not get obsessed with it. Don't have too much lawn, and don't worry about it. Let the weeds do their thing. Let it toughen up in dry weather. The more you baby it, the more it will act like a baby.

Mowing. Don't cut the grass shorter than 3 inches. Leaving the grass a bit longer encourages deeper root growth, so the lawn needs less watering (if any). Use the clippings as mulch or use a mulching mower (there are no negative side effects to just leaving the grass on the lawn, either).

Don't assume your lawn service will "do the right thing." They tend to do "what most people want" and what is easiest and quickest for them (cut the grass short, use leaf blowers). Don't be afraid to say you want the grass cut at 3 inches, and please don't use any leaf blowers, thank you very much. (A leaf blower—that paean to laziness and non-usefulness—pollutes 34 times as much as a car. You are better off driving your car really fast around your yard to grind up and blow the leaves away.) And don't forget, 1 hour of lawn mowing pollutes as much as a car does after being driven for 11½ hours.

Fertilizing. Not necessary, but if you do it, use organic fertilizers. Better to plant the right grass for your climate and area (shade-loving species for shade, sun-loving species for sun).

Watering. If you must water your lawn, do it infrequently but deeply. Water in the morning for the most effective, least wasteful drink. But don't freak out if your grass turns slightly brown. A good rain will make it green again.

Aerating. Aerating is *only* appropriate if the lawn is heavily used or on heavy soil.

Thatch. Thatch is really a buildup of dead grass roots, stems, and leaves. It's caused by using chemicals, which kill the microbial life in the soil that would normally break down the dead grass. Don't use chemicals and don't mow too much, and you won't get it. If you see

There is nothing quite like the silky softness of moist warm **grass beneath your feet** in the summer.

Dandelion greens make a delicious and nutritious spring salad. So, if you can't beat them, eat them (before the flowers appear and they go to seed).

some thatch, ignore it and it will probably go away. If you must do something, rake early in the spring and let the grass recover naturally with the spring rains.

Weeds. Lots of weeds (including the infamous dandelion) are a symptom of a deeper problem—the wrong kind of grass, compacted soil, bad mowing practices. Find and fix the root of the problem and you'll rid your lawn of most weeds (because grass is one of the most aggressive weeds there is). Clover, on the other hand, is good. It's like having an all-natural nitrogen factory right in your lawn.

Diseases and insect pests. Again, most problems occur because of too many chemicals and too much fussing to begin with. If you use health-promoting techniques to care for your lawn, it can fight its own pest and disease problems with a healthy immune system.

5 Ways to
Dig Up Grass

Occasionally, you will find yourself wanting irrepressibly to dig up grass, either to plant a new bed or do some other landscaping thing. There are five basic ways to do it organically.

1. Use a pickax, a shovel, and some elbow grease. It's hard work but good exercise, and you get immediate results. Basically, dig it up and put it on the compost pile.

2. Lay down cardboard or newspapers, compost, and mulch on top (1 layer cardboard or newspaper, 4 inches compost, and 6 inches straw), and water exceedingly well. Wait over winter until the grass dies and things decompose. Plant. This is good if you've got the materials on hand and you are not in any big hurry.

3. Bring in a pig. A pig will dig up anything and everything in sight, and then fertilize the soil with its manure. Pigs will also eat almost all your kitchen scraps while they are visiting. They don't smell if you only have one or two. And, if inclined, you can eat them when they are through.

4. Bring in a backhoe. It's best for the impatient with large-scale plans. You can rent them by the day or hire excavators to do the job. Not recommended for small garden beds,

although you may be tempted if you are in the middle of digging one up by hand.

5. Hire someone with a turf digger. Most landscapers and lawn-maintenance companies have a machine that comes in and scrapes the top layer of soil off. It's more modest than a backhoe and requires more cleanup afterward. But it's still quicker than doing it yourself.

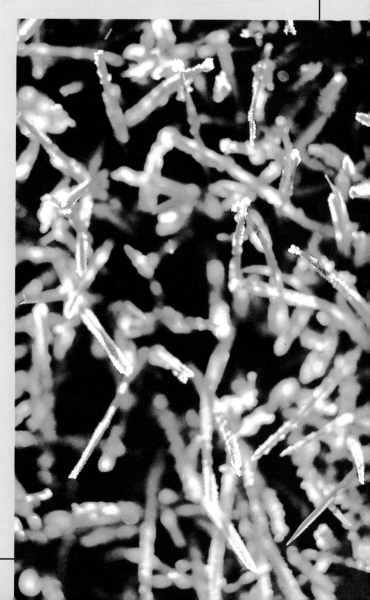

Enjoying the

Spring is so easy to enjoy. Baby birds are being born left and right, and they chirp you awake in the morning. Chipmunks and bunnies wake up and play, chasing each other in circles. Bulbs slink out of the ground, slowly at first, and then boldly braving the extremes of weather. Trees, bushes, and flowers burst out in a decadent display of hallucinogenic passion. And then the first fresh tastes of spring—asparagus, rhubarb and strawberries, lettuces and herbs—awaken your senses and cleanse away the darkness of winter.

Garden-Fresh Delights

Besides rhubarb, which you'll read more about in "Rhubarb Is Good (Really)" on page 180, there are other seasonal treats that you can harvest fresh from your garden. Spring is here!

Spring Fruit

Strawberries are so easy to grow. I grow the *fraises des bois* type (little alpine strawberries) because they don't spread like other strawberries. But I am sure it's just a matter of time before I grow the regular ones. Regular strawberries have to be divided every few years. And you need to cover them with netting while they are ripening if you want to ever eat any of them rather than letting the birds get all of them.

Season

Spring Vegetables

Arugula is a quick spring lettuce-type plant that is great for salads, in pasta, or on pizza. Just plant the seeds and watch it grow almost in front of your eyes. Do not plant wild arugula, however, unless you want it to take over your yard—you'll have to pull it out of everything for years and years. (I made that mistake and I'm still paying.)

Asparagus is a perennial vegetable that takes about three years to get established enough to start harvesting but, once established, provides you with years and years of sweet and fragrant spears. The plant turns into a beautiful bush during the summer, then dies back completely during the winter.

Kale is one of the best sources of calcium besides milk. Kale loves a cold spring and rewards you with a tasty flavor. Cook it with eggs (the same way I recommend for Swiss chard) or eat young kale fresh in salads.

Lettuces of all kinds are essential for spring salads. Lettuce is quick and easy to grow. Plant the seeds, and 40 to 90 days later you can harvest either the leaves or the entire heads. Lettuces prefer cool weather, and bolt (flower and go to seed) quickly in the heat. Don't eat lettuce after it's bolted, since it will be bitter. But if any plants do bolt, go ahead and let them set seed—they will both reseed themselves and provide food for finches and pollen for bees.

Peas are one of the staples of spring. I love peas. But unfortunately, the bunnies that visit my yard love them more and have prevented me from growing my own peas successfully for the last few years. I am now in the process of creating a "beautiful" mini portable bunny-keeper-outer fence so I can grow my peas and eat them, too. There are several types of peas—English or garden peas, snow peas, and snap peas. All are delicious and easy to grow, provided you can stop the bunnies. Not all peas need to be trellised, but for the ones that do, try putting some sticks in the ground where you plant the peas. It's a heck of a lot easier than building a trellis, and it looks cool, too.

Radishes are fast and fun. Pop the seeds in and watch them grow! The challenge is eating them before they get too big and spicy.

Swiss chard is so easy to grow, and it's good for you, too. My favorite way to make it is in a Cinquino family (my in-laws) special recipe: eggs and greens. Just sauté onions, garlic, and fresh chard, add a few eggs (scrambled), cook until done, and add grated romano cheese, salt, and pepper. You can also add any kind of herb, mushrooms, and even mint for a breakfast treat that will send you sailing though the day on a speeding train of energy. You can harvest Swiss chard a few stalks at a time, and the rest will keep growing. Take just enough for breakfast each time, and you'll have plenty for a summer full of yummy breakfasts.

Asparagus ferns are lush and airy.

Since I long ago lost faith in so-called experts, I bought two dozen asparagus roots a few years ago and decided to try planting them by just laying them on top of the ground (in a bed of peonies) and tossing hay on them. And I have had a fine crop from these roots every season. . . . And, of course, it gets no fertilization and no weeding around it; in fact, the grass grows right up against it.

—Ruth Stout, *The Ruth Stout No-Work Garden Book*

Many gardeners have never seen parsley in bloom.

Blooming thyme creates a purple carpet.

Spring Herbs

There are many, many herbs that a gardener can grow. But no garden or window box should be without the basic culinary herbs—chives, oregano, parsley, and thyme. These herbs are among the first to be ready to pick in spring, their flavors awakening winter-dulled senses.

Chives are well-behaved, beautiful, and delicious! Use chives in salads, soups, pasta, and anything else (other than dessert).

Oregano is delicious in salads, sauces, marinades, and pasta dishes. Give it space to grow and bloom.

Parsley is a biennial, producing leaves the first year and flowers and seeds the second. Parsley is delicious in salads and pasta dishes. Once a patch is established, let it reseed itself every year.

Thyme is delicious with poultry, salads, pastas, and meats. Makes a great groundcover, too.

Celebrate Spring!

Here are some of my favorite ways to celebrate spring.

- The daily tour: Take a tour around your yard every day (before work or right after for a special dose of strength and peace) and see "what's up." In those first days of spring, the changes are dramatic and hopeful.

- Plant trees in memory of people or pets. The first tree we planted on our property was a dogwood tree in memory of Kiki, my childhood dog who had just died. Fifteen years later, I still think of her every time I see the tree.

- Take a lounge chair outside, clean it off, and curl up (with a blanket if you must) with a good book or magazine.

- Plan an outdoor picnic or party to give yourself a deadline to get the yard ready and planted for summer.

- On a rainy spring day, put on your rubber boots and raincoat, grab an umbrella, and head to your local nursery for a walk and to peruse the new stock. Buy some plants and get all wet.

- Let your kids pick out and plant a tree or bush from the local nursery. Most kids love to dig, and it gives them something to remember for a long time.

- Give the animals in your yard names and get to know them better.

- Go on a gardooni-harvesting expedition. This is not for the faint of heart. "Gardooni" is the term used by the Cinquino family for burdock, or wild cardoon, a weed otherwise known by the burrs that get on your dog when he or she goes traipsing through the woods and meadows. Here's how to prepare and eat this wild treat. Cut the gardooni stalks when very young. Brush them and scrape off the stringy pieces around the outside. Boil them for about five minutes. Roll them in flour; dip them in scrambled raw egg; sauté in garlic and olive oil; season with salt, pepper, and romano cheese; and enjoy the most delicious treat you can imagine.

- Keep a bird and butterfly journal, and count the species that come to visit (the more the merrier!).

- Set up an outdoor dining area and eat outside on the warm spring days (enjoy the cool evenings before it gets too hot and buggy).

- Make your first spring salad and savor every bite!

Food for

By the end of winter, if you're like me, you're desperate to start eating fresh food out of your garden. So here, as promised, is the rhubarb dessert that will make you a convert to this tangy plant. And, of course, spring isn't spring without an assortment of delicious salads made from garden-fresh greens.

Rhubarb Is Good (Really)

Rhubarb is very easy to grow. It's a perennial plant that grows year after year but dies back completely in the winter. You can't eat rhubarb raw (and you only eat the stalks, not the leaves), but cooked rhubarb is delicious in pies and sauces.

My brother David (who died of AIDS in 1985) was one of my major inspirations when it came to cooking. He once made a recipe close to this one for me, which I loved. He actually served it as a hot dessert with a dollop of sour cream. I have altered the recipe slightly and serve it cold with ice cream.

David's (Sort of) Rhubarb Delight

I call it "sort of" because it's partly mine as well as his, not because it isn't delightful!

> ½ cup water
> I cup pink grapefruit juice
> I cup sugar
> ¼ teaspoon ground cloves
> 10 or more stalks of rhubarb
> I quart strawberries
> ½ cup dry red wine or ¼ cup port

1. Bring the water, grapefruit juice, sugar, and cloves to a boil. Add rhubarb chopped into 1-inch pieces and strawberries that have been cleaned.

2. Cook for about ½ hour or until everything is all mushed together, over medium to low heat.

3. Add the red wine or port. Serve hot or cold with ice cream.

Spring

The Salads of Spring

My favorite food is salad. My mother says I used to sit in my high chair as a child and stuff as much lettuce into my mouth as people gave me. To this day, I still prefer to eat salad with my fingers . . . I know, I'm a beast!

But what I knew then as salad and what I think of as salad today are a far cry from the iceberg-cucumber-tomato-carrot slice-with-goopy-dressing that passes for salad in most restaurants. (This seems to be changing slightly.) I mean *green* salad: romaine, spinach, endive, arugula, 'Oak Leaf' lettuce, watercress, dandelion, and anything else that is flavorful, with a dressing that enables you to taste the sunshine still in the leaves.

For those who don't like salad, give one of these recipes a chance. These are my favorites, and one of them is made nightly at my house for dinner. It's ready in a matter of minutes. The basic vinaigrette salad goes well with anything. The balsamic vinaigrette salad (with or without goat cheese) is delicious with roasted meats and poultry. The faux Caesar dressing is perfect with anything Italian. And the hot bacon dressing is a traditional Pennsylvania Dutch rite of spring.

In all of these recipes (except the hot bacon dressing), the better-tasting the olive oil, the better-tasting the dressing will be. Enjoy them!

Basic Spring Vinaigrette Salad with Violets

Violets add a delightful splash of color and spicy flavor to this salad. Pick some, rinse them off delicately, and sprinkle on top of the salad after the dressing is tossed on.

The Greens

Wash and dry any type of spring greens or a combination.

The Dressing: Basic Vinaigrette

3 parts good olive oil
1 part good vinegar (preferably wine vinegar)
pinch of kosher salt
freshly ground pepper

1. Put all the ingredients in a small bowl (I just use a small cereal bowl), starting with the oil. Emulsify with a fork (whip it up as if scrambling an egg).

2. Pour the dressing on the greens, and toss them.

You can add anything to this basic dressing that you like: herbs, garlic, shallots, spices, whatever. But sometimes it is just good to be simple and let the greens shine.

Balsamic Vinaigrette Salad with (or without) Goat Cheese

I always thought goat cheese was the most disgusting thing until I was served it like this at a dinner party and felt obligated to try it. I haven't been able to stop eating it since.

The Greens

Wash and dry any salad greens, but this tastes best with the darker and stronger-tasting ones, like arugula, spinach, and watercress.

The Dressing: Balsamic Vinaigrette

3 parts good olive oil
1 part balsamic vinegar
chopped shallots
pinch of kosher salt
freshly ground pepper

1. Put all the dressing ingredients in a bowl, beginning with the oil, and emulsify with a fork (whip it up as if scrambling an egg).

2. Pour over salad greens, toss, and serve with a piece of goat cheese prepared as described below.

The Goat Cheese

1. For each person, slice a 2-inch-thick piece of goat cheese.

2. Roll it in bread crumbs (either home-made or store-bought) and place in an ovenproof dish.

3. Spray lightly with olive oil. Heat in the oven at 350°F for about 10 to 15 minutes. Serve warm on the salad plate.

Yum. This is good to make when the oven is already hot from roasting your dinner.

Faux Caesar Salad

I am a wimp sometimes when it comes to eating—I don't like raw eggs and I don't like anchovies. But I love Italian cooking (I have to, since I am married to an Italian). Nothing goes quite as well with a bowl of spaghetti as a garlicky Caesar salad. Well, actually, garlic bread goes best, but salad is second-best. Here's my recipe.

The Greens

Wash and dry the greens. Romaine is the traditional lettuce to use, but anything will do. If you have fresh basil, oregano, thyme, or parsley, add them to either the salad or the dressing.

The Dressing: Faux Caesar

3 parts good olive oil

1 part red wine vinegar

1 clove garlic, chopped or crushed (dried minced garlic makes a milder dressing)

1 part fresh lemon juice

pinch of kosher salt

freshly ground pepper

freshly ground Romano or Parmesan cheese to taste, either mixed into the dressing or served on the side (if you have picky kid eaters as I do)

1. Put all the ingredients in a bowl, starting with the oil. Emulsify with a fork (whip it up as if scrambling an egg).

2. Pour over the salad greens, and toss them.

3. *Mangia.*

Ardie's Dandelion Salad with Hot Bacon Dressing

If you live in Pennsylvania, and it's early spring, and you see some elderly folks walking around with plastic bags and a knife bending over to pick something in a yard or a field, it must be dandelion time. The German word for dandelion is Pissabet, which means something like if you eat this you may wet the bed—it's a diuretic (more fondly referred to as a spring tonic).

Traditionally, dandelion salad is always served with hot bacon dressing, which some people not from Pennsylvania think is an acquired taste. I have acquired it and crave it in the spring. Here's my mother's recipe.

The Greens

Wash and dry the dandelion greens, either foraged when they are very, very new (long before any sort of flower starts to appear) or store-bought if you can find them. This dressing also works well for any sort of bitter green, such as endive.

The Dressing: Ardie's Hot Bacon Dressing

> 5 (or more) pieces of bacon (regular or turkey) and drippings
> 1½ cups water
> 2 tablespoons flour
> 3 tablespoons apple cider vinegar
> 5 tablespoons sugar
> 1 tablespoon yellow mustard
> black pepper
> hard-boiled egg (optional)

1. Fry the bacon and remove from the pan. (If you are using regular bacon, pour out half of the drippings.)

2. Mix the water, flour, vinegar, sugar, mustard, and black pepper together.

3. Add to bacon drippings and cook over medium heat until thick. You may need to adjust sugar to taste—the dressing should be sweet enough to counter the bitterness of the dandelion greens.

4. Pour over the dandelion greens while still hot.

5. Crumble the bacon on top. Add chopped hard-boiled egg if you want.

Calendar

Here's a checklist of garden chores, activities, commonsense tips, and fun for the busy season of spring.

March

Planting

It's time to plant peas, trees, shrubs, and early perennials.

Harvesting

Harvest dandelions for Ardie's Dandelion Salad.

In the South, harvest peas, radishes, and lettuce.

Pruning

Prune dead branches on trees and bushes and dead canes on roses.

Cut back any perennials that look messy.

Doing

Apply compost to your garden.

Get your garden furniture out of winter storage, and clean it off.

Clean up debris left from last year or from winter damage.

Turn under cover crops.

Finalize your orders of shrubs, perennials, and other plants from catalogs.

Preparing

Prepare to plant—get your seeds, seedlings, and plant list in order.

April

Planting	Set out transplants of broccoli, cauliflower, and cabbage.	Plant lettuce, kale, chard, radish, and carrot seeds directly in the garden. Plant seed potatoes.	Plant more new bushes and trees. Plant a strawberry bed.	Keep your seedlings watered.
Harvesting		Harvest asparagus and rhubarb.		
Pruning	Cut back ornamental grasses if you haven't already done so.	Thin raspberry canes. Cut out dead canes.		
Doing	Do your first round of weeding while the weeds are still small.	Dig new garden beds. Edge all your garden beds, or decide once and for all to put permanent edging in.	Wear a wide-brimmed hat when you're outside working on a sunny day.	Mow the lawn for the first time.
Preparing			Put away your snow shovel and other reminders of winter.	Make rhubarb sauce for ice cream or a strawberry-rhubarb pie.

May

Planting	Plant vegetables.	Plant annuals. Use annuals to try out a design scheme. If you like it, plant similar perennials there next year.	Plant perennials.	Plant herbs.

Harvesting

Pick peas, straw-berries, more rhubarb, and let-tuces.

Make sure you eat your vegetables and fruits—they are not just growing to look beautiful!

Pruning

Prune hedges and shrubs.

Don't cut off your daffodils and tulips after they have bloomed. Even though they may look unattractive for a week or two, let them die a natural death, and you will be rewarded with richer soil and better bloom next year. Instead, distract your eyes by planting pretty groundcovers, annuals, or perennials among them.

Doing

Plant containers and window boxes.

Cut lilacs, peonies, and sweet peas for indoor bouquets.

Preparing

Start a new compost pile.

Take an inventory of your canning supplies and freezer containers.

ummer

At what point does spring end and summer truly begin? When the crickets start to sing at night.

When the leaves are truly green and the grass is warm. When the fireflies come out at dusk. When it's warm enough to have dinner outside. When the water's warm enough to swim in (August 15th if you live in Maine).

Summer in the garden goes like this. June: The thrill! Weekends are spent planting, weeding, and primping. July: Things grow out of control, especially if you go on vacation. Fruits and vegetables start to ripen and reward you for your efforts. August: Forget it; the weeds have won, and wouldn't you just rather go swimming?

Summer is an exercise in giving up control and understanding chaos. You simply cannot control nature, and summer proves it to you. But letting go and giving in can be the most joyful experience of all. Suddenly, out of all that chaos will come zucchini, raspberries, flowers, butterflies, and everything that makes the season divine.

Designing

Your Garden

Summer is the time when you will really know if your garden is working for you or you are working for it. You will know if you are working for your garden—symptoms include every free moment spent fighting the onslaught of weeds, a sick feeling in your stomach every time you go outside because there is more work to do than you have time or strength for (or interest in), and most of all, a feeling of physical unpleasantness most of the time you are out there (too hot, too sunny, too buggy, too unattractive).

The way to tell if your garden is working for you is if you actually go outside and enjoy yourself in your yard. Are there shady places to sit and relax? Is there a place to have meals outside that is actually comfortable to use? Do the plants surprise and delight you? Are there good things to eat? Does taking a little walk around your yard to see what is growing give you a thrill of excitement and anticipation?

Every gardener is bound to have that feeling of summer panic every so often—the one where you stand surrounded by the jungle of plants and say to yourself, "Oh my goodness, what have I gotten myself into? I will *never* get all these weeds." That is a very natural feeling that will recur throughout your lifetime. And no, you *won't* ever get all the weeds. But with a bit of work, you'll regain that sense of achievement and reap the rewards of the garden—the fruits, the herbs, the vegetables, the flowers, the comfort of knowing that your patch of land is doing something good for you and the world.

A summer garden bouquet:

hydrangeas, hollyhocks,

and snapdragons.

Planting Compositions

A lot of people I know fret about what to plant where. They have little confidence in their planting design abilities. I say, just get in there and start doing stuff. Pick plants you like and plant them together in ways that seem pleasing *to you.* If you don't know what is pleasing to you, then that is a deeper psychological issue that this book is not really about. Or go back to the "Winter" section and answer the questions in the first section. In your garden there are no rules (except perhaps zoning rules, but even they can be changed).

The beauty of plants is that they are flexible, movable, and often resilient. Even roses can be moved if you don't like where you planted them (provided they are not too old and that you dig down deep enough to get most of the roots). I have some plants in my yard I've moved at least four times. Remember, though, that summer is *not* the time to be moving things around or planting because the plants probably won't handle the stress. But summer is a great time to notice what you like and don't like or what you need to change. You can correct these plantings in the fall or spring, when the plant isn't actively growing.

The **contrast** of cool silver artemisia and blue-flowered love-in-a-mist with the rich hot colors of pinks makes a delightful combination.

The spiky light **shape** of rose campion in the foreground accentuates the darker, flowing, taller **shape** of the ornamental grasses in the background.

Design Basics

If you prefer a little more direction on design, there are a few basic design ideas you can use to make your garden work for you.

Size and scale. Put shorter plants in front, taller ones in back. If your house is really big, plant big things around it. If your house is really small, plant smaller things. (Unless you are going for the Alice-in-Wonderland effect—then do the opposite.)

Pattern. Repeat patterns and shapes to create continuity. Think about a road or long drive lined with the same type of trees and how dramatic that can be. That is an example of repeating a pattern. You can get the same effect on a much smaller scale by using bushes, flowers, or even flower containers in strategic positions.

Shapes. Mix shapes together so that everything doesn't look the same. Round flowers look good with spiky ones. The sweeping, grace-

The different **colors** of these trees make an alluring and mysterious path.

ful arch of grasses with the more sculpted, straight look of a perennial can be a potent combination.

Color. Put together different colors that complement each other. Hot colors (reds, oranges, and yellows) tend to make things appear closer and attract attention. Colder colors (purples, blues, and whites) tend to make things look more distant and calming. There are also many colors of foliage besides "plain" green—from silvery blue-green to dark yellow-green. Combine them in all sorts of pleasing groupings.

Borage has a prickly **texture.**

Texture. Sometimes one texture by itself works fabulously (like wearing all silk). But often, mixing textures works even better. Think how different it is to feel lamb's ears leaves or flowers (which also feel like their namesake, in case you have never felt the flower before) compared to yucca leaves, which are stiff, sharp, and capable of poking an eye out. Mix them together to highlight their uniqueness.

Contrast. Contrast is the difference between darkness and light. It can be applied to colors or to planting schemes. Contrast applied to colors is typified by the blue-and-white garden. The difference between the rich darkness of the purple and blue flowers and the brightness of the whites make a pleasing combination. Contrast applied to overall design is when you have a dark area of your yard or garden that draws you into it like a little mysterious world as well as an area that is bright and open, which welcomes you more brazenly. The combination of darkness and light is a powerful force in the garden (and in the world, too).

I also have a few tricks that help me go from experimenting to feeling satisfied about a planting scheme.

Variegated geraniums really jump out and accentuate the **contrast** when they are in front of a dark background.

Summer Design Tips

- Use annuals to test out color or planting schemes. If you like the way they look, find perennials that are similar to plant next year or in the fall. For instance, if you are looking for a purple flower, try annual purple salvia. If you like the way it looks, switch to a perennial such as lavender, Russian sage, or veronica.

- Don't go hog-wild and buy tons of one type of perennial if you haven't planted it before. I often find that some perennials just don't do that well in my yard or in certain areas of my yard, and then others that I didn't expect to do well really thrive. If one works really well, then the *next* year I'll go back and go hog-wild!

- Don't be afraid to move things around. If you don't like how something looks after it grows, move it somewhere else.

- Be adventurous—try a few new plants if they look interesting. That's the fun of gardening!

- A money-saving tip: Go to nurseries in midsummer and buy perennials on sale. Fill in bare spots with them this year, and then watch them explode with color next year! (Trim them back after you plant them to encourage new growth.)

Nasturtiums are lovely even before they flower.

We couldn't wait for plants to hide Main Street from our view, so we built a wall. It was one of our best investments.

Designing to Hide Eyesores

Sometimes you have unsightly things in your yard that can't be moved. Common problems are pumps and electrical generators, sand mounds (for sewage systems), garbage-can storage areas, compost piles, and unsightly views from windows. There are many ways you can disguise them to make them look as if you actually meant things to be that way.

- Plant evergreens around them like a hedge. Depending on the size of the eyesore you are trying to hide, you can plant either large evergreen trees or dwarf bushes.

- Build a trellis surrounding whatever you are trying to hide, and plant climbing ornamental and vegetable vines on it.

- Build a wall or fence (as a design element) and plant flowers and bushes in front of it.

- Mound up the earth (to make what's called a berm) to hide the eyesore, then plant it with groundcovers and flowers.

- Put a giant rock in front of the eyesore.

Use fast-growing annuals and perennials to hide things quickly.

Designing Especially

When thinking about summer in the garden, certain things come to mind: shady places to hang out on lazy days, peaceful places to de-stress after a hard day's work, low-maintenance gardens (you don't want to spend your whole summer weeding, mowing, and trimming, do you?), a place to picnic or have dinner outside, a place to soak in the sun, a place that's beautiful to look at and be in—whether you're going to entertain or just to enjoy all by yourself.

Structures and Accessories for Your Garden

Plants are wonderful, of course, but for a really great-looking garden—and a garden that's fun to be in—you need structures and accessories, too. Whether it's a deck or patio to relax on, a bench to sit on, a fence to mark a boundary, or an arbor for shade and beauty, you'll get more four-season pleasure from a well-accessorized garden. Here is an overview of your options.

Porches, Patios, Decks, Gazebos, and Pavilions

Usually when you think of outdoor living in the summer, porches and patios come to mind. You can have a thoroughly enjoyable time outdoors without any outdoor structures, but structures can enhance the summer experience.

Porches are fabulous for enjoying the outdoors in all weather. They provide shade from the sun and shelter from the rain. The problem with porches is that they tend to provide shelter for all sorts of other things—bikes, toys, tools, trash. If you can avoid that tendency and make your porch a real outdoor living and relaxing place, you can have loads of fun. If mosquitoes are a problem in your area, screen in the porch.

Patios and decks are great for putting outdoor furniture on, doing container gardening, and creating a sense of an outdoor living room. Make sure that you have some shade or cover, however, because

for Summer

nothing is more unpleasant than a patio or deck that is totally exposed to the sun. And that's especially true if the deck or patio is a bright whitish color that reflects the sun into your eyes. (I had one of those once.) Use soft or dark colors, create shade, and cozy it up with plants and trellises, and you will find yourself spending every moment you can out there.

Good patio surfaces are stone, brick, cement, and gravel. Avoid pressure-treated wood for decks. Use cedar or non–old-growth red-wood instead. Also, avoid the tendency to just build a square structure jutting out from a back door. Create interesting shapes to make a multi-purpose space, leave areas for growing things within the patio or deck, build it around a tree, or make pathways to other areas. Awnings and canvas umbrellas can also make patios and decks more welcoming. Have fun with your outdoor spaces.

Speaking of fun, **gazebos** are an interesting garden feature. The most commonly seen gazebo around here is the pressure-treated or cedar Victorian thing. But I have seen some extremely cool gazebos made of logs and twigs (in Adirondack style), wrought iron, or a combination of materials. You can even make a "living gazebo" out of willow bushes woven together. For the price of a purchased, delivered, and installed premade Victorian gazebo, you may be able to have someone make something really cool just for you, made out of local materials and reflecting your own personal style. Look into it before you rush out to buy something that you will later regret.

Pavilions are like giant gazebos—more for giant parties with kegs of beer (and old El Caminos) than intimate tea parties. My husband threatens to build a pavilion in our yard. We'll just see about that.

Garden Furniture

If you haven't picked up on my primary theme for nonplant gardening purchases, I will reiterate here. The best thing for the environment and for beauty is to buy (or make) good-quality things, and then take care of them and keep them for a long time. Durability is a key require-ment—but so is comfort, as far as I am concerned.

There are two types of outdoor furniture: the kind that stays out-doors year-round, and the kind that would be better off if it were brought indoors. (Although if it were up to me, I'd probably end up leaving everything out all year long out of sheer distraction.)

Furniture that is going to stay outdoors year-round should be able to take it. Stone, teak, and iron furniture are good candidates. Furniture that needs to be brought indoors should be easy to move. Wood is good, but so are wicker, fabric, and lighter metals. I have found that there are many more good choices in mail-order catalogs than in local stores.

One comment: Magazines love to show outdoor photos where the outdoor seating areas are festooned with pillows and couches. If you want that look, you have to be willing to cart everything indoors every

The **best thing** for the **environment** and for **beauty** is to buy (or make) **good-quality** things, and then **take care** of them and **keep** them for a **long time.**

time it rains or put up with soggy, dirty pillows. Or purchase heavy-duty weatherproof cushions. Bring the lovely accent pillows out only when you are going out to sit.

Hedges, Fences, and Windbreaks

All it takes is one nosy neighbor, one escaped dog, or one picnic marred by too much wind (flying hot dogs and such) to desire some protection. Not only is protection in the form of hedges, fences, and windbreaks practical for you, but these items are very useful to plants and wildlife.

Hedges provide essential habitats for birds, beneficial insects, and other animals. And the less you mess with them, the better. Hedges also make it possible for you to revel in the privacy of your own yard without feeling as if you are being spied on.

Fences can keep your dog in and your neighbor's dog out. A fence also makes a great launching pad and resting place for birds, and it provides climbing support for annual, perennial, fruit, or vegetable vines.

Windbreaks are more appropriate for a large-scale area, but you can also create the same effect in a smaller space. If wind is your problem in a small space, plant hedges or evergreens to block the wind either from areas of your yard or from your house. If you have a large area and a lot of wind, let a strip of land "go wild" and plant itself with

Mock orange

native trees, weeds, and bushes. In hardly any time at all, you will have a thriving habitat that is not only beautiful to look at but will also protect your plants and your yard from wind erosion and wind's drying effect on plants (and people).

Just for Pleasure

My garden wish list includes a wood-fired sauna with a solar- or wood-heated outdoor shower and perhaps a lap pool one day. It's good to dream and even think about where you may put things. (Wishes are much more likely to happen if you dream about them than if you just assume they will never happen.) Hot tubs, swimming pools, grottos, and anything pleasurable you can think of should not be excluded just because they aren't completely natural. But if you are going to add things like that, try to do them as naturally as possible, with as little imported energy as possible.

A recent newspaper article on Michael Andretti (the famous race-car driver who happens to live a few miles from my house) mentioned that his new pool is heated by circulating the water under his driveway. The heat from the black driveway macadam passively heats up the water for the pool. Solutions like that take creative thinking—but *life* takes creative thinking. Practice in your garden.

Life takes
**creative
thinking.**
Practice
in
your
garden.

Native wild elderberry
growing in a wooded yard

Cardoon

Designing a Bird, Butterfly, and Wildlife Habitat

Attracting birds, butterflies, and wildlife to your yard is extremely easy and satisfying. (Later in this section, I will tell you how to keep certain critters *out* of your yard.) Basically, wildlife need the same things we need: something to eat and drink, a place to live, a place to raise their children, and a certain sense of security.

Provide food. Flowers, fruits, berries, vegetables, insects, bark, seeds, nuts, and nectar are all good choices. If you plant a lot of different plants in your yard, something is bound to come to eat them.

Provide water. Birdbaths, ponds, puddles, pools, and streams are all great for wildlife. If you have a birdbath, put a few rocks in it to create shallow ledges. Some birds are too little to perch on the edge and reach or stand on the bottom.

Provide a home. Trees, bushes, and grasses are good places for birds to nest. Dead logs or trees, brush piles, and brambles are good for the furry guys. Rock piles, mud holes, and moist, shady places are good for frogs, toads, and lizards.

Leave them alone. Respect the privacy of wildlife and they will respect yours. Don't try to make pets of them. Leave areas of your yard where you rarely go so the wildlife can have some peace and quiet.

This spring, a little brown bird made its nest in a tree rose planted in a pot right on our patio next to the table where we eat dinner. Even though I was tempted to climb up on a ladder to take her picture with her eggs and babies, I resisted since she was already so trusting of us—she would sit in her nest while we ate dinner. We all need a bit of privacy, please.

Cosmos

Birds

According to Harper's Magazine, a woman would have to eat 134 pounds a day in order to eat like a bird.

If you have ever watched birds in the summer for more than a few minutes, you'll be amazed at all the stuff they find to eat—insects, moths, worms, fruit, and seeds. Birds get a bad reputation for eating things like blueberries, cherries, and strawberries—but these are just dessert for them. Mostly they live on the very pests that some people pay tons of money to kill with toxic chemicals. Bigger birds, such as owls and hawks, are key predators of mice, voles, and other garden visitors.

The other day I picked up a big rock from the back of my yard to use in my garden. Underneath was the most hideous giant white grub I had ever seen. I ran off to get an insect ID guide, but before I could come back to figure out what (if anything) to do with it, a robin and its baby—on one of its first dinner outings—had found it and were taking care of it for me. Poor old grub.

Right now it's mid-July and my yard is swarming with little birds out on their own, with their brothers and sisters, and sometimes with their parents. They still have the little tufts of baby feathers sticking out here and there. But they sure do eat. And most of what they are eating is bugs.

All the while they are eating, they are also, shall we say, pooping. Bad news if it's on your car, but great news if it's on your garden. Bird poop is filled with nitrogen and phosphorus, which are very important nutrients for the fertility of your yard. And it's free.

I keep a list of all the species of birds I have seen in my yard. For each new type of bird I see, I feel as if I have achieved something great. If you want to enjoy watching birds without putting out lots of feeders, plant climbing vines like trumpetvine or wisteria outside your window. Not only will you get to watch birds up close all year long but the summer foliage will make a wonderful dappled cooling shade. While I am paying my bills, I can look out onto my front porch and watch a robin who is raising her babies in a nest in the trumpetvine. It's quite pleasantly distracting.

You can also plant nectar-, seed-, and berry-producing plants to attract birds. (See "What to Plant to Feed Birds" on the opposite page.) But more important is a source of water, so make sure you put out a birdbath or shallow bowl and keep it filled with water.

Birds also like to take "dust baths." If you see them fluffing about in the dry dust, it's because the dust keeps their parasites under control. So leave a little dust patch for them.

What to Plant to Feed Birds

Like us, birds have their own food preferences. You'll attract a wider variety of songbirds if you plant lots of different bird-attracting plants. Include trees, shrubs, and smaller plants in your selection (vines and ornamental grasses are special bird favorites). But if you have room for only a few plants, don't worry. Even one or two bird-attracting plants can make a difference. The plants here are taken from *Birdscaping Your Garden* by George Adams.

Trees

Smooth alder
River birch
Sweet birch
Water birch
Boxelder
Cherries
Cottonwood
Wild sweet crab
Oregon crabapple
Flowering dogwood
Balsam fir
Grand fir
Common hackberry
Western hackberry
Possum haw
Cockspur hawthorn
Western hawthorn
Hemlocks
American holly
Rocky Mountain juniper
Larch
Red maple
Sugar maple
Mountain ash
Mulberries

Wax myrtle
Oaks
Lodgepole pine
Piñon pine
Ponderosa pine
White pine
Plums
Eastern red cedar
Allegheny serviceberry
Saskatoon serviceberry
Black spruce
Colorado spruce
Sycamores
Desert willow

Shrubs

Azaleas
Bayberry
Blueberries
Cranberries
Red-osier dogwood
Elderberries
Honeysuckle
Trumpet honeysuckle
Ocotillo
Rhododendrons
Sumacs
Twinberry
Viburnums
Winterberry

Herbaceous Plants

New England aster
Beardtongue
Bee balm
Blackberries
Black-eyed Susan
Big bluestem
Bunchberry
Cardinal flower
Columbine
Black crowberry
Wild fuchsia
Grapes
Jerusalem artichoke
Red shrubby penstemon
Prickly pear
Raspberries
Roses
Saguaro
Scarlet bugler
Wild strawberries
Sunflowers
Trumpetvine
Virginia creeper
Yucca

Rhododendron

What to Plant to Feed Hummingbirds

If hummingbirds are what you're after, provide them with lots of nectar, pollen, and insects. (The best way to attract insects is to plant a variety of nectar-producing flowers, avoid chemical sprays, and let some areas of your garden go a little wild.) Hummingbirds prefer tubular-shaped flowers in vivid colors. Red is their favorite color, followed by orange, yellow, pink, and purple. Design your garden with nectar-producing flowers that bloom through the season. Here are the best plants for specifically attracting those speedy, shiny frequent fliers.

Anna's Hummingbird (California) and Costa's Hummingbird (Southwestern Deserts)

Western azalea

Crimson columbine

Firecracker plant

California fuchsia

Hawthorns

Arizona honeysuckle

Scarlet lobelia

Ocotillo

Red shrubby penstemon

Nootka rose

Twinberry

Desert willow

Soaptree yucca

Ruby-Throated Hummingbird (Eastern United States)

Bee balm

Cardinal flower

Columbines

Trumpet honeysuckle

Scarlet lobelia

Scarlet morning glory

Pineapple sage

Trumpetvine

Butterflies

Butterflies are important and beautiful pollinators. And though in their caterpillar stage they eat the leaves of many different plants, they usually don't do enough damage to make you mad at them. Here's an at-a-glance profile of butterflies.

Butterflies at a Glance

Eat: Nectar.
Are eaten by: Birds, lizards, dragonflies, and spiders.
Live: In fields and meadows; they also migrate.
Other: Butterflies are "solar-powered." The reason you see them basking in the sun is that they have to raise their body temperatures to 80°F to tune their wing muscles to enable them to fly.

Look out for caterpillars and protect them if you want butterflies in your garden.

Butterflies love zinnias.

What to Plant to Attract Butterflies

Like birds, butterflies have favorite food plants. Adults enjoy sipping nectar from nectar-rich flowers like those in the list below. Their caterpillars also have food preferences. For example, monarch butterfly caterpillars only eat milkweed leaves, while black swallowtail caterpillars prefer plants in the carrot family, like dill, Queen-Anne's-lace, and parsley. Butterflies also enjoy such treats as a piece of overripe or rotting fruit and a mineral-rich mud puddle (their equivalent of a multivitamin pill, I guess). Here are the plants most butterflies (and caterpillars) prefer.

Plants to Attract Adult Butterflies

Alfalfa
Alpine pink
Artemisia
Asters
Azaleas
Blackberry
Black-eyed Susan
Bougainvillea
Butterfly bush
Butterfly weed
Candytuft
Cardoon
Red clover
Purple coneflower
Coreopsis
Cosmos
Daisies
Dame's rocket
Dandelion
Dogwoods
Forget-me-not
Gayfeather
Goldenrods
Grape hyacinth
Hibiscus
Honeysuckles
Ironweed

Joe-Pye weed
Lilacs
Mallow
Mexican sunflower
Milkweed
Mints
Mock orange
Passionflower
Phlox
Pincushion flower (scabiosa)
Pulmonaria
Queen-Anne's-lace
Sedums (stonecrop)
Sweet pea
Sweet pepper bush
Sweet William
Valerian
Red valerian
Verbena
Vetch
Viburnums
Violets
Zinnia

Plants to Attract Caterpillars

Apples
Artemisia
Aspen
Beans
Birches
Blueberries
Butterfly weed
Carrots
Cherries
Citrus
White clover
Dill
Dogwoods
Fennel
Hollyhocks
Ironweed
Knapweed
Mallow
Milkweed
Nettles
Parsley
Passionflower
Pearly everlasting
Plum
Privet
Queen-Anne's-lace
Rue

Spicebush
Sumacs
Sweet bay
Sweet pea
Tulip tree
Vetch
Violets
Willows

Butterflies love butterfly
weed, and it's so pretty, too.

Wildlife

While I sit and write this book, I can look out two windows at the garden. It's rather like sitting in front of a fish tank or a one-way mirror because I can see the animals but they can't see me. Yesterday I saw a big mouse sticking its nose out of the garlic patch. There is a baby bunny that goes around nibbling on tasty little things that it can reach, sometimes standing up on its hind legs to reach them. Occasionally a squirrel hops on by.

My favorite chipmunk just brought an alpine strawberry to his special "patio" on the garden wall. He sat on his hind legs, his fat little tummy sticking out, and gobbled down the whole thing in less than a minute in the fast-action manner these little guys have. After he was finished, he rubbed his face with his little hands and scampered off to his next meal. (Which turned out to be the inside of a cherry pit that someone had spit out.)

What a life these critters have . . . if they happen to live in my yard, that is. The one year that our yard was excavated for lead, our neighbor caught 15 rabbits that had come into his yard for sanctuary. He caught them with a "HavaHart" trap and released them somewhere else. It has been two years since the excavation, and we have plenty of rabbits in our yard again.

I have a strong belief that most of the time there is enough for everyone. The animals get some of the food I grow, and in return I get fertilizer for my garden every time they relieve themselves. They eat a lot of the waste products (I wasn't planning on eating the inside of that cherry pit anyway). And, well, they *are* cute.

In the wild, birds and other animals play a critical role in planting the forest. A lot of the nuts and seeds that squirrels bury are forgotten and grow into trees. There are many seeds of important plants that *must* go through an animal's digestive system before they will germinate . . . and the animals coat them conveniently in little pellets of compost.

People assume many animals are bad just because they are "yucky." In truth, they can be your best defense against other pests. Bats are good . . . and so are skunks!

Having just said that, I recognize that some people have had major garden devastation from animals like groundhogs and deer. But even groundhogs and deer have important reasons for existing. Many books and people approach animals in the garden as pests and deal with them by declaring open warfare. But you can control even the peskiest pests in natural, nonharmful ways that won't interfere with the beauty of your garden or with your potential friendship with small furry animals.

Most important of all is to try to understand the complex but dependent relationships we all have with each other—plants, animals, birds, people, and bugs. Truly, we can't live without each other.

Poor woodchuck

How to Keep Animals from Eating Your Plants

Here are five effective ways of dealing with animals in your garden.

1. **Build barriers and fences.** The real reason that people built castles, moats, courtyards, and walled gardens in the past wasn't to keep out warring neighbors, but to keep out hungry animals. Actually, I am just making that up, but it sounds as if it could be true, doesn't it? (Think about invading wolves.) In reality, our predecessors probably ate all the hungry animals that came close to their gardens. The only foolproof way of keeping out the big animals like deer and woodchucks is to fence high (up to 9 feet) and low (3 feet underground—for woodchucks, not deer). But before you go to extremes, try a few of these techniques first.

2. **Introduce predators.** Having dogs and cats can do wonders for keeping away animals. Not feeling as if you have to eliminate every animal you see will also help keep predatory behaviors in balance.

3. **Plant things they won't eat.** If rabbits get your peas every time and you don't want to fence the peas in, then don't plant them. There are many trees and shrubs that deer just don't like, such as azaleas, boxwood, butterfly bush, junipers, oleander, rhododendrons, and smoke tree.

4. **Use HavaHart traps.** Catch the animals and then take them to some other wild place to free them. If you're in doubt about their health or are afraid of them, call your local animal control officer or a wildlife rehabilitator in your area and have them take over.

5. **Try natural sprays, sonic devices, remedies, and repellents.** Many of the things you read about (such as rotten eggs and bloodmeal) or see in catalogs will work, but you have to keep reapplying the sprays after every rain. And some of them, like bags of human hair, just don't pass the beautiful organic garden test (they are ugly).

Ultimately, if you have a diverse mix of animals and plants and an abundance of food sources for everyone, you can live in harmony with each other. The most important thing is to try to understand each other and not panic when you meet face to face.

What Eats What—And Where They Live

You'll enjoy the wildlife in your yard more if you know a little about them. (Knowing the animals' lifestyles makes it easier to keep them out of your garden, too.) So here are at-a-glance profiles of all the critters that are likely to visit your property—including your fellow humans.

Bats

Eat: Mosquitoes, gnats, and small flying insects, including moths. One bat can eat 600 mosquitoes per hour.

Are eaten by: Cats, maybe.

Live: In caves, attics, and bat houses. They only come out at night. If you are going to put up one of those bat houses, make sure you put it up high. Bats need to drop before they can fly.

Other: Bat droppings are a rich source of nitrogen.

Control: No need to control. In fact, you might attract them to control mosquitoes. If you want to rid a bat from your house, open a window and throw sand or gravel out. They'll think it's bugs and go after them.

Moles

Eat: Their favorite food is the earthworm. They will also eat beetle grubs or any larvae of lawn- and ground-inhabiting insects. In fact, their presence indicates that you have good soil.

Are eaten by: Cats and bears.

Live: They dig tunnels underground (from their underground nests) to hunt. Their tunnels can kill lawns (another reason not to have a lawn).

Other: Moles take the blame, unfairly, for a lot of damage that mice really do to tree and shrub roots.

Control: Trap them if you must.

Voles (Field Mice)

Eat: Berries, roots, bulbs, seeds. Field mice have to eat one-third of their own weight every 24 hours.

Are eaten by: Everything! But mainly cats, large birds, and snakes.

Live: In marshes and meadows.

Other: A population explosion of field mice can wipe out entire crops and orchards. Voles can have up to 17 litters a year, which is a good reason to keep some outdoor cats around.

Control: Introduce predators.

Mice (White-Footed and Pine)

Eat: Seeds, nuts, roots, bulbs, and bark.

Are eaten by: Everything, including raccoons, bears, bullfrogs, and snakes. And cats.

Live: In woody or brushy places, tunnels, and nests in mulch.

Other: Mice are assisted greatly by moles. Moles dig the holes; mice use the tunnels to "shop" for food in your garden.

Control: Predators.

Chipmunks

Eat: Dried or raw field corn kernels, nuts (acorns, peanuts, walnuts), bulbs, seeds, and berries. Shockingly, chipmunks also eat meat. They will eat bird and frog eggs (and legs), moles, mice, snakes, salamanders, and butterflies. Chipmunks can store as many as 31 kernels of corn in their chubby little cheeks. They *don't* eat daffodils.

Are eaten by: Large birds, foxes, and cats.

Live: Burrow in the ground.

Other: Gain my vote for cutest garden creature.

Control: Protect bulbs with underground screening, if you insist.

Rats

Eat: Live animals, dead animals (and people—yuck), sleeping animals (and people!), vegetables, and their own children. No wonder rats have such a bad reputation.

Are eaten by: Larger animals—snakes, skunks, bears, and cats.

Live: Unsanitary places (something has got to clean up our mess) and nests.

Other: Rats have traveled everywhere in the world and have adapted to every situation they have encountered. Along the way, they damage billions of dollars' worth of food, and they spread disease.

Controls: The best way to control rats is to keep things scrupulously cleaned up so they eat their own young instead of your trash. Don't put meats, fats, dairy products, and cooked grains on your compost piles.

Squirrels

Eat: Birdseed, seeds, nuts (favorites are hickory nuts, walnuts, and butternuts), fruits, maple syrup, pinecones, and mushrooms.

Are eaten by: Larger animals and cars.

Live: Squirrels build domed roofs inside holes high up in trees— probably the former homes of large birds. They also build large nests of twigs.

Other: Squirrels are great tree planters. They bury nuts for winter cold storage, and many of the nuts sprout into trees.

Control: You shouldn't really need to unless you're a nut farmer.

Rabbits

Eat: *My peas,* dry grasses, evergreen plants, bark, fruits, clover, weeds, oats, barley, pea hay, alfalfa, and vegetables.

Are eaten by: Larger animals, including cats (plus humans and cars).

Live: Anywhere there is shelter and cover near grass, clover, and weeds (the vegetable patch is simply a bonus).

Other: Rabbit is excellent to eat and easy to raise. I love rabbits too much to ever want to eliminate them. To see little bunny brothers and sisters chasing each other around in circles and leaping in the air is one of life's great pleasures . . . even better than eating spring peas.

Controls: Predators and fencing.

Raccoons

Eat: Fruits, vegetables, small water animals (frogs, fish, and so on), and garbage.

Are eaten by: Larger animals.

Live: In hollow trees.

Other: They hunt at night.

Controls: Traps and dogs.

Opossums

Eat: Snakes, including rattlesnakes, copperheads, and cotton-mouths, insects, small animals, birds and their eggs, earthworms, frogs, mushrooms, grain crops, fruits, and carrion. Persimmons, corn, and apples are favorites.

Are eaten by: Hawks, eagles, and larger animals, including foxes.

Live: They make a nest of leaves in hollow trees.

Other: Opossums are immune to rattlesnake venom. Possums play dead when scared, but otherwise they're very smart. They have 50 teeth, which is more than any other North American land animal. (I guess snakes can be rather chewy.) They're the only wild animals in North America that can hang by their tails.

Control: No need to control.

Groundhogs

Eat: The scourge of gardeners everywhere, groundhogs eat 16 ounces of food per meal. They relish garden vegetables, grasses, and greens.

Are eaten by: Foxes, hawks, dogs, and cars.

Live: Dens and tunnel systems. Sometimes their tunneling helps the soil, but it can also wreck gardens and pastures. They also climb trees.

Other: Groundhogs are also called woodchucks and "whistle pigs." They're similar to the marmot in the West. Groundhogs have one specific "bathroom" chamber in their tunneled homes where they relieve themselves. They also have bedrooms and nurseries in their underground labyrinths, as well as two entrances.

Controls: Traps and above- and underground (3-foot-deep) fencing.

Skunks

Eat: June bugs, May beetles (and their larvae), Japanese beetle grubs, ripe fruit, mice, injured or dead birds (they can't catch them otherwise), sweets, and insects that eat the plants you love.

Are eaten by: Cars.

Live: For the night.

Other: If a skunk stamps his or her feet at you and growls, you are about to be sprayed.

Control: Skunks are our friends.

Deer

Eat: Shrubs, vegetables, grasses, evergreen needles, tree buds, and twigs from red maples and many other trees.

Are eaten by: Hunters, bobcats, and cars.

Live: In meadows, forests, and other places that are protected from the wind.

Other: Deer meat is excellent and very low in fat.

Controls: Electric fences 6 to 9 feet high, basil, human hair, and Irish Spring soap (but I like it!). You can also pile lots of dead branches around something you want to protect (like a tree, bush, or garden area).

Porcupines

Eat: Bark, buds, and twigs of ashes, basswood, beeches, firs, hemlocks, oaks, pines, poplars, and spruces; aquatic plants.

Are eaten by: Coyotes, bobcats, and fishers.

Live: In dens. Let's just say they are not as good housekeepers as our friends the groundhogs.

Other: Native Americans used dyed porcupine needles to ornament clothes and moccasins before European beads became widely available.

Control: Stay as far away from them as much as possible—although they can't shoot you with their needles unless you're very close.

Bears

Eat: Fish (salmon especially), berries, roots, bark, grass, ants, rodents, bees, and honey.

Are eaten by: Hunters.

Live: In dens, caves, and hollow trees.

Other: Bears aren't considered garden pests, but they are an important predator.

Control: Bears (especially black bears) can live unobtrusively in suburban areas. If one is on your property or in your neighborhood, call your local animal control officer or your state game commission, and ask for assistance. Don't approach a bear for any reason.

Cats

Eat: Mice, moles, voles, chipmunks, birds, frogs, and Tender Vittles (or household leftovers appropriate for cats).

Are eaten by: Cars and dogs (yeah, right!).

Live: On your couch and on top of your TV. An outside cat will live under porches or in barns or sheds.

Other: I can understand that people don't want their cats to be killed by cars, but laws that insist that cats stay indoors strike me as unnatural and a different sort of cruelty to animals—it's denying them their true nature.

Control: Getting them "fixed."

Dogs

Eat: Groundhogs, garbage, dead animals, leftovers, dog food, and anything else they can get.

Are eaten by: Some people (and not to be confused with hot dogs or corn dogs sold at state fairs).

Live: On the floor (in my house, anyway). In nature, dogs will build burrows and live in caves. That is why they like to hang out under the table (some dropped food is a benefit, too).

Other: Man's best friend (unless you are a UPS delivery person).

Control: Leash laws.

Everything Eats

I accept that all life eats life, and this includes plants and algae that eat bacteria, or legumes that eat nematodes. To live is to live on other life forms.

—**Bill Mollison**, *Travels in Dreams*

There was a recent incident at *Organic Gardening* magazine where a reference to killing a woodchuck caused a deluge of letters, leading to much furor and disagreement. It got me thinking about the way people relate to the animals in their gardens—and on their tables.

On the one hand, you have the vegetarians and animal rights people who believe that no animal should ever be killed for any reason. I confess that I have sympathy with them. Even though I am a meat eater, I would prefer never to kill an animal myself.

On the other extreme, you have the animal-hating carnivores who basically believe that this country was founded on the right to private property and the right to bear arms, and that animals have no right to trespass on their land, so *kapow*. I confess I have sympathy with them, too, since I believe in the rights this country was founded on.

In the middle, you have the self-sufficiency types who say that as long as you eat it after you kill it, then you are doing your part. And there are the hunters who say they are just controlling the population, since most other predators have died out. (This is true, by the way—and besides, I really enjoy venison.) The middle ground is also the home territory of all the others who just don't care one way or the other, but they don't want anything eating their vegetables, so they find all sorts of inge-

nious ways of keeping pests out (from hanging hair balls and soap from trees to spraying pepper and garlic on their plants). I sympathize with these people as well, since I enjoy eating organic and naturally raised red meats, fowl, and fish.

But as Bill Mollison mentions so eloquently in the quote on this page (as a result of seeing a fight at sea, where a sperm whale met its demise from a predator), everything eats. To eat is to live. Even plants are alive and must be "killed" in order to be eaten. Don't believe me? German physicists have actually invented a device that enables them to hear plants "scream." Turns out that the more stress the plants are under, the more they "scream" by giving off shock waves of ethylene gas. Some quantum physicists would probably say that even inanimate objects are alive (their molecules and particles are constantly buzzing), although we tend not to eat them (tables, chairs, computers).

It seems that people's beliefs about these sorts of things are so ingrained and so passionate that I doubt I will change anyone's mind with this book. But I just thought you should know where I stand on the issue.

Humans

Eat: Fruit, vegetables, other animals and birds, fish, grains, milk and eggs, and sugars.

Are eaten by: Other large animals, cars, and diseases. Humans are often destroyed (although rarely eaten) by their own species.

Live: Above- and underground houses built of wood, stone, and other natural resources. Humans are the most destructive of all species, destroying vast forests, natural resources, and other species in order to build homes and businesses.

Other: Like bears, raccoons, and dogs, humans are omnivores—we'll eat anything we can.

Controls: Natural disasters, diseases, and self-destructive tendencies inherent in the species.

Amphibians and Reptiles

Amphibians and reptiles are very sensitive to pollutants in the environment. If you have been reading the news, you might have heard that an alarming number of frogs are either disappearing or are drastically deformed. Even larger reptiles like alligators (which are not really good for the garden) are showing signs of odd deformities. The primary theory currently is that chemicals that mimic estrogens (dioxin, PCBs, and other horrid things) are causing the deformities. Besides being fun to watch, frogs and toads are good garden helpers, eating bunches of bugs. So, to do your part to "save the frogs" (and toads, salamanders, and the like), read on.

Frogs

Eat: Crickets, insects on the ground and in trees, minnows, crayfish, water bugs, spiders, beetles, katydids, and grasshoppers. Bullfrogs will eat (moving) birds and mice.

Are eaten by: Larger frogs, some people, snakes, and large birds.

Live: In ponds, lakes, mud, low bushes or rushes, swamps, and moist spots in your garden.

Other: Frogs are land and water creatures with slimy skin. Frogs hibernate in the winter and lay their eggs in the water in spring. Their legs are good for snacking on, if cooked.

Toads

Eat: Primarily garden insect pests, including cutworms. In three months, a toad will eat up to 10,000 insects. A toad will eat only moving things.

Are eaten by: Dogs, cats, foxes, weasels, and the hognose snake—although once an animal has eaten a toad, it will tend not to try another one because toads secrete a foul-tasting substance to repel predators.

Live: In moist, shady spots in your garden (such as under rocks and pots). They are born in small ponds.

Other: Toads are mostly land creatures with dry warty skin (though they still lay their eggs in the water). Toad warts are not contagious.

Design Tip Attract toads, frogs, and snakes to your yard by building little houses for them. Dig a trench about 6 to 12 inches deep in a moist area of your yard. Cover each trench with rocks. Landscape these "luxury homes" with protective cover, like ferns and shrubs.

Salamanders

Eat: Grubs, worms, and other creatures that live in the soil.

Are eaten by: Larger animals and snakes.

Live: In the woods; in muddy, soggy places; in ponds; and under piles of damp leaves or rotting logs.

Other: Salamanders are nocturnal.

Snakes

Eat: Rodents, insects, frogs, and lizards.

Are eaten by: Opossums, larger animals, and large birds.

Live: Dry lands, woods, fields, meadows, and rock piles.

Other: All snakes are good for gardeners, but not all gardeners are willing to put up with the snake fear factor. Out of the 115 species of snakes in the United States, 17 are poisonous—but most won't bite unless frightened, stepped on, or grabbed. And that leaves 98 "safe" species to help out in your garden.

Some snakes—the pit vipers—actually have a sixth sense that allows them to detect differences in temperature and to perceive wavelengths of the infrared spectrum. This sense is located in pits on their heads and enables them to hunt warm-blooded creatures with perfect accuracy in total darkness.

Lizards

Eat: Butterflies and other insects.

Are eaten by: Large snakes and animals.

Live: Wooded and hilly areas, rocks, and sunny areas.

Other: I have never seen a lizard in the wild in Pennsylvania—they generally prefer the warmer climates of the South and West.

Turtles

Eat: Insects, fish, and frogs.

Are eaten by: Foxes and people.

Live: Near or in water (ponds, lakes, swamps, oceans, rivers and marshes) or the woods (in the case of box turtles).

Other: Some turtles can live to be very old. Scientists can tell the age of a turtle by looking at its shell, much the same way they tell trees' ages by the rings on their trunks.

Water Gardening

If you want to add a pond, fountain, or waterfall to your yard, simply for beauty or to raise goldfish or koi (a fancy and often brilliantly patterned giant goldfish relative from Japan), there are two approaches to larger-scale water gardening. The first and most popular approach is the pond insert and pump system where you dig a hole, insert a black plastic preformed pool and pump, plug it in, decorate, and watch it flourish with either wildlife or algae, depending on your success. I am not an expert (in other words, I haven't done it myself), but I do know that these water gardens are not the simple things they seem to be. However, if you really want to devote yourself to learning and keeping a small pond, two good books are *Low-Maintenance Water Gardens* and *The Pond Doctor,* both by Helen Nash. (In fact, all her water gardening books are good.)

The second approach is more natural. You dig a giant hole, tamp it down really well, and fill it with water. The shape of such a person-made pond should be like an upside-down hat. The deep part in the middle is for the fish to hide in to escape raccoons and other hunters. The shallow edges are for animals and birds to come and drink. There is a whole natural cycle to pond life, just as there is a natural cycle in the garden. Good books on natural ponds and fish farming are Tim Matson's *Earth Ponds* and *The Earth Ponds Sourcebook*.

If you can't be bothered with any of this stuff, but you like the look of a water feature and you have a lot of rocks around, you can build a dry stream bed, which is just what it sounds like—a rocky path that looks like water should be flowing in it. The Japanese tend to do this with very similar pebbles for spiritual and visually harmonious purposes. But if you do it in a way that mimics nature, you can attract all sorts of wildlife and provide many happy homes for them.

Natural **Multi**tasking

Will anyone who has not yet had to learn how to multitask to keep up with the growing speed of life please write to me and tell me how they survive? Multitasking—which is doing things like talking on the phone, paying bills, and watching a TV show at the same time, or answering your e-mail while you are talking on the phone and eating your breakfast—is rapidly becoming a reality for all of us.

Nature is a multitasker, too. A pond, for instance, never does just one thing. Not even two or three things. It is doing thousands of things successfully all at once. Any piece of natural land is the same. You never see Nature, by herself, just growing a field of corn. It's too boring . . . and too unstable.

And yet, that is how we have mainly thought about our yards and gardens (and our lives, for that matter) for hundreds of years. Our yards exist for a few reasons: beauty, pleasure, and perhaps some food, with everything sorted neatly into separate sections. (Of course, Nature is also using our yards for her own purposes at the same time, though sometimes we try to prevent her from doing it.) In Permaculture there is a fundamental belief that every plant or item in your garden should serve *at least three purposes.*

We all need to learn from nature about multitasking—that it is not something to be avoided, but something that is beautiful and inherent in our own nature. Letting it happen naturally rather than fighting it is the difference between stress and joy.

You can multitask in your yard in a number of ways.

If you have a trellis for privacy, shade, or beauty, grow vines that provide food (hardy kiwis or grapes) along with vines that provide beauty (clematis or roses). You can probably stick an annual vine in there, too (like pole beans or climbing nasturtiums).

Plant vegetables, fruits, and herbs throughout your yard. Squash or melons make good temporary groundcovers for late summer (in areas where you don't need to walk). Many herbs also make good groundcovers and ornamental plants.

Let some of your vegetables and herbs go to seed to feed birds and other wildlife (broccoli and lettuces especially).

Choose trees and shrubs for your yard that feed birds and animals, provide shelter, and maybe even produce fruit and nuts for you.

Heritage Gardening: Get in Touch with Your Own Personal and Family History

Summer is often a time of family reunions and vacations spent visiting relatives. Whether this is something you enjoy or something you dread, it is a unique opportunity to delve into your family's gardening secrets and history. Instead of talking about everyone's latest ailments or sports, ask about gardens. Did your grandmother or grandfather have the magic touch with any special plants? Were there any family recipes that depended on the garden patch for produce?

Many of our older relatives—or perhaps you—lived through the Great Depression and the World Wars and remember Victory Gardening. Some of our relatives were so poor that they had to garden just to survive. What was it like back then? What has changed? Sharing stories with your family and passing those stories on to the next generation builds familial loyalty and joy.

Sharing gardening stories with neighbors can also be fun. There used to be a hair salon next door to my house. One of the stylists was Vietnamese. Many years ago she stopped to look at my garden and said, "Oh! We used to grow those plants back in Vietnam and eat them all the time. I don't have a garden, but I wish I could so I could grow those things."

She was pointing to basil and mint. I couldn't imagine eating the two together or what that would taste like. I offered her plants, but she declined because she didn't have a garden.

Since then, Vietnamese food has become quite popular and trendy in New York City, near where we live. We even have a local Vietnamese restaurant. Often when I am enjoying a rice roll with mint and a bowl of pho with basil I think back to that conversation and realize what the stylist was talking about.

As my mother-in-law always says, "Our poor food is now their gourmet!"

Our Mennonite neighbors have grown these poppies for generations (called breadbasket poppies). They use them for cooking.

Interview with Mr. Louis N. Cinquino

As someone who grew up in the family that led the organic gardening movement in America, I find it ironic that I married into a family that is even more passionate about gardening than my own family. On our visits to western New York State to visit the in-laws, we sit around the breakfast table (eating eggs and greens from the garden) and talk about growing fava beans and foraging for wild greens. Over a lunch of homemade soup, we discuss the latest problems with woodchucks and opossums. And over a dinner of spaghetti or manicotti with homemade sauce and salad from the garden, we seriously discuss tomatoes, peppers, and basil.

The Cinquinos' Italian heritage (Abruzzese and Sicilian) is present in their gardens, their food, and in Italian words sprinkled throughout their conversations. Through my in-laws, I've come to see gardening as a heritage and a link to the past and the future.

I have never met anyone who is as dedicated and successful a gardener in a practical, day-to-day way than my father-in-law. Sure, I've met people who have devoted their lives to organic gardening and related philosophies. But that's different from someone who squeezes it in between church, volunteering, Knights of Columbus activities, and grandchildren. Gardening is as much a beautiful tradition in the Cinquino family as it is in mine, and the Cinquino influence on my gardening, preserving, and cooking has been tremendous. Many of the pictures in this book were taken in Louie and Rita's yard. And their recipes and tips are sprinkled liberally throughout this book.

I interviewed Louie early one summer morning (before the household got out of bed) about his experiences and thoughts on gardening.

When did you start to garden?

I didn't get into it until after I was married. My dad was the type of person who liked to do his gardening himself. He had a green thumb and a passion for gardening. He would work real hard all day—he was an iron molder—in sweltering heat, but after supper, he would always head to the garden. For him, it was a release from tensions and probably a good place to get away from his big family.

He started off growing a lot of plants in his cold frame and giving them away to his many friends. Of course, the better the plants he had, the more friends he had—you know how that works. Eventually after he retired, he went to work for a landscaping firm.

I had a chance to get into it, but I think my dad figured 'I want to do it my way.' So I had to be content with just watching him and learning that way.

What did you learn from watching him?

How to plant from seeds. How to transplant them. When to transplant them. How to prepare your cold frame.

He did double-digging without ever reading it in a book—he'd dig down 19 to 24 inches—get all the dirt out. Then he would get some fresh manure and make a bed of 6 inches or so to maintain the heat in the box. Then he would get some good muck and put it on top. He would more or less just scatter the seeds in there, and as the plants grew, he would transplant them to another box. Eventually he even transplanted them into little flats. It was easier to sell them. But he was getting some ridiculously low price for them. It was a labor of love.

What were some of the things that he grew?

Tomatoes, romaine lettuce, and peppers (hot and semihot). He would always like to pick his peppers really red because they definitely have a better taste. We would roast them. Basil—you can't have tomatoes without basil. Parsley, garlic. I still have some garlic that I plant from the seed of his plants. Savoy cabbage—I always remember he would pull it up in the fall. He would make a wigwam with all his tomato sticks around the peach tree. He would pull up the savoy cabbages, turn them upside down, and put them under the "tepee," so to speak. Then we would have them well into the winter. We always had cabbage for our traditional Christmas Eve dinner (with anchovies and hot peppers).

In my dad's day, gardening added a lot to the staples that the family required. Money was scarce. They had more time than money, that's for sure. During the Depression days with a big family, it was almost a necessity. Dad, fortunately, was good at it. He had a green thumb. And we liked to eat, so it went together.

He also grew fig trees, which he kept burying every winter. I think Italian men had a passion for figs, and my cousin from Italy told me why. She said that when she went to visit her grandparents, they would always give her a bag of figs, and it made her feel rich. I think a lot of the men felt the same way because the Italian men always tried to grow fig trees. And now their children are doing it.

Including my own husband. How do you roast peppers?

My mom always roasted them on top of the stove. Basically, no matter where you roast them, you want to roast them so that the skin is actually black. That's a sign that the pepper is cooked, of course. All we ever did was set them in the pan afterward. They tell you to put them in a paper bag, but I've found that the

moisture from the pepper oozes out and all you get is a hole in the bag. But if you put them in a container and put a cover on it, it maintains the heat of the pepper and makes it a bit easier to skin.

Then you take the skin off and core the peppers, removing the seeds and the stems. If you want to prepare them to eat immediately, cut them up in strips and put them in a bowl with olive oil, parsley, and garlic.

If you want to freeze them, leave out the garlic, oil, and parsley. Add them when you prepare the peppers for eating. Just cut peppers up, put them in small bags, and put them in the freezer.

In the last few years that Nana was in the nursing home, she often would look forward to the impossible probability that she would recover and ultimately go back to normal living at home. Often she would tell me and others "Plant a row of parsley for me!" I believe we all did that but we all knew that she would never be able to enjoy her parsley or roasted peppers at home again.

—Mr. Cinquino

How do you make your sun-dried tomatoes?

In my mom's days, they still made paste by sun-drying—cooking down the paste to a certain degree to take the moisture out, then spreading it on a big board and putting it out in the sun to be dried. They would put a lace curtain over it to keep the bugs off. But what I do now is take advantage of technology and put tomatoes in the food dehydrator. I've found that the only trick about that is that you have to be careful not to dry them too much. Then I put them in a jar with some olive oil and rosemary. You can add garlic, too.

Did your dad ever use chemicals?

No, he relied mostly on manure and composting.

Did he ever have problems with bugs?

Not that I recall. I run into the same thing. I've never used insecticides. I believe all the wild garlic I have growing around the place is keeping the bugs away. But I've never had too much of a problem.

What else did you learn from watching your dad?

My dad always saved his own seeds. He would stake out the first plant that had good proper food on it and tie a ribbon around it so that no one would eat it. Then he would save the seed from that plant and perpetuate it. In fact, my brother Joe is still using pepper seeds from descendants of the plants that my dad grew. And he perpetuates the seed that way. Of course, there were no hybrids in those days, so you didn't have to worry about that.

How do you save seeds?

For something like butternut squash, scoop out the seeds and wash them. Lay them down on a blotter or napkin and let them dry out really well. That's one of the bad things about seeds. You can't keep them if they are moist. They have to be good and dry. Then I put them in a container and put them away in a cool, dry place. I've had good luck with butternut squash. I save cilantro seeds and parsley. I let them dry right on the plant and then shake the seeds into a bag. I've gotten seeds from literally all over the world. I've sent seeds to my cousin in Italy. Now I'm getting to the point where I'm growing seeds into plants and giving the plants away, just as my dad used to do.

What's a typical gardening year like for you?

I start around April, working up the cold frame. Then I put the seeds in there. This year I made the mistake of planting too many seeds in there at once. Then my tomatoes took over the whole box. Also, I've had pretty good luck with planting some seeds directly in the ground around the middle of May (near Buffalo, New York). I just throw them in the ground, and then if they are too thick, I transplant them.

Everything else I plant around Memorial Day weekend. What I try to plant are plants my animals won't get. I've given up on corn because the raccoons are plentiful and hungry, and they tear it right down and eat it. I try to stay away from broccoli because the woodchucks love broccoli. And lettuce—I have a little battle going with those woodchucks. I try to plant it early and plant it in differ-ent parts of the garden with the hopes that they will overlook some lettuce and save some for me.

Then of course I always have to plant my garlic in the fall. I tell people if they can't grow garlic, they can't grow anything. It'll grow by itself even. For the last couple of years I've been planting rye in the fall.

What are the most important things you have found necessary for being a successful gardener?

I think you have to do a good job of tilling and loosening the soil. And of course you can't be trodding on it after you've loosened it, especially if there is a lot of moisture in the garden. 'Cause it just stamps down the soil and nothing will grow in there. I think it's important to have compost and manure mixed into your soil. And you've got to have good seed, of course.

Ideally, you should try to hoe around your plants as they come along, and weed them. But I find that I get all hepped up in the spring and try to do all of this, but as the season progresses, every-thing seems to cave in on me and I have to let it go on by itself more or less. But I do water my garden when it needs it.

Growing parsley from Cinquino seed is a family tradition.

What are the biggest problems you have?

My biggest problems are the animals that I share the garden with.

How many animals have you trapped in the garden this year?

This year I got 5 raccoons, 4 woodchucks, 2 possums, and 1 squirrel (but I let him go). Last year I had 11 raccoons, 4 woodchucks, and 4 possums. People tell me they are probably the same ones coming back, but I doubt that very much. I release them out in the country. I don't think they could come back—especially over the highway—without getting hurt. I put them in a quarry because then they won't be in the position of ruining someone else's garden. Last year I caught two raccoons at the same time.

How many years have you been gardening?

50 years.

Has the animal problem gotten better or worse?

I think it's gotten worse. I've become more aware of them and have done something about them since I got a trap. Before that we had a dog. The dog kept them down pretty much. Now that we have leash laws, there are very few dogs on the loose anymore, so there are no predators there for them. And evidently I have the only garden around.

I do have the only garden for quite a distance around me, and that makes a difference. But there is plenty of vegetation out there to eat. They come up here for dessert, I think.

How do you deal with them?

I catch them with a HavaHart trap. The best bait I've found is apples. I slice them up and place them in front of the trap and lead the animals into the trap.

Do they ever get mean?

I usually let them sit around long enough so they are pretty subdued. The raccoons are pretty fierce about getting out—they dig at the bottom of the cage. But I've never had any of them snap at me. I take them out in the country and release them near stone quarries. When I let them go, I usually aim the cage toward the woods about 2 to 3 feet away. Usually they are so happy to get away that they scamper right into the woods.

Do you wear gloves?

I used to. But not anymore.

If you have the last garden on the block and you're constantly battling animals, why do you garden?

> I get a certain amount of pleasure out of it. It is a lot of work. But I love the fresh vegetables and being able to go out into the garden and pick my own. And it really is amazing to me how all these plants grow from little seeds. It's a pleasure to watch them grow and keep them growing. It's a challenge, really.

If you could have only one garden tool, what would it be?

> I would have to say a spade. Now my dad—his era was the era before rotary tillers, and he had a large garden—would spade every inch of it by hand, and this was after work. So you've got to have a passion for gardening to do that. I always suspected, too, that he wanted to get away from his children.

Mr. Cinquino is the oldest of eight children. He also has four of his own children. Some of them love to garden, but all of them love to eat— especially his daughter-in-law: me.

Mr. Cinquino's dad

with his cold frame

Tips, Tools &

Techniques

In summer, gardening can suddenly begin to feel like war. Bugs, weeds, animals, and invasive plants all laugh in our faces. And so we become garden warriors. Brandishing knives, sharpened shovels, and heavy gardening artillery, we do our best to defend ourselves, our families, and our land from the threat of encroaching foreign invasion.

Occasionally in the quiet of the early morning or in the heat of the midday sun, we feel defeat looming like a swarm of gnats up our noses and in our mouths—the sickening, sweaty cold feeling in our stomachs from the deep knowledge that our freedom has been lost and we will have to spend the next 50 years in gardening hard-labor camps, starving because the enemy has taken all our food and refuses to give us anything but a crust of pumpkin.

Oops, wrong book. I am a pacifist, but I also know that conflict and challenge are part of life and not necessarily bad things. If we meet our challenges positively and learn from them, we can't help but grow—even though it's not always a pleasant process. There are many ways to meet the summer's gardening onslaught without resorting to violence. Cultivating a zenlike peaceful heart is a good step toward becoming a better gardener. If you work with your garden instead of fighting against it, your garden can help you grow, flourish, and flower as well.

Sometimes summer can feel out of control. Let's go.

The Art of Weeding

I do not worry about sowing the weeds, they reseed themselves quite easily. . . . You might say that the farmer who tries to control weeds by cultivating the soil is, quite literally, sowing the seeds of his own misfortune.

—Masanobu Fukuoka, *The One-Straw Revolution*

Most people, including me, love to complain about weeding. There are times when, if the truth be known, weeding is a miserable activity. Weeding is, however, one of the best ways to really get to know what is going on in your garden. If done in the right frame of mind and at the right time, it can be downright pleasant.

The best way to approach weeding is as if you are out on a research and exploration mission: "Let's see, what will I find today?" Sometimes it also helps to think of weeding as a parenting process . . . as in, "I've got to go out and take care of the children lest they catch a chill or bug and get sick!" Either way, it is during weeding that you come closest to all of your plants and can see if they are healthy or diseased, bug-ridden or bug-bitten.

I also delight in seeing what sorts of things are growing that I hadn't planted or expected, like wildflowers or tomatoes that have "volunteered" from seeds of fruits that dropped the year before. Sometimes things you thought had died come back to life, or mysterious but nice plants grow where you didn't plant them. Often, you find the living quarters of friends and foes and the signs of their bounty—the shells of a robin's egg, a praying mantis egg mass.

While you are weeding, too, you can let your mind roam in a stream of consciousness and weedy free-for-all. All your thoughts, fears, emotions, and dreams will be listened to willingly by your garden. I often think about my life in terms of weeding. What are the things that I need to remove so that the things I want to keep can grow big and strong? Like people, weeds have different personalities. There are the nice, meek, harmless weeds who not only don't take up too much space and are easy to pick but give things back to you, like nitrogen (in clover). Then there are the mean old weeds who invade your space and make your life generally miserable, like poison ivy.

You might have heard that weeds are just plants that grow where they are not wanted. There is a lot of truth to that. Many things we consider weeds are actually valuable plants. Many weeds such as pigweed (or fat hen), purslane, and burdock can be eaten and are delicious. No doubt people in earlier times ate them regularly without even having to plant them! Other weeds are important for animals or other plants. Inkberry and other wild berries are eaten by birds and animals.

> While you are weeding, you can let your **m i n d r o a m** in a . . . weedy *free-for-all.*

Many weeds are useful plants. The roots of burdock are used in medicine, while the cooked stalks taste like asparagus.

Some weeds are medicinal. And many, I'm sure, serve purposes unknown to us. I often think that one of the roles of poison ivy in nature is what I call the "defender of wildness." Since poison ivy often grows rampantly in the woodlands around here in Pennsylvania, it keeps too many people from trampling through the woods and using it for their playground. I can imagine that the trees and animals are very thankful to poison ivy for that reason.

Weeding is a fact of life if you are going to have a garden. And weed killers cause a lot more problems than they solve. Therefore, you may as well find a way to enjoy the process. Here are my tips.

- **If you remember only one thing:** Pull the weeds out by the *roots*. Just ripping them off at the stem will only lead to stronger, deeper-rooted weeds that are harder to pull.

- **Best time to weed:** Early morning. My favorite time is after I have had a cup of coffee and read the paper. I throw on some old clothes and head out with my flip-flops and basket and go to it. By early, I mean 6:30 to 8:30 A.M. On a weekday I can get a good hour in, take a shower, and still get to work on time (although my nails reveal my habits). On a weekend, I may start later and spend most of the day puttering around and doing stuff in the garden.

- **Second best time to weed:** Late afternoon and early evening. Sometimes after work it is just what the doctor ordered to rip off those darn work clothes, change into something much more comfortable, and get out there and pull. It's the most beautiful, relaxed time of the day in the garden and a great time to enjoy being out there.

- **Worst time to weed:** Anytime it's too hot, humid, buggy, or dry. Thunder, lightning, hail, and hurricanes should also be avoided.

- **Best time for the soil to be weeded:** After a deep soaking rain, weeds pull out of the dirt like ripe apples falling out of a tree. They practically weed themselves for you.

- **Note of caution about weeding when plants are wet:** However, some things should not be touched, picked, or weeded when wet. Weeding carrots when they are wet causes the scent to attract carrot flies. Touching green beans when they are wet can cause rust (a fungal disease) on the beans and leaves.

- **Best tools:** My system is to take two baskets. One large one is for the weeds and the other is for the tools (a trug is what the British call it). In the trug I carry my trusty Japanese weeding knife (the only weeding tool you will ever need), my scissors for deadheading, and raffia for tying things up and back. When the weed basket is full, I dump it on the compost pile.

- **Best weeding system:** Start at one point in your yard and work around from there. Don't go around willy-nilly picking weeds, or you'll just miss things and get frustrated. Set a goal for yourself—from the porch to a certain tree, for example. Even if you feel like quitting, tell yourself, "As soon as I get to that tree, I will quit." For some reason, the closer I get to the tree, the faster and easier the weeding goes, and I usually end up going past my goal.

  Another technique is to start where the weeding is easiest. That gets you warmed up and in the mood. Before you know it, you're weeding the tough spots, and they don't seem that hard after all.

- **Best weeding rule to live by:** Never let a weed go to seed. Ever hear the old saying, "One year's seed is seven years' weed"? It sure seems true. The seeds don't just live on in the ground, but they also get eaten by birds and deposited all over the place.

If you really like it, then it's not a weed.

Even if I don't have time to do a full weeding, if I see a weed about to go to seed, I pluck it out immediately.

- **Best way to keep your hands and nails clean:** Gloves are the easy answer. I tend to hate using gloves unless I'm working with prickly things. Try soap. A friend of mine, Barry Friel, from Zionsville, Pennsylvania, recommends putting soap underneath your nails *before* you go out to weed. I always forget to try it. Actually, I think I'll try it right now—hold on . . .

  It didn't keep my nails clean while I was weeding, but it did make them easier to clean after I was done. Worth a try.

  Having longer nails gives you extra power and protection while weeding. Sometimes if your nails are too short, it's easier to hurt yourself. Some people by their very natures miraculously keep their hands clean. I am not one of them.

When Is a Weed a Weed?

How can I tell a weed from a garden plant? A lot of first-time gardeners ask me that question. Sometimes it really is hard to tell. But you should never be intimidated by gardening just because you don't know what something is. There are very few things that are irreplaceable. Follow these tips and you should be fine.

First, familiarize yourself with common weeds by looking at pictures in books. Try to find books that show the weed seedlings as well as the adults.

Next, look at the way the plants are growing. Are there a lot of them or only one? If you can see a lot of the same kind of plant and they look as if they're growing randomly all over the place, they're most likely weeds. Many things that grow between sidewalk cracks are weeds (but not all—I have mullein, pansies, violets, moss, and cilantro growing between the cracks of my patio). Check them out and see if any of yours match. If there is just one plant and it looks rather exotic, keep it for a while and see what happens. Let it grow and see if you like it. If you really like it, then it's not a weed. If you don't like it, then it is a weed.

Finally, if you're not sure about something, ask. Take a sample to your local nursery, call your local cooperative extension agent or regional master gardener, check with your local garden club, or ask a neighbor.

Controlling Weeds

How do you prevent weeds from growing in the first place? Weeds grow where there is room for them. There are two major ways to control weeds organically.

1. **Plant.** The best way to prevent weeds from growing is to plant things that you want first. For example: If you have a plain square patch of dirt, weeds will grow over the whole patch within a

short time. It's Nature's way of protecting herself—or clothing herself, if you will. But if you plant a tree and some flowers there, fewer weeds will grow. But they will still grow.

If you plant a tree, some flowers, and a groundcover, even fewer weeds will grow. Ultimately, you will never eliminate weeds completely—nor should you want to. But the more you plant, the more Nature's need to be clothed will have been met, and the fewer weeds you will have.

You can notice this when you weed by paying attention to where the weeds seem to grow most of all and where they grow least of all. Usually, where there are lots of plants all planted together, weeds will be less of a problem.

2. Mulch. Mulch is a definite weed preventer when applied at least 2 inches thick. Mulch is a great solution to your weed problems. You don't, however, want to rely solely on mulch, especially if you're using bark chips or fresh sawdust, because too much of it can deplete your soil of important nutrients. Look in "Spring" on page 168 for a complete review of the different types of mulch.

Getting a Grip on Poison Ivy

I've finally discovered the best way to pull poison ivy and other noxious plants. Just follow these simple steps: Get a trash bag (plastic or paper) so you're ready to deposit the plant into it when you've picked it. Put your arm inside a long plastic bag. (A plastic grocery bag works well.) Then put a paper bag on the outside of that. (A paper grocery bag is too heavy, but lunch-bag thickness works well.) Grab the weed and pull as much of the roots of the plant out as you can get. Deposit the weed and all the bags into the trash bag, being very careful not to touch *anything* that has touched the weed. Throw it out. Do not burn, compost, or eat!

If you don't know what poison ivy looks like—this is it!

Two bags are important for double protection, in case one of them rips or already has a hole. It is also easier to grip with the paper bag than it is with plastic—but plastic provides greater protection than the paper. The oils of poisonous or irritant plants can seep through paper bags.

A second technique that I've heard works and have tried successfully so far is just to persistently cut poison ivy off at the stem every time it grows back. Eventually, the roots will die. Make sure you wash the cutting implement with detergent after you have finished. Make sure to wash yourself with lots of *cold water* after you are through!

If all else fails and you have a giant patch that has taken over your life, borrow a goat. Goats love poison ivy and will do a fine job of demolishing it. However, after the goat is through dining, do not, under any circumstances, kiss the goat on the lips.

Scary poison ivy fact The poisonous oil in poison ivy is so toxic that a drop the size of a pinhead could cause a rash in 500 people.

Getting Motivated

When it's time to just get down on your knees and weed, here are a few more tips to help you get the job done.

- **Best weeding motivator.** A deadline. Relatives coming. A garden party. If you need to get your garden weeded and can't seem to get motivated, invite some people over for a backyard barbecue. That will get you moving.

- **How often to weed.** In spring, weeding every three to four weeks will suffice. Once summer hits, go around every week to keep on top of things—depending on your weather conditions. (If it's hot and there is lots of rain, your weeds will go nuts.) Otherwise they will get too big and go to seed. It's much easier to keep on top of weeding by doing it regularly than it is to ignore things for a few weeks and then face a jungle!

- **Bring in reinforcements.** If you can't keep up with it, weeding is a very good job for neighborhood kids looking for some summer spending money. Not only does it help you out but it also subversively plants the gardening seed in the next generation. Spend some time with the kids at first, showing them which plants are weeds and which aren't. Before you know it, you can let them loose.

Ultimately, weeding is not that complicated or hard. Gardening should always be fun, so try to find ways to make weeding fun. Listen to music. Have a nice glass of cold iced tea or lemonade by your side. Take breaks where you just sit on the grass or on a rock and enjoy the beauty around you. Bring a friend or family member out and talk with them while you weed (get them to help if you can). Think how beautiful your garden will be when you are done.

> **Weeding fact** Too much nitrogen in the environment can cause a sort of weed "algae bloom." Acid rain and agricultural pollution release nitrogen into the air and the environment. The excess can cause weeds to grow out of control and choke out native plants, much like nitrogen released into rivers causes algae to grow excessively and choke out fish and plants.

Getting to Know Your Weeds

Weeds aren't just one type of plant, just like "Americans" aren't just one type of people. As I mentioned before, there are no inherently bad weeds. But there are varying degrees of troublesome weeds and varying degrees of useful weeds. I like to break them down into a few categories: edible weeds, medicinal weeds, mystery weeds, and vile, noxious weeds. All of the others being obvious, mystery weeds are the ones whose purpose I simply don't know.

There is also a whole category of "weeds" that are really native plants (but we just don't realize it). And then there are reseeded plants and trees. For instance, I am constantly picking maple and mimosa trees out of my garden. They don't qualify as your typical weeds, but they are weeds to me since I don't want them where they are growing.

Which weeds you have growing in your yard can also tell you about your soil—whether it's fertile or barren, acidic or alkaline. "A Guide to Common Weeds of the United States" on page 246 is a fairly comprehensive list of weeds and contains some interesting things about each of them.

For a complete guide to weeds for identification and more detailed information, there are a number of good books available. My favorites are *Rodale's Successful Organic Gardening: Controlling Weeds* by Erin Hynes and *The Gardener's Weed Book* by Barbara Pleasant.

One word of caution: Don't eat any of these weeds listed as edible or use them for medicine unless you do further research into how to pick, prepare, and use them. Many weeds can be quite deadly if ingested.

A Guide to Common Weeds of the United States

Plant	Annual, Biennial, or Perennial	Soil Indicator	Interesting Facts
EDIBLE			
Burdock	Biennial	Rich soil	Young stems are delicious cooked in batter or in tomato sauce.
Chickweed	Annual	Fertile soil	Chickweed seeds can germinate after being buried for 10 years.
Dandelion	Perennial	Cultivated soil	When battered and fried, flowers taste like mushrooms. Use young leaves for an early spring salad green.
Curly dock	Perennial	Poorly drained soil	Dock can produce 40,000 seeds and remain viable for 70 years. Don't eat the leaves if you have kidney stones.
Wild garlic	Perennial	Sandy soil	—
Barnyard grass	Annual	Poorly drained soil	Seeds make a crunchy topping for breads.
Common mallow	Annual or biennial	Cultivated soil	Seedpods are edible when green.
Black mustard, Indian wild mustard	Annual	Wide range of soil conditions	Seeds can be made into edible mustard; leaves are spicy and slightly bitter; unopened flower buds are a delicacy.
Yellow nutsedge	Perennial	Poorly drained soil	Underground "nuts" (tubers) that grow from the roots are edible. Raw nuts taste like coconut; roasted nuts taste like almonds.
Virginia pepperweed	Annual	Dry, alkaline soil	Tastes like pepper.
Pigweed, spiny amaranth	Annual	Cultivated rich soil	Young leaves can be eaten like spinach.
Pokeweed	Perennial	Rich, deep, gravelly soil	Young leaves can be eaten like spinach. Berries are used for dyes and inks. Roots, mature leaves, and berries are very toxic—although roots have anti-viral properties.
Purslane	Annual	Rich soil	Young shoots are highly nutritious. Add to salad; they turn slimy when cooked.
Red sorrel	Perennial	Poorly drained, acid soil	Young leaves are edible in salads. Leaves also make a delicious soup.
Yellow wood sorrel	Perennial	Stony or acid soil	Leaves are edible.
MEDICINAL			
Ground ivy	Perennial	Rich soil	Reputed to cure heart disease and let you know when witches are near. Leaves can be toxic. Highly invasive.
Mullein	Biennial	Dry, gravelly soil	See page 248.
Plantain	Perennial	Cultivated or compacted soil	Crushed leaves applied as a poultice soothe the itching of poison ivy.
St.-John's-wort	Perennial	Dry, stony soil	Miracle weed used to treat depression.
Shepherd's purse	Annual	Wide range of soil conditions	A poultice of the leaves can be used to stop bleeding, and heal wounds. Tea cleanses the kidneys.

Plant	Annual, Biennial, or Perennial	Soil Indicator	Interesting Facts
SOIL-IMPROVING AND USEFUL			
Black clover	Annual	Infertile or nitrogen-poor soil	Roots fix nitrogen in association with beneficial bacteria.
Queen-Anne's-lace	Biennial	Infertile, dry, alkaline soil	Attracts beneficial insects.
Redroot pigweed	Annual	Cultivated, rich soil	Improves topsoil by bringing hidden nutrients up toward the surface.
VILE			
Bermuda grass	Perennial	Sandy soil	Releases chemicals that inhibit the growth of other plants.
Field bindweed, hedge bindweed	Perennial	Wide range of soil conditions	Roots can go down 30 feet. Seeds live 50 years. Hideous, hideous weed, also known as "devil's guts."
Wild buckwheat	Annual	Disturbed soil	Creepy!
Cocklebur	Annual	Infertile soil	Seedlings are poisonous to livestock.
Dodder	Annual	Dry or moist soil, depending on type	Actually sucks the life out of other plants. A garden parasite.
Greenbrier	Perennial	Moist soil	Scratchy.
Poison hemlock	Perennial	Rich, loamy, or gravelly soil	Highly poisonous if eaten.
Water hemlock	Perennial	Wet soil	A small chunk of the root (which looks like a sweet potato or carrot) is deadly if eaten.
Jimsonweed	Annual	Rich soil	Eating this causes paralysis, convulsions, and death.
Kudzu	Perennial	Wide range of soil conditions	Most famous invasive weed. Pigs will eat it.
Milkweed	Perennial	Wide range of soil conditions	Invasive. Native Americans used seed fluff as disposable diapers for their babies.
Horse nettle	Perennial	Compacted soil	Attracts bugs and carries viruses.
Stinging nettles	Perennial or annual	Rich, damp soil	Touching these plants feels as if you are being stung by bees. Use gloves.
Deadly nightshade	Annual	Sandy, gravelly, or loamy soils	Poisonous—eating this causes paralysis and death. Has recently been discovered as a valuable tool for cleaning up toxic wastes. The roots are especially good at detoxifying and absorbing PCBs.
Poison ivy and oak	Perennial	Wide range of soil conditions	The worst. Don't ever burn them.
Quackgrass	Perennial	Compacted soil	—
Ragweed	Annual	Poor soil	Its pollen is the main cause of hayfever.
Thistle	Perennial	Cultivated soil	Cut back repeatedly. Dig up roots and let them bake in the sun to kill them. Young thistle leaves and roots are edible.

A Weed or a Beautiful & Heroic Adventurer?

Mullein came to America in the ballast of a ship. It wasn't always considered a weed. It was once used as a candlewick (dipped in fat or floating in oil), so it is also known as the candlewick plant. The stalks were dipped in suet and used as torches—hence the names torches, miner's candle, and Our Lady's candle.

The leaves were used as shoe inserts, both for comfort and to increase circulation. Ancient Romans and Europeans used the gold flowers of mullein to add blonde highlights to their hair.

Mullein was also considered a weather predictor. Try it yourself: Blossoms appearing low on the stalk indicate early snow, while blossoms at the top mean there will be a long winter with heavy snow.

In India, mullein is used to ward off evil spirits. The Roman Pliny the Elder used mullein to treat bronchial problems. Other proposed medicinal uses for mullein include curing hoarseness, coughs, gout, hemorrhoids, toothaches, warts, tumors, swelling, dysentery, diarrhea, mental disturbances, and generally thinking bad thoughts.

All this from a "weed."

I cast my vote for the beautiful and heroic adventurer.

All about Bugs

Everything has an intrinsic right to exist. Every time you kill off a species, you're lessening your own chance of survival.

—**Bill Mollison,** *Travels in Dreams*

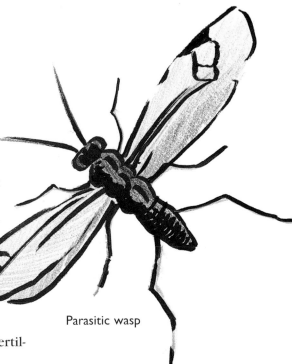

Parasitic wasp

Get your squeamishness out of your system right now because we are about to talk about bugs. Ready? Let's go.

Basically, bugs are everywhere. The more closely you look, the more you will see. Before you freak out and think of reaching for the Raid (which, of course, you would *never really do*), you may want to know a few facts about bugs.

Bugs play a critical role in the garden. They eat waste, break it down into fertilizer, provide food for birds and animals who also fertilize your garden, eat other bugs, and do a lot of soil aeration and improvement. By human standards, there are definitely bugs that are considered good and others that are considered bad. And it has nothing to do with looks. But trying to eradicate all bugs will only give the bad bugs an advantage by making them even more resilient. Yet more than any other aspect of gardening (except perhaps woodchucks), bugs are considered "the enemy."

"It is very important to develop the right attitude toward your enemy," says the Dalai Lama in the book *The Good Heart.* Discussing the Buddhist texts as they relate to Christian texts, he continues, "If you can cultivate the right attitude, your enemies are your best spiritual teachers because their presence provides you with the opportunity to enhance and develop tolerance, patience, and understanding. By developing greater tolerance and patience, it will be easier for you to develop your capacity for compassion and, through that, altruism. So even for the practice of your own spiritual path, the presence of an enemy is crucial."

In many ways, bugs are merely the messengers—they bring us word that there is something in the way we are gardening or growing that needs attention. By just trying to blot out and ignore their message, we are losing a vital opportunity to grow and understand more. But if we listen to them (crunch, crunch) and try to hear and learn what they are trying to tell us, we can grow healthy and strong together with our plants—and even be thankful to those "enemies" for showing us where we need to focus our attention.

Having said that, you may want to know that I have stepped on my share of "messengers." Especially if they are in my house.

When you have a major insect infestation or disease that severely damages a plant or crop, there is usually something wrong with the surrounding environment. Bugs and diseases come when they are called, just as a strong human immune system prevents illness and a weak one attracts illness. The most common causes of bug and disease problems are the following:

- **Poor soil.** Good, fertile soil grows healthy plants that are very resistant to bugs. Bugs hate plants that are really healthy.

- **The wrong soil for the plant.** If an acid-loving plant is planted in soil that is too alkaline, or a plant has too much or too little nitrogen for its most optimum growing conditions, it will reveal its weakness through disease or insect infestation.

- **Plants planted in the wrong place.** A shade-lover in the sun, for instance. You'd get sick, too, if you were fair-skinned and forced to sit in the broiling sun for a full day. An Alpine wild-flower planted at sea level would say it didn't feel too good either, if asked.

- **A sickly variety to begin with.** Some plants are bred to be chemical-dependent. Avoid them as you would a drug addict.

- **A system out of balance.** You'll know that this is your problem if there aren't enough birds, snakes, toads, and beneficial insects in your yard.

- **Same old, same old.** Planting the same vegetables and annuals in the same place every year is an open invitation to pests and diseases. Be sure to rotate your crops.

- **Plants planted at the wrong time of year.** Some vegetables only thrive in the cooler months of spring and fall. Others can't live without the heat of summer.

The first step in working in partnership with bugs is to recognize the ones that are actually garden heroes. These are the bugs we call beneficial insects. You know the typical ones—the ladybugs and honey-bees. But did you know that ants are more critical to the earth's survival than humans?

That's because, while humans use up the earth's resources, pollute the planet, and cause the extinction of other species, ants do the opposite. They help recycle nutrients, hasten the recycling of decaying organic matter, and work the soil. In fact, according to Bert Hölldobler and Edward O. Wilson in their book *Journey to the Ants,* ants are even more helpful than earthworms in moving great quantities of soil, aerating the land, and circulating nutrients. Like earthworms, ants are essential to maintaining life in the soil—and, as a result, life on this planet.

Ants are essential because they plant seeds and aerate the soil. Bees are essential because they pollinate plants—which enables the plants to set fruit for us to eat. But other bugs are pollinators, too—beetles, butterflies, dragonflies, flies, and moths to name a few. Hummingbirds and even bats are pollinators. Some of the plants in your garden that depend on pollinators are cantaloupes, cucumbers, melons, squash, and fruits such as apples, cherries, pears, and plums.

In general, if you are uncertain about what a bug is, leave it.

The Heroes

Here's a rundown of the bugs that every right-minded gardener should want in his or her garden. Look up the ones you don't know in a field guide, then rejoice when you see them in your yard.

Ants. They eat organic matter and honeydew secreted by aphids (which gives them their bad reputation, since they protect aphid colonies and move them to new plants). But they also aerate the soil—in fact, they're more effective at aeration than earthworms—clean up crumbs, and plant seeds.

Assassin bugs. They feed on the larval forms of many plant-eating insects.

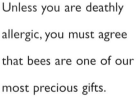

Unless you are deathly allergic, you must agree that bees are one of our most precious gifts.

Bees. By now you might have heard the horrid reports of the decline of the bee population in the United States. A deadly combination of bad weather, mites, viruses, habitat loss, and pesticide use has decimated the bee population. Bees are critical to producing over a third of the food we eat. Through their "volunteer" pollinating efforts, we get fruits, vegetables, and flowers that feed and delight us.

Interesting bee facts According to the National Honey Board:

- **Honeybees tap 2,000,000 flowers to make 1 pound of honey.**

- **A hive of bees flies 55,000 miles to bring you 1 pound of honey.**

- **The average worker honeybee makes $\frac{1}{12}$ teaspoon of honey in its lifetime.**

- **During one collection trip, a honeybee visits 50 to 100 flowers.**

According to the British *Organic Gardening Magazine,* different species of bees like different types of flowers because each species has a different tongue length. Different bees include bumblebees, lawn bees, carpenter bees, and honeybees. Even the stinger-happy yellow jacket wasps (that eat small insects and fruit, too) are useful here. All are important pollinators.

Ground beetles. They consume mass quantities of slugs and snails, cankerworms, and tent caterpillars.

Lady beetles (also called ladybugs). Adults eat aphids, mealybugs, and scale. The black larvae, called spider mite destroyers, eat mites. Vedalia lady beetles eat cottony cushion scale and other soft insects.

Ladybugs are always polite.

Mealybug destroyer beetles. As the name implies, they eat mealybugs.

Soldier beetles (a.k.a. Pennsylvania leatherwings). They eat grasshopper eggs, cucumber beetles, and caterpillars.

Doodlebugs (or antlions). Larvae trap and eat ants and other insects.

Dragonflies. These striking flyers eat mosquitoes and flies.

Earthworms. Though not insects, earthworms are true garden heroes. They eat harmful nematodes and make your soil lush and healthy. Pesticides kill 60 to 90 percent of earthworms.

Fireflies (also known as lightning bugs). They are one of the miracles of nature. They light up summer dusk and early evening like a fairy-tale story, and their larvae feed on snails, slugs, cutworms, and other small insects. (Well, what do you know.)

Green lacewings. These graceful insects eat aphids, mites, thrips, whiteflies, Colorado potato beetle larvae, and insect eggs.

Green lacewings are very good at hiding, probably because they know that they taste so delicious to birds.

Minute pirate bugs. This fierce-sounding predator eats thrips, spider mites, leafhopper nymphs, whiteflies, aphids, and insect eggs.

Praying mantids. These most fearsome-looking beneficial insects eat aphids, beetles, bugs, leafhoppers, flies, bees, wasps, caterpillars, butterflies, and each other. Proof that sex is all in your head: The reason the female eats the male's head during copulation is that something in his brain (his survival instinct, no doubt) actually inhibits his sex drive.

Predatory mites. These tiny mites eat thrips and spider mites.

Robber flies. They eat beetles, leafhoppers, butterflies, flies, and bugs. Larvae prey on white grubs, beetle pupae, and grasshopper eggs.

Spiders. There are probably a jillion types of spiders. Spiders are our friends because in their webs they catch all sorts of other bugs, regardless of whether they are friends of the garden or not. Then spiders suck the living guts out of their prey.

Black-and-yellow garden spiders have very large appetites.

Syrphid flies (flower flies and hoverflies). Larvae eat aphids, and adults eat nectar as well as mealybugs and other small insects.

Tachinid flies. Larvae are the internal parasites of many beetles, grasshoppers, bugs, caterpillars, and sawflies.

Wasps. Parasitic wasps, such as braconid, chalcid, and ichneumon wasps, lay their eggs inside host insects (caterpillars and aphids). When they hatch, the larvae are presented with a living lunch. If you've ever seen a huge green tomato hornworm with white Q-Tip-like heads on his back, they're the cocoons of pupating wasps, and he is not long for this world.

Happy-Go-Lucky Garden Pedestrians

These creatures are neither friend nor foe—they're just along for the ride. Enjoy them for their songs and for adding diversity to your yard—and maybe for providing a meal or two for hungry birds along the way.

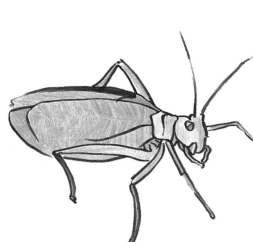

Centipedes and millipedes. These are not insects, but they eat decaying plant matter and some living plant matter.

Cicadas. Some would say these are bad, but since they only come out every 7 (or 13, or whatever, depending on what species they are) years and they are really bizarre-looking, I say, leave them alone and enjoy their weird discarded shells.

Field crickets. Although they eat young vegetable plants, crickets are rarely a garden nuisance, and summer would not be summer without their beautiful night music.

Earwigs. They eat lots and lots of other bugs (including fire ants), which makes up for the fact that they may enjoy some of your zinnias and peppers, too.

Katydids. They eat foliage, but again, there are too few of them to matter, and they're really neat-looking.

Moths. Although many moths are the adult forms of troublesome caterpillars, the main damage moths do is create the next generation of caterpillars. Did you know that the reason that moths flock to the light is that it protects them from their main predator, the bat, who hates light as much as Dracula?

Spittlebugs and froghoppers. These are generally not a problem. If you see what looks like foamy spit on a plant, that is the telltale sign that a nymph is hiding underneath.

Walking sticks. Nymphs feed on foliage, but otherwise they just look cool—like twigs.

Messengers

These bugs are pests. But besides being a problem, they may point to a larger problem in your garden—poor soil, drought stress, weak plants, or whatever. That's why I call them messengers.

Aphids. These little fellows come in many colors and eat fruits, flowers, roses, and vegetables. They include the *bean aphid,* which eats beans, beets, chard, peas, rhubarb, and spinach; the *green peach aphid;* the *pea aphid,* which eats beans and peas; the *spinach aphid;* and the *woolly apple aphid,* which eats apples, pears, and

Aphids love roses.

Just crush them.

quinces. Aphids hate ladybugs and their larvae, other predators, and gar-lic. They also hate being sprayed off plants with a strong jet of water.

Beetles. The pest beetles include the *asparagus beetle;* the *bean leaf beetle,* which eats beans, peas, and soybeans; the *elm bark beetle,* which carries Dutch elm disease; the *striped flea beetle,* which eats broccoli, cabbage, and cauliflower; the *fiery searcher beetle;* the *Japanese beetle,* consumer of apples, cherries, grapes, peaches, plums, quinces, raspberries, rhubarb, and roses; the *Colorado potato beetle,* which eats eggplant, peppers, potatoes, and tomatoes; the *fig beetle,* which eats berries, figs, and tree fruits; the *June beetle* (a.k.a. May bee-tle, dewbug), which eats potatoes and strawberries; the *Mexican bean beetle* (not to be confused with the Mexican jumping bean); the *spot-ted asparagus beetle;* the *spotted cucumber beetle,* which eats corn, cucumbers, eggplant, melons, peas, potatoes, squash, tomatoes, and tree fruits; the *striped cucumber beetle,* which eats beans, corn, cucumbers, melons, peas, pumpkins, and squash; and the *striped blis-ter beetle,* which eats beans, beets, melons, peas, potatoes, and toma-toes. Beetles hate predatory wasps, ladybugs and their larvae, spiders, toads, and birds. They also hate being kept out of succulent crops by row covers.

Borers. This group of pests includes the *Northern corn rootworm,* which eats corn and other grains; the *European corn borer,* which also relishes corn; the *iris borer;* the *peachtree borer,* which bores into the trunks of apricot, cherry, peach, and plum trees; the *pickleworm,* which attacks cucumbers, melons, pumpkins, and squash; the *potato tuberworm borer,* which eats eggplant, potatoes, and tomatoes; and the *squash vine borer,* which strikes plants of cucumber, gourd, melon, pumpkin, and squash.

Bugs. What we call bugs are more properly known as insects. But there is a group of insects that are rightfully called true bugs, includ-ing the *brown stinkbug,* a pest of blackberry, cabbage, corn, peach, and tomato plants; the *cinch bug,* which eats corn; the *harlequin* or *calico bug,* which eats brussels sprouts, cauliflower, cherries, citrus, collards, horseradish, kohlrabi, mustard, radishes, and turnips; the *southern green stinkbug,* which eats beans, citrus, peaches, pecans, potatoes, and tomatoes; the *squash bug,* which eats cucumbers, mel-ons, pumpkins, and squash; and the *tarnished plant bug,* which eats fruits and vegetables.

Besides the true bugs, there are critters that are named "bug" that really aren't even insects. These include the *sow bug* and *pill bug* (actually related to crustaceans), which eat decaying plant matter but can damage living plants in the process.

Grasshoppers. These eat the leaves and stems of vegetables.

A few grasshoppers are not a problem. It's when they come in hordes that you have to be careful.

Leafhoppers and treehoppers. These cute little critters include the *beet leafhopper*, which eats beets, potatoes, and tomatoes and transmits curly top disease in the process; the *potato leafhopper,* which eats beans, celery, citrus, eggplant, potatoes, and rhubarb and transmits viral diseases; and the *buffalo treehopper,* which lays its eggs in slits that injure young fruit trees, potatoes, and tomatoes.

Maggots and flies. Fly larvae are maggots. This "ugsome" group includes *apple maggots,* which eat apples, blueberries, cherries and plums; *cabbage maggots,* which eat broccoli, brussels sprouts, cabbages, cauliflower, radishes, and turnips; *carrot rust flies,* whose larvae chew the roots of carrots, celery, parsley, and parsnips; *leafminers,* whose maggots "mine" the leaves of beans, blackberry, cabbage, lettuce, pepper, potato, spinach, and turnip plants; *Mediterranean fruit flies,* whose larvae tunnel into orchard fruits; *onion maggots;* and *pepper maggots,* which eat eggplant, peppers, and tomatoes.

Mealybugs. Mealybugs look like cotton on your plants. They include the *citrus mealybug,* a pest of avocados, citrus, and potatoes; the *Comstock mealybug,* which infests apples, grapes, peaches, and pears; and the *long-tail mealybug,* which eats the sap of avocado, banana, citrus, and plum plants.

Mites (including spider mites). It's really hard to see mites. Look for the telltale webs to see if your plants have spider mites. Mites can attack fruit tree leaves and fruit but usually aren't a serious problem.

Pear psyllid. This pest eats pears and quinces.

Scale. Scale's a pretty sedentary pest—it just sits on your plant and sucks sap. The types of scale you may encounter include *California red scale,* which attacks citrus, fig, grape, and walnut plants; *cottony cushion scale,* which prefers almond, apple, apricot, citrus, fig, peach, pepper, potato, quince, and walnut plants; and *San Jose scale,* which sucks the sap of apple, cherry, peach, pear, pecan, and quince plants.

Perhaps the most dreaded of all garden messengers, slugs hate salt, copper, and sharp things. But they *love* beer. Just put out a small bowl in your garden and empty it regularly until they're all gone.

Slugs and snails. These are mollusks, not insects, but they're bad garden pests. They eat holes in all sorts of foliage. (Slugs, by the way, are eaten by toads, frogs, ground beetles, and hedgehogs.)

Thrips. These tiny pests eat citrus, dates, grapes, peaches, and flowers.

Weevils. Weevils are actually beetles, but they look so weird with their long snouts that I've given them their own paragraph. They include the *apple curculio,* which eats apples, pears, and quinces; the *bean weevil,* which eats beans and peas; the *black vine weevil,* which eats the leaves of blackberry, blueberry, cranberry, strawberry, ornamentals, azaleas, camellias, rhododendrons, wisteria, and yews; the *cabbage curculio,* which eats broccoli, cabbage, cauliflower, and turnips; the *carrot weevil,* which eats carrot roots, celery hearts, dill, and parsley; the *plum curculio,* which eats apples, blueberries, cherries, peaches, pears, plums, and quinces; and the *vegetable weevil,* which eats beets, cabbages, carrots, lettuce, onions, potatoes, radishes, spinach, tomatoes, and turnips.

Worms and caterpillars. This category includes some of the most pernicious pests, including *beet armyworms,* which eat beets, corn, and peas; *bagworms,* which eat tree foliage; *cankerworms,* which eat apple, beech, elm, linden, and oak foliage; *cabbage loopers,* which eat beans, broccoli, cabbages, cauliflower, celery, kale, lettuce, parsley, peas, potatoes, radishes, spinach, and tomatoes; *codling moths,* whose larvae eat apples, pears, quinces, and walnuts; *corn earworms,* which eat beans, corn, peas, peppers, potatoes, squash, and tomatoes; *cutworms,* which eat seedlings and transplants of garden vegetables; *Eastern tent caterpillars,* which eat the foliage of apple, pear, and other fruit trees; *fall armyworms,* which eat corn, beans, beets, cabbages, cucumbers, grasses, potatoes, spinach, sweet potatoes, tomatoes, and turnips; *fall webworms,* which eat apple, cherry, peach, pecan, and walnut leaves; *garden webworms,* which eat beans, beets, corn, peas, and strawberries; *grapeleaf skeletonizers; gypsy moths,* which eat the leaves of apple, cherry, and oak trees; *imported cabbageworms,* which eat cabbages, cauliflower, kale, kohlrabi, mustard, radishes, and turnips; *navel orangeworms,* which eat citrus and other fruits, figs, and walnuts; *oriental fruit moths,* whose larvae eat almond, apple, apricot, cherry, peach, and plum leaves; *Eastern field wireworm,* which eats beans, beets, carrots, corn, lettuce, onions, peas, potatoes, and strawberries; and *tomato hornworms,* which eat eggplant, peppers, potatoes, and tomatoes.

What the Heck Is a Nematode?

I can never tell whether nematodes are good things or bad things. It seems that they are bad, but then you can also order them by the millions from gardening catalogs as a beneficial. What is the deal with nematodes?

Nematodes are microscopic wormlike creatures without brains or eyes (poor things). It turns out that there are actually two types—the plant parasites and the beneficial nematodes called "free-livers" that feed on insects and pest nematodes.

The plant-parasitic nematodes feed off roots, sometimes killing or stunting the plant in the process. The best way to deal with them is to invite the free-livers and beneficial fungi (both of which feed on plant-eating nematodes) to the party. Rotate your crops, use mulch and compost . . . then, out of sight, out of mind.

Some ornamental plants are nematode resistant, such as butterfly weed, purple coneflower, lilyturf, periwinkle, shellflower, spider lily, sweet William, and yarrow. Ornamental plants that are susceptible to nematode damage include bugleweed, clematis, eulalia grass, lamb's ears, monkshood, and speedwell (veronica).

Marigolds are reputed to rid your garden of the bad nematodes.

Bug-Beating Strategies

Facing an insect infestation can be overwhelming. It's tempting to just freak out and want to rid your garden—and your sight—of any telltale sign of them. But that won't solve your problem at all, and in fact, it will make your garden more vulnerable to future attacks of even greater severity. Here are my best strategies for creating an environment that's inhospitable to bugs.

- Attract or bring birds into your garden. Most garden birds enjoy eating quite a lot of insects. Guinea fowl eat ticks and snakes. Ducks and geese eat slugs. Geese in the orchard are proven to lower insect problems (and to be good "watchdogs").

- If you are going to put in a bat house so bats will come to kill mosquitoes and other bugs, make sure it is at least 18 feet off the ground. A bat has to drop first before it can fly.

- Let your vegetables bloom and go to seed. The seed will attract birds, and the flowers will provide pollen and nectar for beneficial bugs.

- Outwit the buggers. Spread your plants around to fool insects. They may find one patch but not all of them. Rotate your annual flowers and vegetables every year—many bugs have life cycles that depend on plants staying in the same place.

- Plant a diverse mix of plants. Switch vegetable varieties every year or so.

- Plant asparagus, calendula, dahlias, French marigolds, and salvia to repel nematodes.

- To confuse bugs, interplant these plants with your vegetables: asters, chrysanthemums, coreopsis, cosmos, Mexican and French marigolds, and nasturtiums.

- Plant rosemary to repel slugs and snails. Pennyroyal, southernwood, spearmint, and tansy repel aphids and ants.

- Plant decoy crops. For instance, planting potatoes near your tomatoes will keep the Colorado potato beetle from destroying your tomatoes. Then if you see potato beetles on your potatoes, pick them off and "dispose of them properly."

Keep It Clean and Fight Fair

Make sure you target the pests you're trying to control. Don't even use "safe and natural" pesticides like pyrethrum, rotenone, and ryania. They are known as broad-spectrum insecticides, which means they kill every bug, including your garden heroes. Here are some techniques that are effective but harmless to nontarget bugs.

Planting a diverse
mix of flowers, herbs,
and vegetables is
confusing to bugs and
good for your garden.

- **Pick bugs off.** One method often used to kill bad bugs is to pick them off plants and put them in a can of gasoline. A *much* safer way to achieve the same effect is to fill the can with water and then top it with 1 to 2 inches of vegetable oil. Just don't cook with it afterward.

- **Brush them off.** Aphids, for instance, can be decimated in a few swipes—there actually were "aphid brushes" in the old days to brush and crush aphids and get them off plants like roses and fruit trees.

- **Hose them off.** A good strong spray from the garden hose can catapult your bugs to new heights. You can almost hear them scream from the thrill of it.

- **Try a hands-off approach.** Here's one just for carrot flies. Try not to disturb the carrots by touching them once they start to grow. Disturbing them releases a scent that draws carrot flies to carrots like mosquitoes are drawn to me.

- **Get 'em drunk and drown 'em.** What about slugs? There is one simple, tried-and-true trick that works so well you should never need to buy or build any contraptions or use chemicals. Submerge a small dish (plastic yogurt containers or cream-cheese containers work well) into your garden at ground level. Add beer. Check in a few days and dispose of the putrid concoction of dead drunken slugs and beer. Repeat as long as they keep coming.

My father-in-law keeps a jar handy for his collection of Japanese beetles.

Plant Diseases

A plant's health is its own best defense.

—J. I. Rodale

There are so many diseases out there that victimize plants that I couldn't possibly address all of them in this book. However, they fall into four main categories.

1. **Bacteria.** These disease organisms can cause wilting diseases, galls (strange knoblike or knotty growths), rots, spots, and internal blights.

2. **Fungi.** Fungi cause many diseases in the plant world. Most fungi are good because they decompose dead material, but many also live off our garden plants. Whether or not they choose yours depends on weather conditions (wet, stuffy, and humid weather with no air circulation is their favorite) and the general health of your plants. As in everything, prevention is the best cure.

3. **Nematodes.** Of the few thousand species that are problems (as opposed to the many thousand species that are helpful), most cause disease by carrying viruses or letting other diseases enter into the holes they make. (You may wonder why I'm listing nematodes with diseases when I described them as wormlike on page 258, but these microscopic organisms cause diseaselike symptoms, so they're often grouped with the diseases. Really, you can take your pick.)

4. **Viruses.** Viruses are genes in a protein case that are carried and introduced by insects, fungi, nematodes, weeds, people (by touching a diseased plant and then another), tools, and even seeds themselves. Viruses mostly cause yellowing, stunting, and malformations. There is no cure for a plant virus—you just have to pull out the plant and destroy it before the infection spreads.

It is important to keep in mind that bacteria, fungi, nematodes, and viruses are not all bad. They all perform some tasks that are essential to our survival, and banishing all of them would eventually destroy us, too.

As with bugs, diseases are often just a plant's way of trying to tell you that something is not right. If you want to play doctor, a great plant disease book is *Rodale's Pest and Disease Problem Solver.* But before you go getting your scalpels and intravenous feeding tubes hooked up, make sure what you are treating is really a disease. According to a recent article in *Extension Line Lookout* (July 1997),

Bacteria, fungi, nematodes, and viruses are not all bad. . . . and banishing all of them would eventually destroy us, too.

what you think may be a disease could really just be a problem in where or how the plant is grown. For instance:

- If plant leaves are greenish, yellow, and wilted, the plant may be getting too much water.

- If leaves look pale, scorched, and wilted, there may not be enough water.

- If leaves turn yellow and drop off, it may be too cold.

- If a plant wilts, dies, or goes to seed, it may be too hot.

- If plants are spindly, pale, and discolored, you may be growing them where it's too dark.

- If plants are browned, dead, blistered, or discolored, you may be growing them in too much light.

Even overfertilized plants look as if they have some sort of disease. So check your plants' growing conditions before you whip out the sprayer.

Prevention of disease in plants is very similar to prevention of disease in humans, so follow these healthy habits.

- Wash your hands.

- Wash your tools.

- Build a strong immune system.

- Take your vitamins (apply compost).

- Exercise (rotate your plants).

Just because something looks weird doesn't mean it's bad. This "dog stink" mushroom is actually harmless.

Invasive Plants

Besides weeds, insect pests, diseases, and hungry critters, there's one more category of pests we'd all like to keep out of our gardens—invasive plants. But how can you tell if that innocent little plant you picked up at a plant sale is going to consume the garden next season? Read on . . .

The Invaders

Honestly, there are a number of plants that are officially nuisances. But whether they are well behaved or totally out of control depends on where you live. Figs, for example, have to be buried underground in the winter to keep them alive in Pennsylvania. In California, however, they grow as weeds that crowd out native plants.

But just because a plant is invasive in one place doesn't mean it should be completely eradicated. The world would be a very sad and less nutritious place without figs, for instance.

In general, officially recognized invasive plants get that reputation when they are introduced from somewhere else (like another continent) and take over the habitat of native plants, endangering them in the wild. That's why you are not supposed to bring plants into the United States from other countries (that and bugs and diseases, too). It's actually illegal to grow certain plants in some states.

Before you go running out to buy new plants, see if any of the plants you're contemplating qualify as invasive in your region. (Some of these are actually mentioned in this book as good plants and are shown in pictures in my very own garden. I don't think any plant should be completely banished. But if it is a severe problem in your area, avoid it.)

Foxglove

Violets

Paulownia

Information: Your Most Essential Tool (or Weapon)

All gardeners should have a few essential books on their shelf that aid them in their daily skirmishes and discoveries in the garden. Whether it's to identify a bug or weed or to figure out which variety of lilac or tomato is the one for you, there are a lot of books out there. No one book, however, can have everything in it (not even this one—sorry). Here's a list of the basic books you should have and which ones I recommend as essential.

An encyclopedia of organic gardening. *The Encyclopedia of Organic Gardening* was first published in 1959 and recently completely revised and updated as *Rodale's All-New Encyclopedia of Organic Gardening*. It's still the book I go to first when I have questions or problems or just want to know more about anything. I can trust that the information will be comprehensive, clear, and most important, organic.

An insect, disease, and weed identifier. I still haven't found a favorite, but I tend to use *Rodale's Garden Insect, Disease, and Weed Identification Guide*. The problem is that nothing is as comprehensive, detailed, and colorful as I'd like. There are also lots of colorful field guides that are fun to use.

A comprehensive flower, shrub, tree, and herb book. I like the Royal Horticultural Society books for general comprehensiveness, but they stick pretty much to the facts and leave out the more interesting things. For trees, I like *The Trees of North America* by Alan Mitchell and David More and *The Gardener's Illustrated Encyclopedia of Trees and Shrubs* by Brian Davis. But perhaps the best tree books are Michael Dirr's books *Manual of Woody Landscape Plants* and the recently released color version.

A harvesting and preserving book. From how to bottle tomatoes to how to smoke fish, *Stocking Up III* is a Rodale classic, and it gets used rather often in the fall in our house.

A comprehensive garden design book. John Brookes's *The Book of Garden Design* covers all the basics with an eccentric British style. Very how-to without being dowdy.

A bird book (just for fun). Just what is that bird outside your window? Check out *Garden Birds of America* by George Harrison (not the Beatle).

A Permaculture book. I recommend *Introduction to Permaculture* by Bill Mollison in case you need a better understanding of how nature and the world work. Or perhaps you just need a reminder.

For other books I recommend, including the ones I used to help me write this book, see "Recommended Reading" on page 358.

Veronica

Interview with **Eileen Weinsteiger**

If you ever get sick of gardening, which can happen around August or so, think of Eileen Weinsteiger. She has created the quintessential Rodale Institute organic garden and has worked in it daily for over 20 years. And she has a spectacular garden of her own at home.

What I love most about Eileen's garden (and you notice it most at the one at her home) is the variety of vegetables, flowers, fruits, and herbs in a delightful mix that is both beautiful and delicious. Around each corner is a new surprise or an experiment with plants, colors, or form.

In the front of her house is a lemon garden—shaped like a lemon with paths crossing through it—filled with yellow and lemon-scented flowers and herbs. Around back is the water garden and wildlife garden, with little hiding places for toads, birds, and whatever else happens by (including people). On one side of her home is a huge garden that spills over its boundaries in the fading sunlight of summer into a rampant ocean of life. Obviously, Eileen is doing a lot of things right—and all organically.

When you were a kid, did you ever think you would be a gardener for a living?

No, I had no idea, but I have always loved gardening—I've gardened ever since I was about 16. It was a way of getting away from everything . . . just like it is now, but . . . it was just something I really enjoyed. I always loved making flower arrangements, so I would grow my own flowers and make arrangements. We had a country store and hotel. My mother cooked, and I made the flower arrangements for the tables.

I remember you from the Rodale farm a long way back. How long have you worked at the Institute?

I started in 1973. But before that, I had a huge vegetable garden at home. I also worked in a mouse factory.

A mouse factory?

Yeah. I worked there because I could get mouse manure for my garden. Great manure. If you want to see things take off, get some mouse manure.

When people come to the Rodale Institute Experimental Farm, I know one of the main highlights is visiting "Eileen's garden." What are the things they want to know most about? What are the questions they ask most?

Grass clippings. They see the grass clippings and they ask, "Do you put them on green or do you compost them first? I always thought that if you put grass clippings on your beds you would have grass growing in your beds." That is something that I have heard a lot over the years. And also green manures—visitors are always interested in green manures.

Like the clover?

Yeah. Crimson clover, or we use a lot of the buckwheat.

Do you put them in while the bed is fallow?

Usually I have a five-year rotation in the garden, where I never follow the same botanical family in a five-year period. But in that five-year period I usually allow each bed to be fallow, and in that fallow period I'll grow either crimson clover or buckwheat.

Do you move your perennials?

No, I don't. I can't. It's crazy. Some people may, but I don't. Just the vegetable beds.

So, do you have to compost the grass clippings before you put them on your beds?

No. I always use them green. Mow and then dump them wherever they are needed. I find it's a great way to control weeds and conserve moisture, and it also adds a lot of nutrients. You know, some people don't have a lot of time to mess with making compost. So this is really a quick fix. I go out of my way to catch my grass here and at home. It's expensive to go out and buy bark mulch. Plus, I don't think the bark mulch breaks down as well and builds the soil as well as the grass. There is a lot of nitrogen and moisture in grass. And I find that if you have an area where the soil is really bad, grass is a good way to build it up.

In Eileen's garden

at home

Do you even use grass clippings on your ornamentals?

Oh, yes. Some people don't like to use grass clippings on their ornamentals. They would rather go with the different bark mulches or cocoa mulch, which smells really nice—like chocolate. But I use what I have, and I tell that to gardeners. If you have a lot of grass, use that; if you have straw, that's another type of mulch material you can use.

How often do you put compost on the beds?

Here, we put it on in early spring. And if I am going in with a succession crop, then I may put more on if we have time. Usually we use it as a means of keeping the beds raised and to build up the soil rather than as a mulch because there are a lot of weed seeds in compost just as there are in your soil.

In Eileen's garden

at work

What are the most important steps to having a successful flower and vegetable garden?

One would be the rotation schedule. I think that is very important.

Garden sanitation is important. If you have plants that look as if they're diseased, get rid of them. Or if there is a lot of diseased dead matter around a plant, take that out. Keep things as clean as possible. If you have an insect-infested area, try to control the infestation.

Soil is really important. Build your soil either by adding compost, green manures, or clippings into your beds.

Mulching matters, especially in a dry year. Use whatever material you have. I like to go with things that build up the soil as well as control moisture.

Select varieties that do well in your region so your plants are not stressed out all the time. Some varieties definitely do better here than south of here. But I am always looking for new varieties.

What about companion planting?

When I garden, I look for color and texture, so I'll mix vegetables, flowers, and herbs together. If the soil is really good and rich and you have enough moisture, I think most things are compatible.

What else do you recommend?

I think it's great if you can have water in the garden so you can attract things like toads because they do eat a lot of insects. And birds. Somewhere you should have birdhouses. And water doesn't have to be anything elaborate or expensive. You can take a dishpan and just put rocks around it. You can put goldfish in to eat the mosquitoes. They can even survive over the winter if you poke a hole in the ice. Or you can bring the fish in over the winter.

What are the biggest challenges that you face in gardening organically?

Insects can be a challenge at times. But I am so used to doing things without chemicals because I hate chemicals. I would even get an allergic reaction to rotenone, a botanical insecticide. In a greenhouse situation especially, insects can be a problem, so we release beneficial predators in the greenhouse. But the problem there is you have to keep scouting and examining plants to make sure that you don't get large populations.

In early spring, watering is another challenge. If you don't water and plants stress out, insects and disease can be more of a problem.

Those are the main challenges. Water and insects . . . and weeds.

Which do you think are the best-behaved plants in the garden?

There are a lot of alliums that are quite spectacular. Foxtail lilies grow to 6 feet high. Yarrows and culinary sage look great all summer long. Verbascums and penstamons (beardtongues) are also favorites.

What about naughty plants?

Purple loosestrife. Some of the grasses can be invasive. Common mints. At home I have my mint in a ceramic flue so it can't spread. But in other areas, I let it spread to use for tea all summer long.

How do you control those plants?

If I see something is getting out of control, I just yank it out and give it to a friend (ha, ha) . . . or throw it in the compost. It depends on your garden situation. You may *want* a plant that's going to spread and fill in an area that you don't want to worry about.

What do you think people should know about organic gardening?

Start small. The smaller the better, because if you do too much at one time, you're just going to be overwhelmed and get tired of it. And unless you really love it and stick with it, you may just say, 'Oh, forget it. I can just go to the store and buy produce.'

From a health point of view, I think people should grow their own food because you don't know what your food contains or has been sprayed with or how it's grown. By growing your own food, you can choose varieties that you can't find in your local grocery store. And there is so much out there.

So you haven't gotten tired of it after all these years?

No. In fact, I'm doing more all the time. Mainly because I just love plants and I'm curious to see how things grow. I look at these flowers and they really intrigue me. Even though I garden here at work full-time, I still like doing it at home. I find it relaxing. It's just so much fun to see something grow from a little seed to this beautiful plant.

If you could have only one tool for working in your garden, what would it be?

It's called a gooseneck. It's a hand tool. It looks like a hoe. I use it for planting and cultivating around the plants.

The Garden Oasis: Water and Watering

A lack of good, clean water may be one of the biggest problems we have to worry about in the future. Much of our food in the United States is grown in warm southwestern states, where water has to be shipped or piped in. Massive use of irrigation both wastes water and poisons the soil with salt. Then you have groundwater contamination with pesticides and fertilizers that have infiltrated most of the wells and reservoirs in America. And then you have Alpine water shipped from France and Italy quenching our thirst—for a price.

Whether you are worried about water or not, there are a lot of very good reasons to avoid heavy watering situations that don't even have anything to do with saving life on this Earth (human life) as we know it. Things like time, energy, the hassles of watering and hoses, and cost.

Most people overwater anyway. This summer, for example, we had near-drought conditions, but aside from a small bit of watering at the last desperate moment (which, by the way, is almost always followed by rain), we were just too busy to water. Guess what? I still have more tomatoes than I can cook and can, giant cabbages and beets, watermelons everywhere, and the usual array of produce, which didn't seem to suffer one bit. (Of course, I do live in Pennsylvania, which in near-drought conditions is still wetter than, say, New Mexico or southern California.)

In fact, many vegetables and fruits taste sweeter in dry conditions because their flavor is concentrated rather than being literally watered down. The very last thing you want to do is water tomatoes in August.

Avoiding the hassles of watering starts with a few basics.

- Begin by planting the appropriate plants for your region, climate, and natural water levels.

- Mulch well, and let the plants mulch themselves (with their own leaves). Stones also make good mulches in dry areas because they keep the soil underneath quite moist.

- If you want to grow moisture-loving plants, plant them close together so you can water them and forget the others.

- Water only when you first plant something (unless you time your planting just before or after a rain) or in severe drought.

- Collect rainwater and roof runoff, or channel it into areas where you want it to be absorbed by building swales and runoff pools.

Swales are trenches built on the contour of your slope that stop the runoff and force it to be absorbed into the ground rather than skittering down the hill, carrying all your good soil and nutrients with it. If you are going to build a swale, make it at least 1½ feet deep and 2 to 3 feet wide. Locate swales at the top and middle of any slope in your yard, following the slope's contour. Then plant the trench with perennials or annuals (or a mixture of both) so that the swale stays in place.

- Plant trees! Trees actually help to create rain—they "seed" the clouds and enable them to condense into raindrops. They are also essential water recyclers. And their shade preserves moisture and protects plants from the worst sun of the day.

- Create rock circles around plants to collect dew for your plants at night and to keep the soil moist.

- Keep a watering can by your kitchen sink. Whenever you are going to pour out excess cooking liquid from vegetables, empty water glasses, or rinse organic (but bug-free) vegetables and fruit, pour the excess in the watering can and use it to water your potted plants or garden.

- Pour excess coffee, tea, and natural juices right into your compost pile. In fact, pour leftover coffee right onto the soil around your acid-loving plants, such as azaleas and rhododendrons. It will perk them right up.

- Don't water grass. It turns brown but always comes back to life after a good rain. If the drought does kill it completely (which I have never seen happen), consider yourself lucky—you don't have to dig it up for your next garden.

Scary watering fact Up to 50 percent of all irrigation water is wasted—it doesn't even reach the crop. Why the inefficiency? Because farmers only pay 2 percent of the "real cost" of water and receive government subsidies for irrigation.

Enjoying the

When you walk with naked feet, how can you ever forget the earth?

—Carl Jung

Summer seems an obvious time for enjoyment. But all too often, Labor Day arrives and we haven't gone swimming, we haven't had a picnic, we haven't worn white shoes, and we haven't stepped outside our air-conditioned existence for more than a few minutes. Before that happens to you again, read my tips for enjoying the summer garden.

- Go out after dinner and lie down on your beautiful chemical-free green grass and breathe in the scents of your garden. Listen to the crickets coming awake as the sky darkens. It's better than a martini.

- Catch fireflies in a jar to make a fairy-tale lantern. Release them at the end of the evening.

- After working in the garden, get a big bucket and fill it with either warm or cold water and some herbal bubble bath. Soak your feet (or hands) in it at the end of the day.

- Use found objects to decorate your garden and home. Found rocks, wood, and old equipment, if used creatively, can really create an unusual and cool look.

- When dining outdoors, use nice clean tea towels to protect food from flies and other flying pests.

- Make sun tea with fresh mint or herbal tea bags. Refrigerate for a refreshing, inexpensive, and delicious summer drink.

Eve the baby lounges in the grass beneath the old willow tree.

Season

Climb a tree.

Hire musicians to serenade at your outdoor brunch.

- Wherever you go on vacation, visit the gardens.

- Have a family reunion, and ask everyone to bring their favorite "heirloom" family recipes, gardening secrets, or even seeds.

- Try going outside with bare feet and doing a walking meditation. Walk slowly and feel your feet touch the earth with every particle of the soles of your feet. Smile slightly as you are doing it. Feel the planet humming beneath you and your rootedness to it.

- Play "freestyle" badminton without a net.

- Have a bocce tournament on the lawn.

- Take a walk in your local woods. Carry along a little tree identification book, and try to identify your native tree species.

- If you can't grow enough vegetables and fruits—or simply don't want to—look for a local CSA to join. CSA stands for Community-Sponsored Agriculture, which usually stands for buying directly from a local organic farmer on a subscription basis. So you pay a weekly amount and they deliver whatever is ripe and ready to your door. It's a fabulous way to try new vegetables, fruits, and herbs and to support your local farmers.

- Take a "summer sick day" from work when you are just plain sick of missing out on summer. Hang out in your yard all day. If your yard is no fun to hang out in, then make it fun.

- Have someone look in on your garden while you are on vacation. Or invite your neighbors to harvest from it while you are away. There's no sense in letting things go to waste.

- Have a garden party!

Entertaining in the Garden

So many books and magazines these days present such a perfect vision of entertaining in the garden. Perfect food, perfect light, perfect people, perfectly weeded, perfectly designed, perfectly boring. I love entertaining in the garden, and I love those books and magazines. But I have a sneaking suspicion that all of us spend more time hunched over in our living rooms reading about it and intimidated by it than actually doing it and living it.

Being in the publishing business, I know it takes a host of stylists and prop people to create that look. Plus photographers with cameras as big as baseball bats, filters, fancy lighting. . . . For people who work for a living, the idea of putting together a party like that can be downright frightening.

Here's what I recommend. Put this book down right now and have a party. Nothing fancy—cook whatever is ripe, uncork a bottle of wine, light some citronella candles in jelly jars. Talk about things. Important things. Silly things. Take off your shoes. Let the dishes go until tomorrow. Invite someone you would like to get to know better. If there isn't anybody you'd like to get to know better, have the party for yourself or your family. The crickets will be sure to come.

My sister's campfire pit is always busy in the summertime.

I'll never forget my father telling me about the best party he ever attended. It was in the rundown courtyard of an old house in Germany. There were a few friends, some cold simple foods, bread and cheese and wine. They stayed up very, very late, singing.

I remember his story because a few years later, I visited that same courtyard after his death. I could picture it perfectly. The grass was unmowed and soft and long (as if you could make a bed of it). Dusty old label-less bottles of wine were lined up on rusted equipment. A few mismatched old chairs were strewn around an old wooden table. The air smelled of sweetness and smoke. You could almost feel the conversations, laughter, and singing stored in the stone walls of the house. I smiled to myself in that courtyard because my father had known the true meaning of a good time, and it had had nothing to do with fancy cooking and elaborately staged events.

But I have to admit, I often fantasize about having a huge, elaborate party with a giant dance floor, a big band or orchestra playing waltzes, gowns, punch, and the whole shebang. One day.

Meanwhile, here are my tips for entertaining in the garden.

- Have as much done beforehand as possible.

- Provide shade and protection from rain.

- Provide games for the kids (and adults). Bocce, croquet, scavenger hunts, tag, badminton, and volleyball are good. Avoid lawn darts and gun games—the world is already violent enough.

- Relax!

Enjoying the Fruits of Summer

And the herbs and vegetables, of course! In summer it seems as if everything's ripe at once—a fiesta of flavor, color, and fragrance.

Best Herbs for Summer

Some herbs just mean summer to me—especially basil. (Think basil and tomatoes.) Here are my summer favorites.

Basil. Put it in everything (salads, soups, chicken, fish or meat dishes, pasta, desserts . . . anything!). Basil varieties come in all colors, sizes, and flavors. Try all of them. You can either plant basil directly from seed or transplant seedlings. It's an annual herb.

Cilantro (coriander). The fresh leaves of this annual herb are essential in salsas and Latin foods. When young, the herb is called cilantro, but its seeds are called coriander. It's best planted directly from seed. It's quick to bolt.

Fennel. Fennel is a tall, fluffy perennial that has licorice-flavored leaves and seeds. Leaves are great in salads, soups, and pasta. Seeds are great in sausage, tomato sauce, and salad dressings.

Lemon verbena. I never knew what to do with lemon verbena until I had this dish. Try it! Rinse a can of cannellini beans and add a small bunch of chopped lemon verbena. Toss with a little vinaigrette and freshly ground pepper. If you want to, add some grilled shrimp. Goodness gracious, it's good. Lemon verbena is a tender perennial, so bring plants indoors in the winter if you live in a cold climate. Expect the plants to look as if they've died around February, but they will come back if you keep them warm and watered.

Lovage. Lovage looks like giant celery. Use it as a celery substitute. It goes great with potatoes. I love lovage because in German it's called *Leipschtick,* which roughly translates to love stick.

Rosemary. Rosemary is essential when cooking roasted potatoes and chicken—at least as far as I am concerned. A tender perennial (bring it in over the winter), it is a hearty herb with a strong flavor best suited to breads, meats, and olive oils. A rosemary tomato sauce has an interesting and delightful flavor.

Best Vegetables for Summer

Assuming that you are gardening for pleasure rather than for survival, the first goal of growing vegetables in the summer should be to grow the things you love to eat and that simply taste better when picked right off the vine (which is everything, really). If you are growing for survival—or to augment your year-round pantry—you also want to grow things that preserve well and easily and provide lots of nutrition for the garden space they take up. Here are a few of my favorite vegetables that meet both criteria.

> *Nature is eternally young, beautiful, and generous.*
>
> —George Sand,
> *The Haunted Pool*

What's for dinner? Salad Niçoise—with everything but the olives from the garden.

Green beans. Green beans are very easy to grow. Just watch out to make sure that the rabbits don't get them, and *never* touch a green bean or green bean plant when it is wet, or it will get rust (a fungal disease). Green beans freeze really well after they're blanched for about three minutes.

Peppers. The varieties and colors are seemingly infinite. If you go for hot ones, you can base your whole garden on them. I prefer the big, sweet, juicy red ones (in the grocery store they go for a fortune and often taste like rubber). For preserving, I roast them and then freeze them. Peppers do need to be started indoors for earliest harvest, but they transplant well.

Fresh peppers are awesome. They literally pop with flavor and juices.

Potatoes. Potatoes are another very easy crop to grow. Buy "seed potatoes" and stick them in the ground. After they flower and the tops start to die back, dig up the tubers (carefully) with a pitchfork. At one time, there were special potato pitchforks with little balls at the end (I saw one at the Garden History Museum in London) so that you didn't skewer the potatoes when you were digging them up. Potatoes keep very well right in the ground. Dig as you need them and eat them the same day. If you dig them all up, keep them in a dark place so they don't turn green; green potatoes are toxic. Exposure to sunlight causes them to turn green, forming solanine, a nightshade-family poison. Also, don't keep potatoes in the refrigerator. It really ruins the flavor.

Garlic. As my father-in-law says, "If you can't grow garlic, you can't grow anything." Plant individual cloves of garlic in the fall (October here in Zone 6). Watch them grow in the spring and summer. When

the tops start to turn brown and bend over, pick the garlic (the bulb is the root). Garlic and onions have to "season" a bit. Leave garlic out in the sun in a dry spot for a week. This really just lets the skins dry out so that they don't get moldy when you store them. Once the garlic is seasoned, you can either braid the bulbs like a French braid, or just cut off the tops and put the bulbs in a basket in a dark place in your house. Garlic will last you all year if you plant enough. I can't remember the last time I had to buy any, and we eat a lot of it.

Squash, pumpkins, zucchini. Easy, easy, easy. Stick the seed in the ground and watch it take over your whole garden. I didn't plant zucchini this year, but I missed it. I didn't plant my usual pumpkin-pie pumpkins this year either, but they are growing like gangbusters in my compost pile. (We devoted our whole pumpkin patch this year to

You can fry up these squash blossoms for a southwestern treat. Just pick before the bees get locked inside them at night.

growing a giant pumpkin for a contest—the seeds were from a 600-pound pumpkin that came to Emmaus, Pennsylvania, last year. We'll see just how heavy an organic pumpkin can get.)

I love to plant squash and pumpkins because they last so long and well. I stick them on a shelf in my kitchen and eat them for months.

Corn. I never plant enough corn to have more than a few meals from it, but it is fun to grow even though it often attracts all sorts of insect and animal varmints. Last year I caught a chipmunk climbing a cornstalk to munch on the ear. When planting corn in your home garden, don't plant it in rows—plant it in blocks (the plants pollinate each other better that way). Interplant pumpkins or squash underneath the corn and you won't have to weed all summer. Plus you get the extra crop.

Red beets. Unfortunately, I am the only one in my house who likes red beets. Otherwise we would be eating borscht and pickled beets once a week. So I eat them myself. I wrap them in tinfoil or parchment paper and bake them in the oven for an hour and a half (at about 350°F, or at

whatever temperature I'm cooking anything else). Then I slip them out of their skins, chop them up, and put a light vinaigrette on them. I will eat that with lunch, dinner, and another lunch. By myself, of course. But they are terribly simple to grow. The main thing to remember is to thin them out so the beet has room to grow a big root.

How can you not love a vegetable this color?

Tomatoes! No other fruit or vegetable better exemplifies the reason to have a garden of one's own than the "love apple" itself—the tomato—which is, technically, a fruit. Tomatoes are very easy to grow. Here are the basics. Start them indoors in April (not too soon, or they will be too big to transplant happily), or buy transplants. Plant them outside as soon as the last frost date has passed. Mulch them with straw (optional, but it's been proven to increase yields and improve the health of the plants). Stake and tie them up as they grow. Await their ripening. Eat.

Other easy summer vegetables to grow: cucumbers, eggplant, onions, and carrots.

Easiest Fruits for Summer

There's more to summer fruits than peaches—but just picture a ripe, fragrant, juicy peach. Or a handful of just-picked red raspberries or blueberries. Or a big, red slice of watermelon . . .

Blueberries. A blueberry bush is lovely year-round—a nice addition to your landscape. (Just remember that blueberries need acid soil.) If you want to harvest a significant portion of the blueberries, however, you'll have to cover them with netting when they get ripe. Birds have a knack for knowing about three hours before you do that a blueberry is perfectly ripe.

Sour cherries. Sour cherries grow on pretty trees that have short life spans (about 20 years), but they give you lots of joy in the meantime. Sour cherries are exactly the kind of fruit you should plant in

Baby watermelons are easy to grow in your home garden.

your yard. They are difficult, if not impossible, to find in a store or even at a farmers' market. They are easy to preserve in sauces, jams, and pies. And what you don't eat, the birds and other wildlife will be happy to clean up for you.

Peaches. Peaches are actually not that easy to grow—they seem to be prone to all sorts of fungi, cankers, and insect infestations. But, oohh, the taste of a homegrown organic peach, ripe from the tree. Millions of Americans of my generation have no concept of what that means. A peach to most people is an out-of-season, mealy, bruised, flavorless, chemicalized thing from Chile. (Either that or a schnapps flavor.) It's worth the effort to try to grow a peach tree just so you can attempt to bring back the true flavor and joy of peaches. Consider it a humanitarian project.

Raspberries. Raspberries are good and easy to grow, especially if you have a back corner of your yard where you can let them proliferate. Wild black raspberries are even better (if you ask me). They taste better than anything you have ever bought in a store and last only briefly. The best thing to do is either eat them directly or the same day, or bake a nice juicy pie with them. Raspberries are high in fiber, too. They tend to attract Japanese beetles, but just pick them off, and put them in a jar.

Watermelons. Baby watermelons (yellow and red) are fun and easy to grow and delicious to eat. They ripen at the end of summer into juicy balls of sweetness. You'll have a hard time eating store-bought watermelon ever again.

Other summer fruits to try: Nanking cherries, currants, elderberries, gooseberries, hardy kiwis, mulberries, and pawpaws.

Extend the heat of summer for your melons by using cloches.

Food for

10 Ways to Eat a Tomato

1. **Warm right out of the garden.** Pick. Rinse. Eat. Wipe the juice off your face.

2. **Tomatoes, mozzarella, basil, olive oil, pepper.** Slice tomatoes, slice fresh mozzarella, and layer them on a platter. Sprinkle with basil leaves, extra-virgin olive oil, and freshly ground pepper. *Mangia!*

3. **Bruschetta.** Make toast with crusty bread. Cut a clove of raw garlic in half and rub it onto the bread. Chop tomatoes, garlic, herbs, and a bit of olive oil, and pile this mixture on the bread.

Summer

4. **French-roasted tomato.** Slice tomatoes in half. Sprinkle bread crumbs, cheese (cheddar, Gruyère, parmesan, or other meltable cheese), chopped onions, and a bit of butter or oil on top. Bake until everything is melted and golden for a hot, soft, delicious side dish, or broil until melted and golden for a fresher-tasting treat. (This is my mother's recipe.)

5. **Pasta with marinara sauce.** This is my mother-in-law's recipe. Sauté five or more cloves of garlic in olive oil. Add a bunch (10 to 20) of chopped tomatoes. (You can peel tomatoes if you want by submerging in boiling water for a few seconds until the skins crack.) Add all sorts of chopped herbs—primarily basil, but also oregano, thyme, rosemary, or whatever. Add a pinch of salt, a pinch of sugar, and a few twists of freshly ground pepper. Allow the pasta to sit in the sauce for a while before serving (to absorb the juices).

6. **Tomato sauce from scratch.** This is another of my mother-in-law's recipes. Wash tomatoes and slice in half. Put them in a giant pot and boil until they look like stewed tomatoes. Put them through a tomato peeler and seeder machine (hand-cranked). Or you can put the whole mixture in a food processor. Or you can leave the skins and seeds in, too. (Taking the seeds and skins out makes a sweeter sauce.) Sauté as much garlic as you can handle in olive oil. Add the tomato puree (or chopped tomatoes for a chunkier sauce). Boil and simmer for as much time as it takes to get to the desired thickness, which is usually about three hours. Add salt and pepper to taste. Add herbs to taste. Try to use a lot of paste tomatoes, since they are very meaty. Eat directly or freeze. If you want to make a meat sauce, add a chunk of meat and a chunk of pork to the garlic and oil. Brown a bit, then add the tomatoes.

7. **My father's spaghetti sauce.** My father was not Italian, but one of his specialties was spaghetti. My daughter has refused to eat most tomato dishes her whole life, but she eats this spaghetti voraciously. I suppose it's more of a Bolognaise type of sauce, and of course, there are no measurements. But here is the general scheme of it.

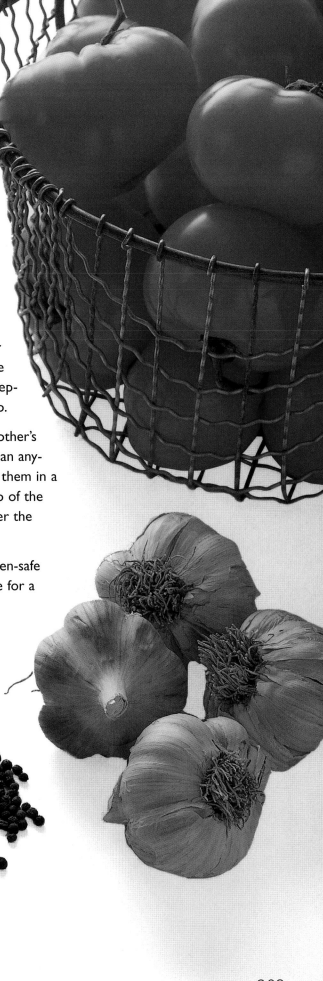

In a large pot, sauté garlic and onions with olive oil. Brown ground beef in the mixture. Add your favorite tomato sauce (4 parts) and tomato paste (1 part). Add oregano, basil, salt, and pepper.

Here's the secret part: Add one dash of maple syrup and three dashes of dry red wine. Be careful with the maple syrup, since it's hard to correct too much sweetness in the sauce. But you can be liberal with the wine, since it just makes the sauce better. Be sure to use a good, dry red wine.

8. **Fresh salsa.** Chop and drain four tomatoes. (Let them sit in a colander for an hour or so, or for faster results, press some of the juice out of them.) Put in a jar. (Use the drained tomato juice for flavoring soups or poaching fish.) Add two cloves chopped fresh garlic, one chopped hot pepper, one chopped onion, vinegar, salt, pepper, and tons of chopped cilantro. Shake it up. Dip a chip.

9. **Sweet and sour tomato salad.** Another one of my mother's recipes. This one evokes summer in Pennsylvania more than anything. Slice up a few tomatoes, peppers, and onions. Layer them in a pretty dish (my mother prefers cut glass). Sprinkle the top of the tomatoes with sugar, then sprinkle apple cider vinegar over the sugar. Add salt and pepper to taste.

10. **Slow-roasted.** Put washed and cored tomatoes in an oven-safe dish. Add a bit of olive oil, rosemary, salt, and pepper. Bake for a whole day at about 250°F. Very unusual.

Calendar

Here's a checklist of garden chores, activities, and fun things to do in summer.

June

Planting	Plant succession plantings of beans, carrots, summer lettuces, and cilantro.	Fill in any bare spots with annuals, perennials, or left-over seeds.	Plant brussels sprouts transplants for fall harvests.	
Harvesting	Harvest whatever is ready—herbs, beans, peas, straw-berries, greens, and beyond.			
Pruning			Prune hedges.	Prune spring-flowering shrubs—if you need to.
Doing	Visit garden stores to buy perennials on sale. Keep birdbath clean and filled with water.	Weed now before August hits and things really get out of control. Thin carrot rows.	Pull out spent veg-etables from your garden, and plant a second round. Thin fruit on apple and peach trees to 6 to 8 inches apart.	Make sure every-thing is mulched. Start a new com-post pile. Put out beer traps for slugs.
Preparing	Prepare to move all of your living out-of-doors.	Cut bouquets of roses and perenni-als to prepare for guests.		

July

Planting	Plant last-minute purchases of plants on sale. (Water them well for the first week or so if it doesn't rain.)	Plant succession crops of cilantro and heat-tolerant lettuces.	Plant broccoli, cabbages, and cauliflower seedlings for fall harvests. Sow kale.	
Harvesting	Harvest herbs for drying. Make herb vinegars for Christmas gifts.	Make onion and garlic braids.	Pick the first tomato! Harvest blueberries, cherries, currants, and gooseberries.	Remember to harvest beans, cucumbers, and squash before they get humongous.
Pruning	Deadhead flowers that have already bloomed to stimulate new blooms.	Prune wisteria both to control its spread and to encourage spring blooming.		
Doing		Take a daily tour of your yard and garden to check for ripeness, problems, and surprises. Weed, weed, weed!	Find a neighbor who doesn't have any zucchini—and likes it. Remove diseased plants. (Don't compost them.)	Handpick pests—especially Japanese beetles from grapevines and roses.
Preparing	Blanch and freeze extra Swiss chard.	Preserve fruits in jams, sauces, and desserts. Make a batch of dill pickles.		

August

Planting	Sow final fall succession plants: Chinese greens, lettuces, peas, radishes, spinach and turnips.		
Harvesting		Harvest beans, melons, potatoes, and tomatoes.	Harvest early apples, blackberries, elderberries, peaches, and peppers.	Harvest everything!
Pruning	Continue to deadhead annuals and perennials.			Prune diseased or broken branches on trees and shrubs.
Doing	Try not to give up.

Watch out for heat stroke! | Take notes on which varieties performed well. | Pull weeds before they go to seed. | Save seeds from your heirloom tomatoes.

Order fall bulbs for planting. |
| **Preparing** | Freeze corn.

Make pesto.

Roast peppers and freeze. | Make tomato sauce to freeze.

Can salsa.

Can peaches. | Find a new recipe for zucchini. | Enjoy the first new potatoes from the garden. |

all

Autumn is so bittersweet. Gone for another year are the lazy days, bare feet on warm grass, fireflies, swimming, and the hot sun on your skin.

At first, fall intrudes on our dreams of an endless summer. (What? The leaves are turning already?) Then gradually fall arrives, fresh and annoyingly perky, with sweaters and the sweet smell of falling leaves. Plants relax, animals get drowsy, and the rest of us start hunkering down for the dark season ahead.

On early fall mornings, the flowers, grasses, and leaves are candied with dew. Later on in the season, the dew turns to silvery frost. Plants die back and burn with cold autumn fire. Leaves fall, tentatively at first, and then later with abandon. Get out the rakes. Jump in the pile.

Toward the end of fall, the small, gentle mountain in front of my house is tinged with golden orange leaves that look like the burning embers of a dying fire. Then, finally, the yard becomes a cold mass of naked trees. Fall is a great time to garden. It's the last glorious scene before the long intermission known as winter. Enjoy the show.

Designing

Fall is the time to make any corrections, changes, or additions to your garden before winter comes. Doing it now gives you one more reason to look forward to spring, and it gives plants a chance to get an early start next year. It's also a more relaxing time to garden than in the spring. Can't get to it this year? Oh, well. It can wait till spring.

Take a walk around your yard with a notebook. What worked this year and what didn't? What did well and what failed (or rather, wasn't well adjusted)? Where are there bare spots you may want to fill with bulbs, groundcovers, perennials, bushes, or trees? What spaces were a frenzy of weeds—and can you do anything to prevent that next year?

A lot of things can look diseased by the time fall rolls around, whether it's a "fungus among us" or something that looks like an insect infestation. Don't freak out. Sometimes a good cold winter is just what a plant needs to snap back to good health.

Refining Your Design

I don't think we gardeners are ever satisfied. There's always something we want to try or change in our yards. Thank goodness! And fall is a great time to review and refine your landscape design. Ask yourself the following questions every fall—it will help your garden get better and better each year.

Are things planted in the right location? This year, I'm moving my azaleas to a shadier spot. I could tell they were getting too much sun because their leaves turned yellow and burned. I am also going to move two upright yews that just didn't work out the way I wanted them to and that have those poisonous berries on them. Once when I was a kid, I ate a poisonous yew berry. My cousin said, "Don't eat that!" So I ate it. I still remember throwing up into a stainless steel bowl in the hospital emergency room after having received a dose of syrup of ipecac. So those berries bring back bad memories, and I'm going to move them to where I don't have to look at them all the time. And now that I have a little one around (who might have inherited my belligerence), I don't want to take any chances.

What did really well? I planted just a few rose impatiens this year—but I'm going to town with them next year. They are stunning and absolutely carefree. The Mexican sunflowers were veritable feasts for butterflies, bees, birds, and who knows what else. But they grew so large (over 7 feet tall) that I think I'll plant them somewhere out of the way next year. I also planted far too many nasturtiums, and they did far

Your Garden

too well. Someone who will go unnamed planted too many pumpkins, and we needed a machete to keep them from consuming our neighbor's yard and our own. We have enough pumpkins to line all of Main Street with jack- and jill-o'lanterns for the Halloween parade. (Hey, that's not such a bad idea. Martha Stewart would do it. I'd rather make pie, though.)

What weren't you satisfied with? My raspberries were out of control. I think I'm going to have to submit to trellising them next year. I also want a better table for eating outside. (I'll save the folding picnic table for when I have parties and need the extra space.) Make *your* list. You may not be able to do everything you want to do, but you can think about it all winter and plan for it if you wish.

Where did you end up weeding too much? If an area got too weedy too many times, that calls for a management change for next year. Either you need more mulch, more groundcovers, more flowers, or more bushes and trees. Macadam should not be an option unless it's necessary (if you are going to put in a basketball court, for instance). And of course, herbicides are out of the question.

What else was too high maintenance? I am in the process of removing all hedges that need pruning. Personally, I think it's a waste of time when there are plenty of plants that do just fine without pruning. Certain bushes, like privet and forsythia, are commonly used for hedges. But if you see them when they are allowed to become full-grown, they are often 20 feet high and just as wide. Why would you want to fight that year after year? You'll never win. And those plants will never be truly happy. There are tons of varieties of arborvitae, holly, and boxwood that don't need anything other than an occasional trim (unless topiary is your thing). The right plant in the right place—that's my motto.

What didn't do well? Sometimes you can plant things and they just seem to disappear. Bulbs forget to come up. Wads of perennial roots evaporate into dust. Bushes and even trees shrivel and sink back into the earth. Since I am forgetful, I often just never realize that things didn't grow. Referring back to my garden notebook really helps. If you pick up on my handy system of cutting out catalog pictures and descriptions and pasting them in a sketchbook to refer to when your plants arrive, it will be easy for you to go back and check on what did and didn't really grow. If you are stubborn and persistent, you may want to try the same plant from a different catalog or nursery, or find a more tolerant variety. Or you may just want to avoid that plant in the future.

In the garden, each year is a learning experience that stays with you for a long time. You can study from a book, but there is no substitute for trying things out and learning for yourself. Nature is very forgiving, too (or a lot more forgiving than your neighbors). She's the ultimate teacher. But luckily (or unfortunately), Nature doesn't call you to parent-teacher conferences or send report cards. She keeps mistakes between you and her . . . unless you tell somebody (like me and *my* big mouth).

Nature is very forgiving.

Planning for Next Year

When the snow starts to fall, you'll have a hard time remembering where you needed to plant those spring flowers or what plants you wanted to get to fill in your garden. Don't forget about vegetable rotation, too. You don't want to plant your potatoes in the same place you planted them in the previous year, or the bugs will be eating them before you.

So take notes now. Sit outside with a nice hot mug of tea and observe your yard. Soak up some vitamin D (don't wear sunscreen). Make a list.

Don't limit your planning to plants or products. Think about how you want to use your yard differently. This year, for example, I was really pleased that we ate dinner outside almost every night. But I wish we had entertained more. Next year I swear I am going to get to that back area and discipline it a bit more. Or maybe I'll let it become the downtown Emmaus nature preserve.

Think about paths and walkways. Are they in the right spot? Check where the grass or plants have been worn away to the dirt . . . think about putting a path there next year. Go with the flow.

Or perhaps you want to try some new techniques or projects in your yard. Here are two to consider.

Rosemary is more than an aromatherapy plant. It flavors chicken nicely, too. Put a sprig behind your ear if you want to remember something.

Lavender is a small bit of the south of France in America.

Planting and Using an Aromatherapy Garden

Aromatherapy is the use of scents and essential oils to create emotional and physical responses in a person. You can buy essential oils (they are difficult to make). Or you can plant the plants around you and enjoy their living fragrance in your life. Doctors can see the results of smelling certain scents by studying brain waves. You may already have aromatherapy plants in your garden because you like them, and many of them are popular garden plants—roses, for example. Or you may want to create your own aroma-apothecary garden specifically to manage your (and perhaps your family's) moods. These plants will get your garden off to a good start.

To get rid of a bad mood: citrus (grow in pots and bring indoors in cold climates)

For relaxation and stress relief: floral scents—geranium, lavender, rose

For invigoration: eucalyptus, juniper, pine, rosemary

For memory improvement: rosemary

For first aid (soothing cuts and bruises): lavender

For mental stimulation: jasmine, peppermint

Planting and Using a Healing Herb Garden

Traditionally, gardens have been places for both healing and growing food. Before aspirin, there was willow bark. Before Pepto-Bismol, there were chamomile and mint. Some of the loveliest garden plants also have powerful healing properties. Echinacea, otherwise known as purple coneflower, has been proven to boost people's immune systems and prevent colds.

Glossary of Aromatherapy and Herbal Healing Terms

Most herbs are used medicinally by drying them, making them into a powder with a mortar and pestle or coffee grinder, and then making a tea with them. But there are many different ways you can use them. Here is a glossary of some of the ways to use and preserve herbs.

Capsules. Powdered herbs can be put into capsules.

Compress. Soak a clean cloth in an herbal tea, and place it on your skin. (The compress can be either hot or cold, depending on the problem.)

Decoction. Make an extract from roots or bark by simmering the roots or bark in water for about 20 minutes. (The simmering time will vary depending on the herb.)

Essential oils. These oils are better bought than made, since it takes pounds of flowers or herbs to make even a small bit of oil. (It takes 600 pounds of rose petals for 1 ounce of essential oil.) Essential oils are very powerful and are best used to add scent to potpourris and other inedible things.

Infusion. This is prepared like a tea but steeped longer (10 to 20 minutes) to create a strong medicinal brew. If you're using fresh herbs, double the amount of herbs.

Ointment. To make an ointment, add an herbal tincture to lotion or oil.

Potpourri. A potpourri is any combination of dried flowers, herbs, and spices. Add orrisroot or sweet flag as a fixative (1 tablespoon for every 3 to 4 cups of dried flowers or plants).

Poultice. Make a poultice from chopped herbs that have been lightly cooked or mashed. Place them directly on the skin.

Tincture. A tincture is an extract made with alcohol (vodka or brandy) or vinegar. More potent than an infusion or decoction.

When you harvest, always store your herbs and concoctions in a dark, airtight container.

Eucalyptus

When choosing herbs to grow in a medicinal garden, you can grow herbs that were historically grown for healing, like foxglove (for heart disease), or you can grow herbs that you can safely use in homemade preparations. Either way you'll have a delightful and fragrant garden with an intriguing history.

But if you're actually planning to make home remedies from your herbs, use caution when choosing and preparing the herbs. A good reference book is essential. The best that I have come across is *The Healing Herbs* by Michael Castleman.

And please, be careful! Pregnant women and small children should not use herbs for healing. Certain herbs, such as angelica, calamus, mugwort, pennyroyal, sage, and wintergreen, can cause a miscarriage. Basil, hyssop, myrrh, marjoram, and thyme can also cause problems.

Miracle flower purple coneflower (echinacea) boosts immunity, prevents colds, and makes a nice bouquet, too.

Designing

Especially for Fall

Making your yard and garden look beautiful in the fall is not too difficult. September, before the first frost, is one of the most beautiful months of the year in Pennsylvania—everything is still blooming
and just beginning to become tinged with gold, red, and orange. The
dying plants seem more tragic and dramatic than dead.

September is like the final scenes in an opera, where you know
that at least one person, and maybe two or three, is going to die (either
by suicide, consumption, or murder), but the singing is so beautiful it
doesn't really matter. It's expected. The singing is the point. (Speaking
of opera, it makes good gardening music. Turn on the "Saturday at the
Met" opera radio show and head out to the garden. The story and

Hydrangeas are one of the
all-time best summer and fall
landscape plants. And when
they have finished blooming,
you can make a lovely everlasting bouquet.

music keep you distracted from the bother, and I think the plants like it—especially the Italian varieties.)

When designing especially for fall, there are a few easy tips and design themes to remember.

- Choose a few trees and shrubs for your yard that stand out just because of their fall color. (See "Best Plants for Fall" on page 339.) But plant them where their color is highlighted by the surrounding plants. Maybe the color is set off by a background of evergreens, or the color adds a subtle differentiation to neighboring plants.

- Mums are nice, but don't overdo it. There are lots of other flowers that are beautiful in the fall . . . and other ways to get color into your landscape. Pumpkins add bright orange punctuation marks to the dark fall landscape. Hydrangeas and asters are especially nice. Don't overdo it on the ornamental kale, either.

- Keep planting cool-season vegetables, such as arugula, corn salad, kale, radishes, spinach, and turnips, into September. Lettuce mixes not only do very well in September and October (until the first frost), but they also add that fresh green color to your landscape.

- Don't forget to include fall fruits in your plantings. There are many apple varieties that are disease-resistant. Quinces are beautiful and delicious in the fall. 'Fallgold' raspberries are my favorites. (I just ate some luscious red raspberries today, and it's mid-October.) The American persimmon was my father's favorite fruit. It tastes divine, but only after being kissed by frost. (If you eat it before that, it will taste as if you've been French-kissed by a sour, bitter, fuzzy, poisonous frog—blech!)

Visiting Gardens

Fall is a great time to visit public and private gardens. The air is fresh and cool. The light is perfectly golden. Plus, the ideas you get from looking at other gardens can germinate all winter and sprout in spring—your own hybrid variation. Local public gardens and arboretums can give you great ideas about plants that will grow well in your area and give you fascinating new perspectives on your own garden potential. Visiting gardens in other countries can give you great design ideas and inspire you to try new things.

There are also some beautiful and fascinating organic gardens to visit that can show you how to grow your own beautiful and delicious organic garden. On the East Coast, there is the Rodale Institute Experimental Farm in Maxatawny, Pennsylvania. On the West Coast, Cascadian Farms is open to the public. To find others, check with your state's organic farming and gardening association.

The annuals, having gone through their more or less successful little lives, die peacefully, perhaps even willingly.

—Ruth Stout,
The Ruth Stout No-Work Garden Book

Interview

with Anthony Rodale

The person I know who has traveled the most is my younger brother, Anthony (that dirty rat). He is truly a world traveler and a global gardener. Since 1987, he's traveled through 23 countries, learning, observing, and experiencing first-hand how people grow, market, and trade foods and crops. He is currently the Vice-Chairman of the Rodale Institute. I asked him about his global perspective of gardening.

Which country has the best gardens?

There are two types of gardening. There's gardening for survival and gardening for pleasure. France has the best gardens for pleasure. For survival? I'm not sure. But South Africa is by far the most beautiful country in the world.

In the countries that garden for survival, it's more of a community effort. People are still relying on the extended family and on social interaction. Gardening for pleasure is a personal thing, but gardening for survival is a community concern.

Tell me your impressions of the different countries.

In Africa, you have different climates, from tropical to arid. Tropical areas are more suitable for Permaculture methods and need a more integrated approach to gardening. Arid areas are more like here [Pennsylvania], with vegetables, fruits, and animals more separate.

Russia has community gardens and weekend gardens. The rich and the middle class have weekend homes and gardens. The city dwellers have community gardens.

Since China is still a communist country, they still have community gardens surrounded by high-rises. They raise fish in the irrigation lanes, then they scoop out the bottom of the fish water to fertilize their raised beds. They put canopies over the crops to protect them from the sun.

In Japan, space is so limited that people grow vegetables around stop signs. Everywhere you look, you see food growing. You sense they have no limitations to where they will grow food.

I've heard that people in Russia grow potatoes in their front lawns. Is that true?

They grow all sorts of vegetables. A lawn is a very American thing. Around the world, if there is a lawn, it's usually a grassy patch with in a courtyard.

You have also visited some of the great garden masters. What was it like to visit Masanobu Fukuoka?

Fukuoka goes way beyond gardening for pleasure or survival. He is pushing human thought to its outer limits. The Japanese have taken over the nature farming movement, which he founded. But others have commercialized it and made it part of their religious thinking. There are many different groups who are using nature farming to keep going. They use it to fund their groups and attract others—sort of like communes.

What about Bill Mollison?

People either hate him or they like him. He's not in it for fluff, he's in it for the commitment. He's experienced other things and is totally self-educated and self-motivated. There are not many people in this world who can just follow and do and learn as much as he's done.

He is like Fukuoka in that they both have a much higher spiritual perspective—it's the understanding of cultures around the world. Understanding different people's cultures in the world has pushed him to a higher level.

In all your travels, what's the most important thing you have learned?

That there is a lot of unnecessary stuff in this world.

America is the only country in the world that does not have a direct connection to the soil. Every other country in this world has a cultural aspect that respects the land and nature. There are a lot of people who garden, but our agricultural industry has led people away from believing that we need to have direct contact with the soil. It's the way we see food. It's produced cheaply. Everything is produced in a way that misleads or misguides you to believe that it's not important for humans to be connected to this earth. But people do need to have direct contact with the soil.

Every chance that I get to leave this country I take because I appreciate learning from others and being a part of other cultures that have respect for the earth.

What do you see as the biggest barriers in America to organic gardening?

There are no barriers, other than the chemicals and fertilizers on the store shelves. But there's a lack of knowledge of how to plant a seed and watch it grow, and a lack of patience. Because you don't need all the chemicals. There is a perceived immediate need to want things to grow in this culture. You want it tomorrow, when it really needs a week to grow.

Plus, Americans are overequipped. We are victims of our marketing culture. Socially, if you don't have the right equipment, you look out of place. We have major social problems in this country. It's all marketing.

What memories do you have of growing up on the farm?

I remember tasting things like carrots, broccoli, asparagus, grapes, and 'Seckel' pears. The farm was my playground. I still carry the memory of those tastes. But I never really enjoyed food until I spent some time in France.

Do you garden for pleasure or survival?

I do very little for pleasure. After losing many parts of my family (our father in a car accident and our brother to AIDS), I've learned that life is not here for pleasure, it's here for living and learning. The pleasure comes from your hard work.

If you could have only one garden tool, what would it be?

A hoe, because my wife, Florence, plants and I weed.

Gardening for survival in Senegal, Africa

Photo by Anthony Rodale

Study How Nature Landscapes Herself

Fall is a fantastic time to go for walks in the woods or countryside and study the natural landscape. Understanding nature will make you a much better gardener. You will work less, while providing more benefit to the environment and your furry and feathered friends.

Did you ever go into a pine and moss forest and get off the path for a moment? I know you aren't supposed to, but here's why. You sink down about 5 inches as if you are walking on feathers. Why? Nature never rakes. She just piles and piles. And everybody and everything loves it. Leaves and pine needles create a natural mulch that is the perfect habitat for native plants, mosses, insects, and animals. And all that is required is for you to do nothing. Although I admit that sometimes nothing is the hardest thing to do.

And another thing about nature in her wildness: Did you ever notice how closely trees grow together in the wild? Americans seem fixated on thinking that every tree "needs its space." If you are going for an arboretum-quality English eighteenth-century sweeping lawn with specimen trees, then by all means, give each tree the space it

If everyday was exactly what we would order, life would become too, too serene, predictable, and without much challenge, even dull.

—Ruth Stout,
The Ruth Stout No-Work Garden Book

deserves. But otherwise, if you are going for a low-maintenance, natural look, pile them in.

The greatest complexity, diversity, and growth happens at the edges of things—the edge of the forest, the edge of the pond, the edge of the garden. You can get a lot more than you think into your yard by maximizing the edge spaces.

The woods have this strange primal relationship with people. We love them, yet we fear them. I find that I fear the woods most before I go into them—the thought of it scares me. But then I pass through the thick and shielding edge and into the cool and shaded interior, and it's like home—like nothing could feel safer in the world. Of course, we don't have lions, tigers, or bears too often in the Pennsylvania woods where I live (though there are bears in Pennsylvania).

In Maine it always feels like fall. Unless it's winter.

The 7 Tendencies of
Regeneration

Find yourself in your place. You are connected to the earth—even if you don't know the land.

—Robert Rodale

When I worked for my father many years ago, he was deep into developing his philosophy of regeneration. He was fixated on trying to apply the process of natural regeneration to communities and even to people's own personal and spiritual lives. Nature can't help but heal herself. He believed that communities and people had that same power. By studying natural regeneration, he thought that perhaps we could learn how to transform our own lives.

At the Rodale Institute Experimental Farm, the scientists studied natural regeneration and came up with a list of seven things that tend to happen in nature when regeneration occurs (the healing process after a disturbance). Together, my father and I expanded the list to include communities and people. We never tested our theories on people and towns, but it was fun to think about, and in a way it is common sense.

The very nature of the word regeneration implies the healing process that takes place after some sort of disturbance. In nature, it could be a forest fire or an earthquake. In your community, it could be a depressed economy, the decline of businesses on Main Street, or a mass exodus to other places. In your own life, it could be an illness, a tragedy, or simply a deep-seated desire for change (which is a form of depression). The key in all of these areas is prevention. How can you prevent illness and tragedy by making regeneration happen naturally? Don't wait for something horrible to happen to wake you up and force you to heal. Be proactive.

Some things can't be prevented, but still, using the concept of regeneration, you can learn and grow from the experience, rather than be consumed by bitterness and unhappiness. Nature is known for giving gentle reminders. But if we ignore her, the reminders get more serious and cause more harm.

At the same time, regeneration in nature just happens as a result of "leaving things alone." In your own life and community, the challenge is more one of "going with the flow" and not fighting and resisting what life, and nature, have to offer you.

Here's what happens in nature when regeneration occurs, and what may happen in your town and your life if you would let it.

1. **Pluralism.** One of the first things that happens when regeneration starts in nature is an increase in diversity of plant species. Often, the same thing could be said for communities. As diversity of people and cultures increase, businesses and entertainment start to thrive.

In your own life, diversity happens when experiences that you might never have expected in your life start happening or new people enter your life. You begin to change, to learn, and to heal. New opportunities may open up that you never expected.

2. **Protection.** Regeneration in nature causes the soil to be protected by plants and beneficial organisms, preventing erosion. Regeneration in communities builds stronger relationships among people, which inhibits crime and other social problems. Strong relationships and good health build protection and immunity in your life, giving you the ability to withstand crisis and illness.

3. **Purity.** When you allow nature to regenerate by stopping the use of chemicals, a greater mass of plants and life exist in the soil. The equivalent in a community is to stop trying to control everything. Focus more on natural and softer businesses and less on industry and manufacturing, which pollute the environment and decrease the quality and variety of life in a community.

   Ending the use of chemicals—whether it's tobacco or cocaine, douches, or air fresheners—in your own life enables you to experience and enjoy life more fully.

4. **Permanence.** The less chemical and human involvement in the soil, the more perennials and plants with vigorous root systems begin to grow, creating a deeper and stronger ecosystem. Likewise, when communities are allowed freedom and are given support, businesses and institutions are more stable, long-lasting, and valuable.

   In your own life, when regeneration happens, life takes on a deeper meaning, and relationships grow stronger. Think about the phrase "putting down roots," which implies committing to a community, your family, and a certain piece of land.

5. **Peace.** The more nature is allowed to regenerate, the fewer weed and pest problems there are. The more your community is allowed to regenerate, the less violence and fewer problems there will be. The more you allow yourself to

regenerate, the fewer negative emotions and problems you will have.

6. **Potential.** When you let Nature go, she feeds herself quite nicely. Nutrients accumulate near the soil's surface and are easily used by plants. Communities also rise to the occasion when given the chance and opportunity. The daily papers are filled with stories of people rushing to the aid of those in need during a crisis. That's our genetic predisposition toward regeneration.

   And if you believe that things can happen and allow them to happen, they will happen a lot more often than if you never believe or never try. You have the resources and the power within you to do whatever you want to do.

7. **Progress.** Finally, when regeneration happens, the soil structure improves. More water is retained in the soil and is purified by the soil. Community progress is measured when the quality of life improves, and people and businesses stay and thrive. You will know when regeneration happens in your own life because your whole life will improve, good things will happen more often, and good people will stick around.

   Regeneration is ultimately about the joy of letting go, the power of and need for recovery and rest in our lives, and the natural cycles of nature, of which we are an inextricable part. Tap into it, and your life will never be the same.

Interview with **Ardie Rodale**

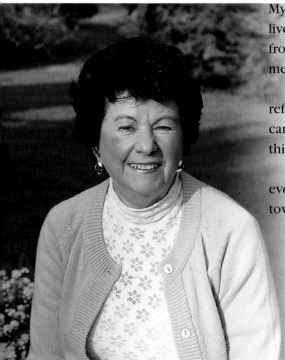

My mother, Ardie Rodale, knows about regeneration first-hand. She has lived through the death of a son from AIDS, the death of her husband from a car crash in Russia, two bouts with breast cancer . . . not to mention dealing with me!

But she never stopped gardening. In fact, gardening has been her refuge. Even now that she is chairman and CEO of Rodale Press, you can still find her out in her garden in the spring, "trying to get everything planted and weeded before the Indy 500."

My mother has learned how to garden with spirit. Before I could even ask her a question, she started telling me about her feelings toward gardening.

I guess I was destined to be a gardener. My name comes from the Apocrypha: "So I went into a field called Ardath and sat among the flowers and ate of the fruit of the field and was satisfied." And somehow I believe your name plays a tremendous part in your destiny. I was led into this family and I have learned so much, through working with Nana all those years, ordering the seeds (Nana was very much against using hybrid seeds because she said they weren't as good as the old varieties), and getting out by St. Patrick's Day to plant the peas. And I grew to really love it.

I found that touching the soil brought me so much peace—especially when I was all stressed out, and I would go out and dig hard, and after a while I saw myself relaxing. It turned out to be such a pleasurable experience that this is something that I not only needed to but wanted to do. It created a balance in my life. And the ability to create beautiful gardens and bring the flowers into the house was very, very important to me.

Tell me about your gardens.

Over the years the gardens have changed. When we first moved here, we decided to create a spring garden under the tree by the driveway. So we gathered the stones and the big rocks and planted all the spring flowers. And it turned out to be my first beautiful garden. And then it changed. After a while, we planted things other than spring flowers so it would change with the seasons.

I am always trying new things. Two years ago I decided to plant the butterfly garden, which was a wonderful experience. This year, I wanted to create a medicine wheel garden, but I could never quite get that together, so then I found out about mandala gardens, which turned out to be really fantastic.

What was gardening like in your family growing up?

My father had roses. This was the love of his life. What brought him peace was to take the hose and just watch the water sprinkle out while he watered his roses. They were his pride and joy. In the blooming season he always wore a fresh rose on his lapel.

Then I got involved in cutting the grass, since this was a way I could earn money. My father paid 25 cents a cut. The neighbor boy was cutting his grass two times a week, but my father said, 'If you think I am going to pay you more than 25 cents a week, you are wrong. You can cut it as many times as you want, but you're still just going to make 25 cents a week!

Then we moved during World War II. Everybody had a victory garden. We were always busy harvesting, planting, and preparing the vegetables.

When and why did you become a serious gardener yourself?

To try and make this house more beautiful. And my first garden was the spring garden when Bob and I moved to the farm after we were married. I wondered if I could create my own Eden.

What motivates you the most to garden?

To create. To be inspired and to discover. I'm inspired when I start to clean the garden in the spring, push the weeds back, and see the little sprouts coming up. I feel as if they are my children.

I also really enjoy harvesting all my beautiful flowers and sharing them with other people. This year I started growing herbs with the flowers, and that's a pure delight because it gives you extra enjoyment. As you are doing your gardening, you can smell the herbs—rosemary, thyme, and parsley.

What plants do you think are the most beautiful?

I love roses, but I haven't had much luck, so now I am going to the old-fashioned roses. And it may not qualify as "beautiful," but I am wild about arugula.

What are the most important things to you to being a successful organic gardener?

First, you have to love it. Second, it's similar to being a shepherd. You are caring for your little plants and watching them grow. It's a real joy to see them flourish.

Color is important to me. I envision how I want it in my mind. I need to create beauty, to surround myself and the people who come here to the farm to enjoy this place as a treasure.

And it is.

It is.

Do you do any preserving anymore?

Yes. I just freeze tomatoes whole—I even leave the skins on—and use them for soup. One thing I really love is to dice up green, yellow, and red peppers. I put them in a plastic bag and freeze them. That's what I use all winter long—I don't buy any peppers at all. I don't blanch them or anything. I use them in anything cooked.

You obviously have the option of having gardeners do everything for you in the garden, and yet you still do much of your own weeding, planting, and harvesting. Why do you do it?

I do it because I enjoy it. And because when I come home from a stressful day, I like caring for the plants and making things look orderly and neat.

Another reason I don't give everything to the gardeners to do is because they pull up my plants!

Nobody can do it as well as you do it!

Right. I've had that happen too often.

What does gardening mean to you?

Gardening to me is a way of life. It's a way of connecting the life circle.

What's in the circle?

Seeds. Good fertile soil. Water. Anticipation. Encouragement. And then comes the fruit and the sharing. And then it all goes back into the soil and rests a bit, and then it rears up again.

If you could have only one gardening tool, what would it be?

My Japanese weeding knife.

Like mother, like daughter?

Yes.

My mother's
butterfly and
cutting garden

Tools, Tips &

Fall is a time of preparing for the darkness ahead: "putting up" food, cleaning up, and then preparing to slow down and relax. So in this section, I'll discuss one of my favorite activities: preserving my own food. Though this form of cooking may seem time-consuming and old-fashioned, I'm setting out to convince you that it isn't. If you do it my way, it's fast, flavorful, and healthy. And I've added a few tips on winter-izing your garden and raising backyard livestock. But let's start with the most exciting part—buying plants!

Buying Plants in the Fall

The same things I mentioned in the "Spring" section about the pros and cons of mail-order versus nursery buying still apply for fall. The only difference is that fall planting catalogs start arriving in summer, when nurseries are still selling perennials and annuals.

Taking a trip to a nursery in the fall to buy trees and shrubs can be frustrating. They tend to sell plants with nice fall foliage rather than a selection of plants for all seasons. And even though fall is a great time to plant all sorts of trees, nurseries will have sold out of many of them last May.

As much as people tend to drool over the spring mail-order catalogs that arrive in winter, the fall catalogs actually may be a better bet for ordering. First of all, bulbs should almost all be planted in the fall. You'll find all those fabulous spring- and summer-flowering trees and shrubs, too. Fall is when ornamental grasses are in their glory, so it's a natural time to check out the catalogs and see what's available. And catalogs offer a much larger selection of plants with no difference in quality—in fact, quality is often better in catalogs.

A lot of perennials also do better if they are planted in the fall. Such luscious things as poppies and peonies (both regular and tree peonies) are almost always sold only in catalogs, unless you have a very unusual nursery nearby. And fall catalogs offer the best selections.

However, nurseries often offer great bargains in the fall. Wilted perennials are 50 percent off but will still return to their full glory with a minimum of care. Herbs and groundcovers are priced to sell, sell, sell. If you like a good bargain or have a "rescue" complex, fall nurseries are your friends. As long as you are buying a perennial and the roots seem healthy and strong, you can reap the benefit of fall bargains.

Ornamental grasses such as blue fescue are great to purchase and plant in the fall.

Techniques

How to Buy Plants in Fall

Here's my mini-guide to seasonal plant buying for fall. Just as in spring, some plants are best ordered from catalogs, while others are just fine from the local nursery or garden center.

Best things to buy from catalogs in the fall

Bulbs

Peonies

Poppies

Other perennials

Spring-blooming trees

Best things to buy from nurseries in the fall

Mums (you can't avoid them)

Other perennials

Shrubs

Ornamental grasses

Trees

Herbs

Preserving the Bounty

There is no better feeling than heading into fall with food from your garden nestled in the freezer, lined up on the shelves, and dried or canned in your pantry. But it's amazing how much knowledge has been lost about how to grow and preserve your own food—and in just one or two generations.

Although it can be time-consuming to spend an evening after work making tomato sauce for the freezer or canning fruit, the rewards of eating them later are well worth it. And in reality, it takes a lot less time to make things yourself than it does to get in your car, go to the store, and buy stuff that was made in giant vats and trucked for hundreds or thousands of miles. (Mmmmm good.) Plus, you have the satisfaction of knowing that your food is fresh, organic, and good for you and your family.

An excellent book that I use as a source of information for all my freezing, canning, drying, and preserving is *Stocking Up III*. There have been three versions over the years, and they are all good. You can look up any vegetable, fruit, meat, or fish and find out the different ways to preserve it. It will even tell you which varieties of fruits and vegetables are good for canning or freezing.

Harvesting and Preserving Simplified

You don't need a Ph.D. in home economics to preserve your home-grown fruits and vegetables. It's just easy step-by-step techniques combined with a little common sense. Freezing is easiest of all, but drying and canning aren't challenging, either. So go ahead—choose a technique and try it! It won't be long before you're looking forward to the preserving season each year.

Freezing

Freezing is one of the simplest ways to preserve food. You can freeze produce raw (like grapes, berries, and cherries), freeze it blanched by dipping it briefly in boiling water (like peas, corn, and spinach), or freeze it fully cooked (like sauces, soups, and casseroles). The best vegetables for freezing are the ones you normally cook. For example, vegetables like celery and onions do not freeze well. If foods are prepared properly and sealed well, they can last a year or slightly more. Of all the preserving methods, freezing preserves the highest vitamin C content in your foods.

Blanching is important because it preserves the color, texture, taste, and nutritional content of your vegetables. To preserve vitamins, steam-blanch your vegetables, freeze as soon after harvesting as possible, and eat the foods quickly after they are frozen. (If food has been in the freezer longer than a year, it may taste OK, but you probably won't be getting many nutrients out of it.) Thaw foods in the refrigerator to preserve their nutrition and texture.

I've found these techniques work really well—and they're so easy! Try them and see for yourself.

- Spread berries or grapes out on a tray and put them in the freezer (covered) until they freeze, then put them into a freezer bag.

- Be sure to leave space in the freezer container because as things freeze, they expand. A jar filled right to the top will crack open.

- If you are freezing pesto, cover the top of the container with a layer of olive oil. It will help to seal out the air and preserve the green color of the basil.

- Corn is one of the most rewarding vegetables to freeze since home-frozen corn tastes so much better than store-bought for some reason. Get a fresh batch and steam it till it's cooked. Cut it off the cob. Put it in freezer bags. Serve at Thanksgiving with a little bit of salt, pepper, and butter, and you will be thankful.

- Roasted peppers also freeze famously well. Freeze them in their own juices, then add olive oil, garlic, and parsley when they thaw.

- Rather than steam-blanching root vegetables, sauté them in a bit of butter or oil and they will taste better.

- Fruits should be really ripe if you are going to freeze them. Add lemon juice to preserve color and flavor.

- To preserve herbs in your freezer, add them either raw or blanched to butter or oil, and freeze them in small containers (or rolls, if you're freezing herb butter). Thaw as needed for cooking or serving. The best herbs to freeze this way are basil, dill, garlic, rosemary, sage, tarragon, and thyme.

Canning

I was always a little bit afraid of canning. I thought I might inadvertently poison myself or my family if I did something wrong. But then I took a tomato canning class and I felt much better about it. If you follow instructions carefully, your sauce, pickles, or jams will be fine. You will know if a jar was not properly sterilized by looking at the lid or the color. A lid that is bowed or rounded on top is a sign of botulism. *Don't* eat the contents! A lid that doesn't "pop" when you open means that it wasn't sealed properly to begin with. If the liquid looks brownish or blackish, something went wrong and you should throw the food away. If the food is slimy, moldy, or frothy, throw it out.

The most important thing in canning is following the instructions exactly. A good book (like *Stocking Up III*) is essential.

The benefits of canning are that you don't need a large freezer, and some things, including pickles, sauerkraut, and some fruits (like peaches and pears), just taste better canned. High-acid foods can be canned easily and will be very unlikely to spoil. They include pickled vegetables, fruits, and tomatoes. Low-acid foods need to be pressure-canned at a very high temperature in order to kill dangerous bacteria. Low-acid foods include meat, poultry, fish, and all vegetables except tomatoes.

Canning is the most complicated preserving process and also preserves the least amount of nutrients. The amount of cooking needed to seal a jar cooks lots of nutrients right out of the food.

Drying

Dried foods are nutritionally concentrated and great sources of energy. Drying can be done the old-fashioned way (hanging the herbs, fruits, or vegetables in a dry, warm place to dry, or laying them out in the sun), or the newfangled way (either with a dehydrator or in the oven). Blanching vegetables before drying helps preserve them better, just as it does when you're freezing them. Slice, dice, or otherwise cut the produce into thin pieces (think of apple rings or pineapple slices) so they'll be easier to dry.

To dry food outdoors, use a screen and cover the drying produce with cheesecloth (a bit of tulle or chiffon works well, too). Bring the screen indoors at night. Keep taking it outside until the fruit, herbs, or vegetables dry. Store them in the refrigerator or in a cool, dark place.

To dry food in a dehydrator, which will give you the most consistent, reliable results, follow the directions that come with the dehydrator, or check *Stocking Up III*.

To use your oven for drying, put the fruits or vegetables right on the rack (or place a screen or cheesecloth on the racks) and set your oven on warm. The temperature shouldn't exceed about 125°F. Leave the oven door slightly open to keep it from overheating and cooking your food rather than drying it. Drying in the oven can take anywhere from 4 to 12 hours. It's not economical, however. So if you plan to dry a lot of food, buy a dehydrator.

General Preserving Tips Here are three more tips to help you become a preserving pro. And don't forget that homemade jams, jellies, pickles, applesauce, and so on make cherished gifts.

- Only preserve your best, most perfect foods. A bad piece of fruit or vegetable will taste just as bad frozen, canned, or dried, and it can spoil the whole batch.

- If you want to make jams and jellies, use fruit that is not quite ripe because it has a higher pectin content.

- Another method of storing foods is called root cellaring. If you have one of those cellar doors with an underground covered entrance, you can use the inside cold area as a cold-storage room during winter months. Just put your cabbages, potatoes, carrots, and other roots and fruits in mouse- and pest-proof containers. Store your apples and pears in a separate area from the vegetables because the ethylene gas released by the fruit will cause your potatoes to sprout.

Raising Backyard Livestock

Just in case you get the hankering to raise farm animals in your backyard (as I do every day, though I still have not succumbed), here's a quick look at what it would involve.

But first, allow me to complain. It seems that every week there is another article in the paper about someone having to fight to keep a pet pig in their town or their suburb. I think pet pigs are great. But all too often, they are fed store-bought "pig food." Americans love their pets, but like dogs and cats, pigs and other pets have lost their value in the cycle of life.

It's tempting, I know. But honestly, pets feel happier when they are doing something to contribute to their family. Dogs love to defend their territory and protect their families. Cats love to rid their hosts' homes of rodents. Pigs love to eat kitchen scraps. Cows, sheep, and goats love to keep your lawn mowed and provide fertilizer for your garden. Does it mean you love them any less? No. In fact it often means you love them *more* because you understand their needs, they understand yours, and together you are partners in the beautiful cycle of life.

John Seymour, author of *The Self-Sufficient Gardener,* would do an angry Irish jig if he knew about the folly of Americans and their "pets." Yet I never saw happier animals than his Fudge and Smudge (God rest their porky souls), Polly the cow and her daughter Padrigene, and the dog Noula who was as free as a dog could ever be. In return for the animals' keep, the Seymours got protection, milk, cheese, meat, and bacon.

Pets have lost their value in the cycle of life.

One day, I swear I am going to have chickens, geese, and maybe a cow on Main Street.

Game birds can also be raised in a backyard. Guinea hens can roam freely, eating grubs and insects, and they won't destroy your garden like chickens. Pheasants are managed game birds here in Pennsylvania, much prized for their delicious meat. And quail are raised like chickens, and their meat and eggs are a gourmet treat.

Warning: Do not try to raise farm animals based on the descriptions in this book. This is just to give you an idea of what is involved. Further study and research should be done to meet your and your animals' exact needs. Never buy a farm animal including a potbellied pig on impulse.

Rabbits

What they eat: Grains (oats, wheat, barley, sorghum), hay (alfalfa, timothy, clover), salt, greens, and roots.

What they need: Rabbits need good ventilation, plenty of fresh feed and fresh water, room to roam and raise bunnies, separate cages, and shade from hot sun. Don't let them live on wood floors. (They will eat the wood and get sick.) Give them lots of clean, dry bedding.

What they give: Meat, fur, fertilizer, and cuddly cuteness.

Bringing in the cows is a daily joy at John Seymour's smallholding.

Chickens

What they eat: Corn, soybeans, wheat, oats, fish meal, meat scraps, alfalfa meal, dried whey, brewer's yeast, insects, weeds, and vegetables.

What they need: Fresh water, a clean place to live, a "coop" (a small hut or shed) to live in, which should contain a "roost" (a long board off the ground) to hang out on at night and nestboxes for egg laying. Fence them in to keep them from eating your garden vegetables—and to keep predators from eating them.

What they give: Meat, eggs, and fertilizer that's high in nitrogen. Chickens will start laying eggs when they are about six months old and will lay well for several years. They will also do a grand job of controlling pests in orchards if you let them.

Geese

What they eat: Pasture grasses, clover, alfalfa, weeds, oats, corn, wheat, barley, and other grains.

What they need: Unless you live in extreme cold, geese don't need anything more elaborate than an open shelter to protect them from the sun. They need water and fine grit. Fence them out of your vegetable garden, however.

What they give: They make great "watch geese" and also provide eggs, meat, and weeding and bug-eating services. They are even better than chickens at keeping orchards healthy. Plus: Down for pillows and comforters.

Turkeys

What they eat: Grains, corn, greens (lettuce, cabbage, alfalfa, and clover), weed seeds, insects, milk, and water.

What they need: Domestic turkeys need a lot of management because they are not very smart and are more susceptible to disease than chickens. They also need a house with a raised wire mesh floor (to keep them off the ground) and a covered area for sleeping and eating. If you let them roam, an acre can support about 50 turkeys, but they need additional food. They still need shelter at night to protect them from predators.

What they give: Thanksgiving turkey, quill pens, and stuffing for pillows.

Pigs

What they eat: Alfalfa, clover, grains, garden wastes, table scraps, eggs, milk, vegetables, corn, seeds, and rotten fruit (in orchards).

What they need: Pigs are one of the easiest animals to keep. But they need a covered shelter for protection from snow and rain and for shade in summer. They can be raised either in pens or in a pasture (with

Pigs are smart and clean and eat all sorts of
kitchen scraps. But they do squeal quite a bit,
especially when they are excited.

a very strong or electric fence), but at minimum they need some mud to root around in. Rotate their pastures to prevent parasite infestations.

What they give: Ham, bacon, sausage, meatballs, chops, leather, chew toys for dogs (dried pigs' ears—yuck!). Pig stomach is a Pennsylvania Dutch delicacy, although you couldn't pay me enough to try it.

Sheep

What they eat: Pasture grasses, grains, hay, salt, and water.

What they need: A well-ventilated shelter with about 15 square feet per sheep, fresh straw bedding, and pasture (rotate their pastures to prevent parasite infestations).

What they give: Meat, wool, and organic fertilizer.

Goats

What they eat: Hay, grain, grass, salt, and water (not to mention clothing, buttons, and poison ivy).

What they need: A clean, dry place free of drafts, but well ventilated. They can withstand lots of cold and lots of heat. Straw bedding.

What they give: About 2 quarts of nutritious and delicious milk (a day for eight to ten months of the year, which is easy to digest and naturally homogenized), chèvre cheese, meat, leather, and lawn mowing.

John Seymour and Polly the cow—milking is a form of meditation.

Cows

What they eat: Hay, alfalfa, soybeans, clover, ground corn, wheat bran, salt, water, and pasture grass.

What they need: A well-ventilated and draft-free place to live and spend the night in winter. Cows can live on pasture during the summer, provided they have shade from the hot sun. Two acres of grazing pasture (I guess I *won't* have a cow on Main Street). Milking cows need to be milked twice daily and produce about 1,800 gallons of milk a year!

What they give: Milk, cheese, butter, meat, leather, and a reason to get up in the morning.

Horses

What they eat: Hay, grasses, salt, and grains.

What they need: A stall, daily exercise, pasture, water, grooming, and shoeing.

What they give: Transportation, work, companionship, and organic fertilizer.

Getting Your Garden Ready for Winter

Fall is the time to walk the fine line between letting things completely go and trying to get the garden so "cleaned up" that you end up killing your plants. Some people are so fastidious that every leaf is picked up and packaged in a nice bag, bushes are wrapped up, the soil is combed of all debris. *Remember this*: Leaves fall because Nature wants them on the ground. If you want beneficial bugs and animals, they need a place to live. However, there is some basic fall maintenance that needs to be done. Here's my list.

- Clean up rotting vegetables and fruits from your garden. (Traditionally, we had domestic and wild animals to do this for us, and then we would eat them—but that doesn't seem to work any more.) Put the gleanings on your compost pile.

Don't fret too much about cleaning up. By spring it will be gone.

My friend Pat's fig
trees and his cat

- Do one last weeding if you have the strength.

- Rake leaves where they land thickly enough to suffocate the grass over the winter—but only there.

- In late fall, add an inch or two of compost on garden beds that need some extra vigor.

- Pile straw or leaves around plants that need extra protection (like roses and lavender).

- Don't cut back ornamental grasses. Cutting them back in fall exposes them to rotting at the roots. Wait till spring to cut them back. Besides, they add a nice touch to a winter landscape and provide food for birds.

- Let some of your perennials, herbs, and other plants remain uncut to provide food and shelter over the winter to animals, birds, and beneficial bugs.

- Put your toys, tools, and movable garden furniture away.

A **Special Message** to the **Men** of America

Read any men's handyman or gardening magazine and you will find tons of references to gadgets, chemicals, lawn potions, power tools, and machinery. Often it's in a voice of stern command and control, as if Nature were an unruly child who needs to be reprimanded and sent to his room.

I have a theory. The theory is that because women have kept men out of the house because of our perfectionistically high cleaning standards (and because for thousands of years that was the only area women could remotely call "their own"), men have been "kicked outside" to find stuff to do. It's the adult version of "Well, that's sweet, honey, but now go outside and play." So, not wanting to actually play too much because most religions and societies value hard work, their wives are inside working very hard, and there is probably some hard outdoor work gene left over in us from when we actually needed to work outside to survive, men have gone outside to "work."

Here is what these men do. They apply unnecessary fertilizers and chemicals to things. They drive machines around their yards. They seal their driveways (when in fact sealing driveways actually damages them). They stake trees. They rake and vacuum leaves and put them into plastic bags to be hauled away by giant polluting trucks and then dumped in some trash pit where they will never be free to contribute to the soil, for criminy's sakes. They put on their protective goggles and earplugs and whack weeds, blow leaves around, and chainsaw anything that looks as if it's even thinking of causing trouble. It's the John Wayne/Clint Eastwood ideal of gardening.

Men of America: Relax! Hang a hammock. Lie in it. Weed. Grow vegetables, not potbellies. Or you could come inside and work . . . or play. Come on—make my day.

> *We work so hard at driving ourselves mad, extending neat and clean to nature, extending clean fields to the horizon. And there we sit, in a square box in a square and limitless field. Mad.*
>
> *—Bill Mollison,*
> *Travels in Dreams*

Do You Need Cover Crops in Your Backyard Garden?

Cover crops—crops that you grow over an entire area, then till or dig into the soil to enrich your garden—have a big following. Lots of books tell you they're the ultimate garden fertilizer and soil builder.

There are three reasons to plant cover crops. First, to add organic matter to the soil. Some cover crops will also add nitrogen. Second, to reduce weeds. Third, to prevent erosion.

Many cover crops need to be grown during the full growing season, so that in effect you are letting your garden bed go "fallow" for a year. You may want to fit a cover crop into your vegetable garden rotation. A good choice for that would be clover. Red clover can actually be seeded into existing crops to make a nice, nitrogen-rich groundcover for the vegetable garden.

Crimson clover is one of the most versatile and easy cover crops to use. It will put nitrogen into your soil.

Hardy annual winter cover crops like rye vetch can be planted after the growing season. Then mow them down or till them under in the spring. The best plants are winter rye and hairy vetch. Some cover crops, like buckwheat, can be planted during the growing season as a temporary crop. Perennial crops like asparagus, rhubarb, and strawberries can't be rotated with cover crops; in their case, compost is your best choice.

The bottom line is you don't *really* need to use cover crops as long as you keep your soil well mulched and enriched with lots of compost.

Environmental Tip Don't get "fixated" on nitrogen. According to a recent study by an ecologist at Stanford University, the world has too much nitrogen in it already. Too much nitrogen causes toxic algae blooms, urban smog, tree death, leaching of nutrients from the soil, and the loss of heath lands. As the study puts it, "As the world struggles to boost crop yields, the amount of industrial fixed nitrogen applied to crops during the decade of 1980 to 1990 more than equals all that applied previously in human history."

Enjoying the

Fall is the most beautiful season, when the world comes alive with color. Don't let it pass you by as you rush about your usual routine. Besides admiring the colors, here are a few of my favorite autumn activities.

- I know it's a cliché — but when was the last time you jumped in a pile of leaves and got them stuck in your hair and sweater? It's really rather fun. Dogs love it, too.

- Before you put your chaise lounge away for the winter, go outside with some blankets and a cup of tea and read a book or write in your journal . . . or just watch the leaves fall.

Season

- Be thankful. Too often we forget to give thanks—to each other, to Nature, to whatever intelligent being is behind this thing we call life.

- Did you know that by planting bulbs, you communicate your faith in the future? According to Dr. G. Coltaire Rapaille, the act of planting is a ritual that ensures spring will come. Which is why Americans planted over 1.3 billion bulbs in fall 1997.

- Give yourself a natural day spa experience: Start the day with a long walk. Have a light breakfast of fruit and toast. Do yoga, go for a bike ride and/or more strenuous hike. Eat a good lunch followed by a luscious nap. Take an herbal salt bath in the afternoon. Get a massage and/or a manicure. Try Tai Chi Chuan, Qui Ghong, or meditation at the end of the day. Do it outdoors in your aromatherapy garden. Have a light dinner with only food from the garden. Go to bed early. The world can wait for just one day.

The health of soil, plant, animal and man is one and indivisible.

—Lady Eve Balfour,
The Living Soil

Best Plants for Fall

Trees

White ash

Crabapples

Sour gum

Sweet gum

Japanese maples

Red maple

Sugar maple

Red oak

Scarlet oak

Callery pear

Shrubs

Northern bayberry

Japanese beautyberry

Beauty bush

Burning bush (dwarf or regular)

Fothergilla

Heavenly bamboo

Winterberry holly

Hydrangeas

Pyracantha

Viburnums

Witch hazel

Groundcovers for Shade

Ivy

Lamium

Partridgeberry

Periwinkle

Violet

Groundcovers for Sunny Spots

Ajuga

Heathers

Plumbago

St.-John's-wort

Sedums

Creeping thyme

Wintercreeper

Perennials

Japanese anemones

Asters

Boltonia

Goldenrods

Helenium

Hellebores (foliage)

Heucheras (foliage)

Joe-Pye weed

Mums

Sedum 'Autumn Joy'

Perennial sunflowers

Toad lily

Herbs

Chives

Parsley

Rosemary (in the South and West)

Sage

Thyme

Fruits

Apples

Cranberries

Grapes

Hardy kiwi

Olives

Pears

American persimmon

Pomegranates

Quinces

Fall-bearing raspberries

Vegetables

Arugula

Broccoli

Brussels sprouts

Cabbage

Carrots

Cauliflower

Endive

Kale

Kohlrabi

Leeks

Lettuce

Oriental greens

Pumpkins

Radishes

Spinach

Turnips

Winter squash

Food for

Fall brings to my mind birds roasting in the oven, baked squash sweetened with maple syrup and butter, mashed potatoes, and a few delectable vegetables brought out from the freezer (corn, spinach, and foraged cardoon). And with so many fruits ripening in the fall, it almost forces you to make pies and desserts.

Giving Thanks

Thanksgiving is one of my favorite holidays. No gifts need to be exchanged other than the sharing of food and company. It crosses all religious and political boundaries to bring together a nation (for a four-day weekend, no less) in a few potentially heartfelt moments of thanks. And feeling thankful can feel really good. When Thanksgiving is also blessed with food grown by you, made from scratch in a simple or elaborate feast, the thanksgiving feels even more true.

Surprisingly, many people have lost the knowledge of how to make the basic foods that comprise a Thanksgiving feast. Cooking is like gardening in that way. Though it's taught in some schools, the knowledge is usually handed down from generation to generation, or people are self-taught out of an internal need to know.

There are as many ways to roast a bird as there are to create a garden, and each reflects the personality of the cook and gardener. But ultimately it doesn't matter how you do it or which way you learn. Knowledge means survival. Knowledge ensures the perpetuation of our species. Knowledge instills in your soul a confidence that grows as deep and as wide as an ancient beech tree. Knowledge is the living connection to your past and your future. Knowledge is good.

That is why I am now going to tell you how to make a complete and utterly simple Thanksgiving dinner. No fancy decorative elements like Martha would do. No list of 30 ingredients like you can read in a magazine. But a humble feast, cooked with love. Feasibly one that the Pilgrims and Native Americans might have shared—but more important, one that you can share with your family and friends and feel thankful about.

Knowledge means survival.

Fall

Roast Turkey, Roast Chicken, or Roast Goose

Roasting a turkey and a chicken are fairly similar, except that the size of the turkey means more roasting time. By now, if you have read this whole book, you know I'm not going to go in for fancy trussing. Basically, here is all you need to do.

1. Start with a fresh, plump, organic bird. Figure on about a pound per person.

2. Clean the bird out (pull out its guts, which will probably be wrapped in nice little paper bags for your squeamish pleasure). You may choose to use the giblets. Our forefathers and fore-mothers probably used them, but I don't.

3. Wash the bird off with water, and put it in a roasting pan (breast side up) with plenty of room so the juices are caught in the pan and not on the bottom of your oven. Now is the time, if you want, to rub the bird down with spices (sage, garlic, and salt are nice) and butter or oil. But you really don't need to. Plain is also good. You can also put fruit (apples or lemons) or onions inside the bird to infuse it with flavor and moisture while it is cooking. Some people cook the bird upside down first so that the breast is juicier. If you want to try that, go ahead. But unless you put water or oil at the bottom of the pan, the skin will probably stick and rip when you try to turn it over.

4. Put the bird in a preheated oven (400°F for the first hour; 350°F after that). Figure on 20 minutes per pound. Plan on its being done a half-hour before you are ready to serve it so it has time to settle. Your bird will be juicier if it has a half-hour to rest before carving.

5. Baste! Probably the most critical step is to baste the bird occa-sionally with fat and juices from the bottom of the pan. Basting with pan juices makes the skin crispy and the meat juicy.

6. Cook until done. The bird is done if a meat thermometer reads 180°F when inserted deep in the thigh, 170° to 175°F in the thick-est part of the breast, just above the rib bones, and 160° to 165°F in the center of the stuffing. Also, the juices should run clear, and one of the bird's legs should be loose when you wiggle it.

7. Carve and serve.

Goose is fattier than turkey and chicken, so you'll need to take it out halfway through, dump the fat, turn the bird over, and then put it back in. Put whole apples or pears inside to absorb the fat.

Gravy

People make gravy all sorts of ways, but my mother taught me how to make it this way, and it's graced many a pile of mashed potatoes. It only takes five minutes.

1. After the bird has finished cooking, take it out of the pan, and put it on a platter to rest.

2. Put the roasting pan on two burners on top of the stove. Skim off as much of the fat as you can, and leave the juices.

3. Add ⅓ cup flour to ⅔ cup water, and stir with a fork.

4. Bring the pan to a boil (turn both burners on high). Scrape away the brown bird stuff, from the sides and bottom of the pan. When the juices are boiling, stir in the flour-and-water mixture, and keep stirring until the gravy is the thickness you want. If you need to add more flour or more water to get the consistency right, go ahead. Just taste to make sure it's the right amount.

5. Add salt and pepper or other herbs and spices to taste.

6. Serve right away in a warm gravy bowl.

Mashed Potatoes

Mashed potatoes make me happy. And they really aren't hard to make.

1. Peel potatoes, and set them in a pot of cold water. Cover the potatoes with water.

2. Put the pot on the stove, and bring to a boil.

3. Boil for 30 to 45 minutes, depending on the size of the potatoes. You can make mashed potatoes really quickly if you cut them up into small pieces. To tell if they are done, poke them with a fork or knife. If you meet no resistance, then the potatoes are done.

4. Drain the water.

5. Mash with a hand masher.

6. Add some butter or olive oil—as much as you want. You don't need to add any if you don't want to.

7. Add milk to reach the desired consistency. If you want creamy, fatty mashed potatoes, use cream or whole milk. If you want lighter mashed potatoes, you can add skim milk. They're all good.

8. Add salt and pepper to taste.

Baked Maple Squash

What's Thanksgiving without that traditional New England specialty, baked winter squash? I'm sure the Pilgrims ate squash, and I enjoy it, too.

1. Wash butternut or acorn squash, and cut it into halves so you have "bowls" for the filling to sit in. Scoop out the seeds, and put them in your compost pail. Figure on a half squash per person.

2. Pour a teaspoon or two of maple syrup into each squash "bowl." You can also add walnuts, raisins, fruit, and butter.

3. Bake for about 45 minutes at 350°F.

Corn

Corn—fresh from your garden to your freezer to your table—is a wonderful autumn reminder of the summer just gone. It adds a lighter touch to the Thanksgiving feast.

1. Bring some corn from summer out of your freezer. Put it in a saucepan with a bit of water.

2. Boil the water, steaming the corn until cooked (about 10 minutes).

3. Add a bit of butter, salt, and pepper to taste.

Tangerine Cranberry Relish

Most families serve some kind of cranberry concoction with the Thanksgiving dinner. Here's my favorite.

1. Wash a bag's worth of cranberries, and grind them up in your food processor or with a hand grinder.

2. Do the same with a washed and cut-up organic tangerine (the whole thing, peel and all).

3. Add sugar or maple syrup to taste. (In my experience, you'll end up using ½ to 1 cup.)

4. Put the relish in your refrigerator so the flavors can mingle for a few days.

Mixed Greens with Apple Cider Vinaigrette

Don't overlook salad at Thanksgiving. This apple cider vinaigrette adds a distinct hint of fall to the flavoring.

1. Wash organic salad greens. Add carrots or vegetables if you wish.

2. To make the apple cider vinaigrette, add 3 parts olive oil to 1 part apple cider vinegar. A dash of real cider also is good.

3. Add salt and pepper to taste.

4. Add shallots if you feel like it.

5. Toss the salad with the apple cider vinaigrette.

Hot Spiced Cider

Put some cider in a pan on the stove on low heat. Squeeze one whole orange or tangerine into the pan and throw the rinds in, too. Add a dash of nutmeg, some cinnamon sticks, and a few cloves. Let it simmer. Enjoy the aroma and the warm, sweet spicy flavor.

Roasted Chestnuts

I wouldn't dream of serving Thanksgiving dinner without chestnuts. But I do often forget to get them out of the oven. Set a timer to remember.

1. Cut Xs in the chestnuts so they don't explode in your oven.

2. Bake at 350°F for about a half hour.

Pumpkin Custard

Pumpkin is one of those legendary foods—people either love it or hate it. In my family, it's love every time. To make an elegant low-fat alternative to pie, take any pie filling—pumpkin, apple, quince, or pear, for example—and cook in individual-size custard cups (called ramekins). Lightly butter each ramekin before filling, and bake until warm and bubbly. Serve in the ramekins garnished with fresh fruit, whipped cream, or frozen yogurt.

Prepare the Pumpkin

This part is slimy, but it's easy.

1. Cut the pumpkin into manageable pieces.

2. Take out the seeds, and set them aside.

3. Cut off the skin.

4. Chop into 2-inch pieces, and steam until tender.

5. Mash by hand, or mix with a blender for a smoother texture.

6. If you have extra pumpkin, freeze it or add it to risotto, muffins, or cakes. Or just eat it mashed with butter and maple syrup.

Prepare the Custard

Here's what you'll need to make first-rate pumpkin custard.

2 cups mashed pumpkin
1½ cups whole milk (use milk for a low-fat pie, cream for an extra-rich one)
¼ cup brown sugar
¼ cup maple syrup
¼ cup molasses
2 small eggs
1 tablespoon mixed pumpkin pie spices (ginger, cinnamon, cloves, and nutmeg)
pinch of salt

1. Mix all the filling ingredients together, and fill the ramekins.

2. Carry them *very carefully* to the oven, and place it in a pre-heated oven.

3. Bake at 350°F for 30 minutes or until a knife stuck in the middle comes out clean.

Cook the Seeds

Even the pumpkin seeds get served (if they last that long).

Once the custard is in the oven, coat the unwashed pumpkin seeds with olive oil. Add salt, soy sauce, and if you want them, other spices like chili powder, garlic, or cumin. Add a dash of maple syrup.

Spread the seeds out on a cookie sheet, and bake them with the custard until brown and crispy.

Thanksgiving Timetable

There's so much to do to get ready for Thanksgiving dinner that it's easy to forget something, or worse, spend hours getting the meal ready, only to let it burn in the last-minute rush. So I've devised a timetable to make sure everything gets done in the most hassle-free way. Using a timer comes in handy, so you don't forget something that's in the oven—like the chestnuts. Here's my schedule.

- Make the cranberry sauce a few days before the feast.

- Get the pumpkin ready the day before.

- Put the turkey in the oven.

- Peel the potatoes and keep them in cold water.

- Baste the bird.

- Wash the salad greens and make the salad dressing. Prepare other salad ingredients, if desired.

- Cut the chestnuts.

- Baste the bird.

- Prepare the squash and put it in the oven.

- Boil the potatoes.

- Baste the bird.

- Mix the pumpkin custard. Fill the ramekins.

- Take the turkey out of the oven.

- Put the custard in the oven.

- Prepare the seeds and put them in the oven.

- Mash the potatoes.

- Cook the corn.

- Toss the salad.

- Carve the turkey.

- Make the gravy.

- Put the chestnuts in the oven.

- Give thanks.

- Eat!

- Don't forget to take the chestnuts out of the oven!

Fall Finale

The older I get, the less patience I have with perfection. Why obsess over so many things that the passage of time will make irrelevant? Of what good to me is a perfectly elaborate cake or a fancily wrapped present? After an "ooh" and an "ahh," its beauty is destroyed (or devoured). I would rather spend time laughing and talking with family and friends than trying to impress them.

My idea of beauty changes, too. What is beautiful is that which is lasting and sustainable. Things that work well become more beautiful than things that simply look good. Give me my old shovel any day rather than some newfangled shiny tool. A weathered well-worn gate speaks of history and passages much more beautifully than something new and without experience.

The fleeting beauty of nature is an exception. Every moment, from the last golden dusky sunlight on the burning mountain leaves to the foggy cold morning clinging to bare tree trunks, seems both temporary and eternal. New and ancient. The utter beauty and sweet sadness is that fall will come and go, come and go, and come and go long after we are gone. Nature is imperfectly perfect, secularly divine, and the ultimate chronicler of our times.

Let us give Nature a chance; she knows her business better than we do.

—Michel Eyquem de Montaigne

Life is like a 'Fallgold' raspberry—it's best eaten right off the vine.

Calendar

Here's a fall checklist of garden chores, activities, and preparations for the cold season to come.

September

Planting

Put in a last planting of corn salad, lettuce, and radishes.

Plant quick-growing cover crops like crimson clover, hairy vetch, or buckwheat.

Plant garlic cloves and multiplier onions.

Harvesting

Continue to harvest tomatoes and peppers.

Dig carrots and beets.

Harvest winter squash.

Enjoy the last fall raspberries.

Cut dried sunflower seedheads or leave in the garden for the birds to enjoy.

Pruning

It's too soon to prune!

Doing

Order fall bulbs and perennials from catalogs.

Take notes on what did well in your garden.

Make a dried flower wreath.

Preparing

Prepare foods for your freezer and pantry.

Prepare your basement, toolshed, and storage areas to store your tools and furniture for the winter.

Make tomato sauce and salsa.

Roast peppers.

October

Planting	Plant fall trees, shrubs, perennials, and bulbs.		
Harvesting		Harvest the last chard, kale, broccoli, and cauliflower.	Harvest grapes.
Pruning	Cut back perennials if you must, but don't cut back ornamental grasses until spring.		
Doing	Put away your hoses. Take cuttings of geraniums and coleus to root for next season.	Play in the fallen leaves. Make jack-o-lanterns.	Pot rosemary, thyme, chives, and parsley plants for your kitchen windowsill.	Dig tender bulbs like cannas and store them, if they don't overwinter outdoors in your area.
Preparing	Divide perennials.	Pile light mulch around tender perennials, herbs, and shrubs (lavender, roses, and so on).	Clean up the garden and start a new compost pile.	Make applesauce.

November

Planting

Move bushes and other plants in your garden once they go dormant.

Harvesting

Check the garden for the last harvest of brussels sprouts and leeks.

Pick American persimmons.

Pruning

Use pine-bough prunings to decorate for the holidays. (When you're finished with them, spread them around your acid-loving plants.)

Doing

Raid your freezer and pantry for Thanksgiving treats from the garden.

Preparing

Clean and set out bird feeders. Buy seeds and other bird-feeding supplies.

Mulch the strawberry bed with leaves or straw.

Prepare fig trees for overwintering in cold areas.

Epilogue

I think you can spend your whole life looking or waiting for something else—and then you miss it because it was right in front of you the whole time. For some reason, gardening forces me into the present. It inspires me to make the most of what I have, enjoy it while it's happening, and anticipate the future as a pleasant surprise rather than an escape or some distant fantasy.

Still, it is always good to take time out to reflect and think about the past and what you want to do in the future. Set goals, make promises to yourself and others, and seek ways to get ever closer to the elusive goal of satisfaction and happiness.

Resolve to try. Try to make a difference in the world. Try to get closer to the things that make you happy and further from the things that don't. Try to simplify and live with all your senses awake and alert. Try to make your garden a haven for you, your family, the birds and the bees, and the animals with whom we share the world.

New Year's Resolutions

New Year's Day is a great time to think about all this—after all, you're supposed to be making resolutions anyway. Here are few I think are worth making.

Resolve: To try to buy all your seeds and plants from certified organic sources.

Resolve: To spend less time buying and more time doing.

Resolve: To compost and recycle.

Resolve: To buy and eat as much organically grown food as you can.

Resolve: To garden!

Resolve: Never to use chemical fertilizers, pesticides, and insecticides ever, ever again.

Resolve: To change the world.

Never doubt that a small group of thoughtful, committed citizens can change the world. Indeed, it is the only thing that ever has.

—Attributed to Margaret Mead, Institute for

Intercultural Studies brochure

Nobody knows what the future costs will be of so much officially sanctioned use of organophosphates and organochlorines, or of the routine dosing of livestock with antibiotics. . . . These hidden costs have never been linked to the price of conventionally grown food. The illusion has been maintained that intensive farming practices have, at least, given us cheap food. But the real sums are never done. If you add in the production subsidies, the degradation and loss of our environmental capital, and all the costs of cleaning up, then what started out looking like cheap food is actually nothing of the sort.

—HRH the Prince of Wales from "The 1996 Lady Eve Balfour Memorial Lecture"

Resources

Annuals, Perennials, and Bulbs

W. Atlee Burpee & Co.
300 Park Avenue
Warminster, PA 18991-0001
Phone: (800) 888-1447
Fax: (800) 487-5530
Web site: http://garden.burpee.com

Carroll Gardens
444 E. Main Street
Westminster, MD 21157
Phone: (800) 638-6334
Fax: (410) 857-4112

Forestfarm
990 Tetherow Road
Williams, OR 97544-9599
Phone: (541) 846-7269
Fax: (541) 846-6963

The Fragrant Path
P.O. Box 328
Fort Calhoun, NE 68023

Goodness Grows, Inc.
Highway 77 N
P.O. Box 311
Lexington, GA 30648
Phone: (706) 743-5055
Fax: (706) 743-5112

Greer Gardens
1280 Goodpasture Island Road
Eugene, OR 97401-1794
Phone: (541) 686-8266
Fax: (541) 686-0910

Milaeger's Gardens
4838 Douglas Avenue
Racine, WI 53402-2498
Phone: (800) 669-9956
Fax: (414) 639-1855

The Natural Garden
38W443 Highway 64
St. Charles, IL 60175
Phone: (630) 584-0150
Fax: (630) 584-0185

Pinetree Garden Seeds
P.O. Box 300
New Gloucester, ME 04260
Phone: (888) 527-3337
Fax: (207) 926-3886
E-mail: superseeds@worldnet.att.net

Prairie Nursery
P.O. Box 306
Westfield, WI 53964
Phone: (608) 296-3679
Fax: (608) 296-274

Roslyn Nursery
211 Burrs Lane
Dix Hills, NY 11746
Phone: (516) 643-9347
Fax: (516) 427-0894
E-mail: roslyn@concentric.net
Web site:
http://www.cris.com/~Roslyn

Southern Perennials and Herbs
98 Bridges Road
Tylertown, MS 39667-9338
Phone: (800) 774-0079
Fax: (601) 684-3729
E-mail: sph@neosoft.com
Web site: http://www.s-p-h.com

Thompson & Morgan, Inc.
P.O. Box 1308
Jackson, NJ 08527-0308
Phone: (800) 274-7333
Fax: (888) 466-476

We-Du Nurseries
Route 5, Box 724
Marion, NC 28752
Phone: (704) 738-8300
Fax: (704) 738-813

Woodlanders, Inc.
1128 Colleton Avenue
Aiken, SC 29801
Phone/fax: (803) 648-7522

Herbs

Nichols Garden Nursery
1190 North Pacific Highway
Albany, OR 97321-4580
Phone: (541) 928-9280
Fax: (541) 967-8406
E-mail: nichols@gardennursery.com
Web site:
http://www.pacificharbor.com/nichols

Richters Herb Catalogue
Goodwood, Ontario L0C 1A0
Canada
Phone: (905) 640-6677
Fax: (905) 640-6641
E-mail: orderdesk@richters.com
Web site: http://www.richters.com

The Sandy Mush Herb Nursery
316 Surrett Cove Road
Leicester, NC 28748
Phone: (704) 683-2014

Well-Sweep Herb Farm
205 Mt. Bethel Road
Port Murray, NJ 07865
Phone: (908) 852-5390

Ornamental Grasses

Kurt Bluemel, Inc.
2740 Greene Lane
Baldwin, MD 21013-9523
Phone: (410) 557-7229
Fax: (410) 557-9785
E-mail: kbi@bluemel.com
Web site:
http://www/bluemel.com/kbi

Greer Gardens
1280 Goodpasture Island Road
Eugene, OR 97401-1794
Phone: (541) 686-8266
Fax: (541) 686-0910

Limerock Ornamental Grasses, Inc.
70 Sawmill Road
Port Matilda, PA 16870
Phone: (814) 692-2272
Fax: (814) 692-9848

Prairie Nursery
P.O. Box 306
Westfield, WI 53964
Phone: (608) 296-3679
Fax: (608) 296-2741

Tools and Supplies

Gardener's Supply Company
128 Intervale Road
Burlington, VT 05401
Phone: (800) 863-1700
Fax: (800) 551-6712
E-mail: info@gardeners.com
Web site: http://www.gardeners.com

Gardens Alive!
5100 Schenley Place
Lawrenceburg, IN 47025
Phone: (812) 537-8650
Fax: (812) 537-5108

Harmony Farm Supply
P.O. Box 460
Grafton, CA 95444
Phone: (707) 823-9125
Fax: (707) 823-1734

Kinsman Company, Inc.
River Road
Point Pleasant, PA 18950
Phone: (800) 733-4146
Fax: (215) 297-0450

A. M. Leonard, Inc.
241 Fox Drive
P.O. Box 816
Piqua, OH 45356
Phone: (800) 543-8955
Fax: (800) 433-0633

The Natural Gardening Company
217 San Anselmo Avenue
San Anselmo, CA 94960
Phone: (707) 766-9303
Fax: (707) 766-9747

Ohio Earth Food, Inc.
5488 Swamp Street NE
Hartville, OH 44632
Phone: (330) 877-9356
Fax: (330) 877-4237

Peaceful Valley Farm Supply
P.O. Box 2209
Grass Valley, CA 95945
Phone: (916) 272-4769
Fax: (916) 272-4794

Smith & Hawken
2 Arbor Lane
Box 6900
Florence, KY 41022-6900
Phone: (800) 981-9888 *catalog requests only*
Fax: (606) 727-1166

Worm's Way
7850 N. Highway 37
Bloomington, IN 47404
Phone: (800) 274-9676
Fax: (800) 316-1264

Trees, Shrubs, and Vines

Carroll Gardens
444 E. Main Street
Westminster, MD 21157
Phone: (800) 638-6334
Fax: (410) 857-4112

Forestfarm
990 Tetherow Road
Williams, OR 97544-9599
Phone: (541) 846-7269
Fax: (541) 846-6963

Greer Gardens
1280 Goodpasture Island Road
Eugene, OR 97401-1794
Phone: (541) 686-8266
Fax: (541) 686-0910

Raintree Nursery, Inc.
391 Butts Road
Morton, WA 98356
Phone: (360) 496-6400
Fax: (888) 770-8358

Roslyn Nursery
211 Burrs Lane
Dix Hills, NY 11746
Phone: (516) 643-9347
Fax: (516) 427-0894
E-mail: roslyn@concentric.net
Web site:
http://www.cris.com/~Roslyn

Wayside Gardens
1 Garden Lane
Hodges, SC 29695-0001
Phone: (800) 845-1124
Fax: (800) 457-9712
E-mail: catalog@waysidegardens.com
Web site:
http://www.waysidegardens.com

Woodlanders, Inc.
1128 Colleton Avenue
Aiken, SC 29801
Phone/Fax: (803) 648-7522

Vegetables

Abundant Life Seed Foundation
P.O. Box 772
Port Townsend, WA 98368
Phone: (360) 385-5660
Fax: (360) 385-7455
Web site:
http://csf.Colorado.edu/perma/abundant

W. Atlee Burpee & Co.
300 Park Avenue
Warminster, PA 18991-0001
Phone: (800) 888-1447
Fax: (800) 487-5530
Web site: http://garden.burpee.com

Bountiful Gardens
18001 Shafer Ranch Road
Willits, CA 95490-9626
Phone/Fax: (707) 459-6410

The Cook's Garden
P.O. Box 535
Londonderry, VT 05148
Phone: (800) 457-9703
Fax: (800) 457-9705
Web site:
http://www.cooksgarden.com

Ferry-Morse Seeds
P.O. Box 488
Fulton, KY 42041-0488
Phone: (800) 283-3400
Fax: (800) 283-2700

Gurney's Seed & Nursery Co.
110 Capital Street
Yankton, SD 57079
Phone: (605) 665-1930
Fax: (605) 665-9718

Johnny's Selected Seeds
Foss Hill Road
Albion, ME 04910-9731
Phone: (207) 437-4301
Fax: (800) 437-4290
E-mail:
homegarden@johnnyseeds.com
Web site:
http://www.johnnyseeds.com

Native Seeds/Search
2509 N. Campbell Avenue, #325
Tucson, AZ 85719
Phone: (520) 327-9123 *no orders*
Fax: (520) 327-5821 *orders welcome*
Web site:
http://desert.net/seeds/home.h

Geo. W. Park Seed Co., Inc.
1 Parkton Avenue
Greenwood, SC 29647-0001
Phone: (800) 845-3369
Fax: (800) 275-9941
E-mail: catalog@parkseed.co

Pinetree Garden Seeds
Box 300
New Gloucester, ME 04260
Phone: (888) 527-3337
Fax: (207) 926-3886
E-mail: superseeds@worldnet.att.net

Seeds Blüm
HC 33 Idaho City Stage
Boise, ID 83706
Phone: (800) 528-3658
Fax: (208) 338-5658
E-mail: 103774.167@compuserv.com

Seeds of Change
P.O. Box 15700
Sante Fe, NM 87506-5700
Phone: (888) 762-7333
Fax: (888) 329-4762
Web site:
http://www.seedsofchange.com

Shepherd's Garden Seeds
30 Irene Street
Torrington, CT 06790
Phone: (860) 482-3638 *CT location*
(408) 335-6910 *CA location*
Web site: http://www.shepherds.com

Recommended Reading

Cooking

Creasy, Rosalind. *Cooking from the Garden.* San Francisco: Sierra Club Books, 1988.

Hupping, Carol, et al. *Stocking Up III.* Emmaus, PA: Rodale Press, 1986.

McClure, Susan, ed. *Preserving Summer's Bounty.* Emmaus, PA: Rodale Press, 1995.

Shepherd, Renee, and Fran Raboff. *Recipes from a Kitchen Garden.* Vol.II. Felton, CA: Shepherd's Garden Publishers, 1990.

Landscaping

Adams, George. *Birdscaping Your Garden.* Emmaus, PA: Rodale Press, 1994.

Brookes, John. *John Brookes' Natural Landscapes.* New York: DK Publishing, 1997.

_____. *The Garden Book.* New York: Crown Publishing Group, 1992.

_____. *Garden Planning.* New York: The Reader's Digest Association, 1992.

_____. *The Book of Garden Design.* New York: Macmillan Publishing Co., 1991.

Cox, Jeff. *Landscaping with Nature.* Emmaus, PA: Rodale Press, 1991.

Creasy, Rosalind. *The Complete Book of Edible Landscaping.* San Francisco: Sierra Club Books, 1982.

Davis, Brian. *The Gardener's Illustrated Encyclopedia of Trees & Shrubs.* Emmaus, PA: Rodale Press, 1987.

Dirr, Michael A. *Manual of Woody Landscape Plants.* Champaign, IL: Stipes Publishing Co., 1983.

Harrison, George H. *Garden Birds of America..* Minocqua, WI: Willow Creek Press, 1996.

Hart, Robert. *Forest Gardening: Cultivating an Edible Landscape.* White River Junction, VT: Chelsea Green Publishing, 1996.

Kourik, Robert. *Designing and Maintaining Your Edible Landscape Naturally.* Santa Rosa, CA: Metamorphic Press, 1986.

Lindegger, Max O. *The Best of Permaculture: A Collection.* Maxatawny, PA: Rodale Institute, 1990.

Mars, Ross. *Getting Started in Permaculture.* Maxatawny, PA: Rodale Institute, 1994.

Matson, Tim. *Earth Ponds Sourcebook.* Woodstock, VT: Countryman Press, 1997.

_____. *Earth Ponds.* Woodstock, VT: Countryman Press, rev. ed. 1992.

Mitchell, Alan. *The Trees of North America.* New York, NY: Facts on File Publications, 1987.

Mollison, Bill. *Introduction to Permaculture.* Berkeley, CA: Ten Speed Press, 1997.

_____. *Travels in Dreams.* Tyalgum, Australia: Tagari Publications, 1996.

_____. *Permaculture.* Washington, D.C.: Island Press, 1990.

Nash, Helen. *The Complete Pond Builder.* New York: Sterling Publishing Co., 1996.

_____. *Low-Maintenance Water Gardens.* New York: Sterling Publishing Co., 1996.

_____. *The Pond Doctor.* New York: Sterling Publishing Co., 1994.

Roth, Sally. *Natural Landscaping: Gardening with Nature to Create a Backyard Paradise.* Emmaus, PA: Rodale Press, 1997.

Organic Gardening

Organic Gardening magazine
Rodale Press, Inc.
33 E. Minor St.
Emmaus, PA 18098

Bradley, Fern Marshall, and Barbara W. Ellis, eds. *Rodale's All-New Encyclopedia of Organic Gardening.* Emmaus, PA: Rodale Press, 1992.

Bradley, Fern Marshall, ed. *Rodale's Garden Answers: Vegetables, Fruits and Herbs.* Emmaus, PA: Rodale Press, 1995.

Bubel, Nancy. *The New Seed-Starter's Handbook.* Emmaus, PA: Rodale Press, 1988.

Coleman, Eliot. *The New Organic Grower.* White River Junction, VT: Chelsea Green Publishing Co., rev. 1995.

_____. *The New Organic Grower's Four-Season Harvest.* White River Junction, Vt.: Chelsea Green Publishing Co., 1993.

Cox, Jeff. *Jeff Cox's 100 Greatest Garden Ideas.* Emmaus, PA: Rodale Press, 1997.

Ellis, Barbara W., ed. *Rodale's Illustrated Encyclopedia of Gardening and Landscaping Techniques.* Emmaus, PA: Rodale Press, 1990.

Ellis, Barbara W., and Fern Marshall Bradley, eds. *The Organic Gardener's Handbook of Natural Insect and Disease Control.* Emmaus, PA: Rodale Press, 1992.

Gilkeson, Linda A., Pam Peirce, and Miranda Smith. *Rodale's Pest & Disease Problem Solver.* Emmaus, PA: Rodale Press, 1996.

Hynes, Erin. *Rodale's Successful Organic Gardening: Controlling Weeds.* Emmaus, PA: Rodale Press, 1995.

Jeavons, John. *How to Grow More Vegetables Than You Ever Thought Possible on Less Land Than You Can Imagine.* 5th ed. Berkeley, CA: Ten Speed Press, 1995.

Kowalchik, Claire, and William H. Hylton, eds. *Rodale's Illustrated Encyclopedia of Herbs.* Emmaus, PA: Rodale Press, 1987.

Martin, Deborah, and Grace Gershuny, eds. *The Rodale Book of Composting.* Emmaus, PA: Rodale Press, 1992.

McClure, Susan, and Sally Roth. *Rodale's Successful Organic Gardening: Companion Planting.* Emmaus, PA: Rodale Press, 1994.

Olkowski, William, Sheila Daar, and Helga Olkowski. *Common Sense Pest Control.* Newtown, CT: The Taunton Press, Inc., 1991.

Pleasant, Barbara. *The Gardener's Weed Book.* Pownal, VT: Storey Communications, 1996.

Rodale, J.I. *Pay Dirt.* Emmaus, PA: Rodale Press, 1941.

Seymour, John. *The Complete Book of Self-Sufficiency.* London: Dorling Kindersley, Ltd., 1975.

Smith, Miranda, and Anna Carr. *Rodale's Garden Insect, Disease & Weed Identification Guide.* Emmaus, PA: Rodale Press, 1988.

Perennials and Other Ornamentals

Appleton, Bonnie Lee, and Alfred F. Scheider. *Rodale's Successful Organic Gardening: Trees, Shrubs, and Vines.* Emmaus, PA: Rodale Press, 1993.

Benjamin, Joan, and Barbara Ellis, eds. *Rodale's No-Fail Flower Garden.* Emmaus, PA: Rodale Press, 1994.

Bradley, Fern Marshall, ed. *Gardening with Perennials.* Emmaus, PA: Rodale Press, 1996.

Burrell, C. Colston. *A Gardener's Encyclopedia of Wildflowers.* Emmaus, PA: Rodale Press, 1997.

Cox, Jeff. *Perennial All-Stars.* Emmaus, PA: Rodale Press, 1998.

Holden Arboretum Staff. *American Garden Guides: Shrubs and Vines.* New York; Pantheon Books, 1994.

McKeon, Judith C. *The Encyclopedia of Roses.* Emmaus, PA: Rodale Press, 1995.

Phillips, Ellen, and C. Colston Burrell. *Rodale's Illustrated Encyclopedia of Perennials.* Emmaus, PA: Rodale Press, 1993.

Proctor, Rob, and Nancy J. Ondra. *Rodale's Successful Organic Gardening: Annuals and Bulbs.* Emmaus, PA: Rodale Press, 1995.

Roth, Susan A. *The Four-Season Landscape.* Emmaus, PA: Rodale Press, 1994.

Index

Note: Page references in **boldface** indicate photographs.

CREDITS

Excerpts from the following are reprinted with permission by the publisher or copyright holder:

Page 44: "Work" excerpt ©1987 by the Estate of Brenda Ueland. Reprinted from *If You Want to Write: A Book about Art, Independence and Spirit* with the permission of Graywolf Press, Saint Paul, MN.

Page 77: Lui Collins, "Awaiting the Snow," ©Molly Gamblin Music, P.O. Box 4005, Ashfield, MA 01330.

Page 115: Warren Schultz, "Re: Cycling Your Lawn–The Crackdown on Mower Pollution." *Garden Design* magazine, August/September 1996, pages 21–22.

Page 211: George Adams. *Birdscaping Your Garden.* (Lansdowne Publishing Pty Ltd.) Emmaus, PA: Rodale Press, 1994.

Page 164, 223, 249, 334: Bill Mollison, Founding Director, Permaculture Institute, and Founding Director, Tagari Publications, NSW, Australia. *Travels in Dreams.* Tyalgum, NSW, Australia: Tagari Publications, 1996.

Page 249: *The Good Heart: A Buddhist Perspective on the Teachings of Jesus.* ©1996 His Holiness the Dalai Lama and World Community for

Christian Meditation. Courtesy of Wisdom Publications, 199 Elm Street, Somerville, MA 02144.

Pages 262–263: "Impersonators in Your Garden," *Extension Line Lookout,* July 1997, Cornell Cooperative Extension, Erie County, NY.

Page 335: (Stanford University study) *Issues in Ecology* #1, Spring 1997. Reprinted with the permission of the Ecological Society of America.

Page 338: Lady Eve Balfour, *The Living Soil* (New York: Devin-Adair Co., 1950). The Literary Executors of Lady Eve Balfour Estate, c/o Elm Farm Research Centre.

Page 355: From "The 1996 Lady Eve Balfour Memorial Lecture" given by HRH The Prince of Wales. The Literary Executors of Lady Eve Balfour Estate, c/o Elm Farm Research Centre.

All of the photographs in this book are by Maria Rodale except for the following: Photographs on pages 44 (bottom), 46 (left), 69, 70, 79, 80, 181, 183, 184, 232, 272, 286, 287, 288-289, 341, 342, 343, 344, 345, and 347 are by Kurt Wilson/Rodale Images; photographs on pages 14, 16, 81, 121, and 235 are courtesy of the Rodale Family archives; other photographs throughout the book are credited with the photo.

USDA Plant Hardiness Zone Map

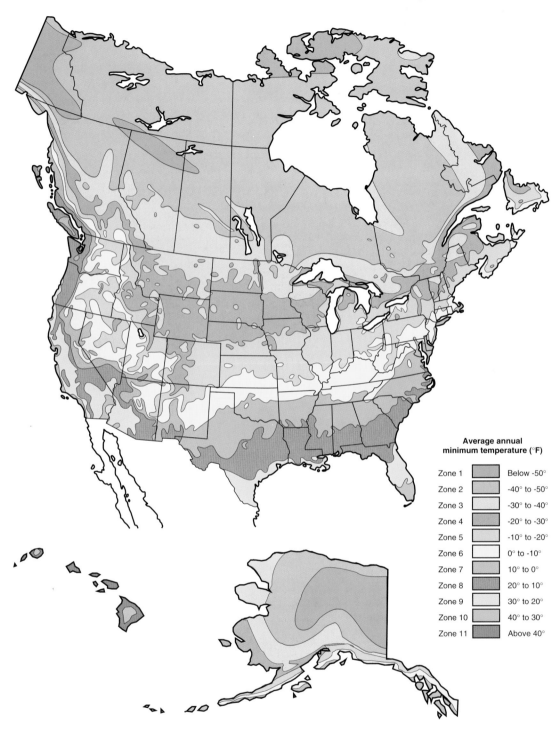

Average annual minimum temperature (°F)

Zone 1		Below -50°
Zone 2		-40° to -50°
Zone 3		-30° to -40°
Zone 4		-20° to -30°
Zone 5		-10° to -20°
Zone 6		0° to -10°
Zone 7		10° to 0°
Zone 8		20° to 10°
Zone 9		30° to 20°
Zone 10		40° to 30°
Zone 11		Above 40°

This map was revised in 1990 to reflect changes in climate since the original USDA map, done in 1965. It is now recognized as the best estimator of minimum temperatures available. Look at the map to find your area, then match its pattern to the key on the right. When you've found your pattern, the key will tell you what hardiness zone you live in. Remember that the map is a general guide; your particular conditions may vary.